What the caterpillar calls the end of life,
the butterfly calls the beginning.
Richard Bach (amended)

Panic Attacks
five steps to freedom

Lorraine Mason

E3 Publishers

First edition published in 2006 by E3 Publishing House Ltd

Second edition published in 2014 by E3 Publishing House Ltd

This third edition published in 2015 by E3 Publishers
Email: info@e3publishers.com

Medically Edited/Verified by Dr. Carmel Casserley M.B., B.Ch, FF Hom
Illustrated by Brian Mason

A CIP catalogue record for this title is available from the British Library.
ISBN: 978-0-9551868-4-4

Please note

All suggestions of help and advice in this book were founded on the suffering and recovery of countless panic attack sufferers, including the author. The author has been an adviser and mentor to panic attack sufferers for over 35 years. Throughout this book, every piece of medical information was verified by the highly respected Dr. Carmel Casserley M.B., B.Ch, FF Hom.

Despite the vast experience and credibility stated it must be noted that, as symptoms of stress can vary enormously from person to person, before commencing this or any other stress related self-help book, programme or practice, you are strongly advised to seek medical advice regarding the particular book, programme or practice from a qualified medical doctor.

Also, regarding the experience and credibility pertaining to this book, it must be noted that, a) as it is impossible to predict the countless circumstances in which the information within may be used and b) as the interpretation of information by one person can be quite different to that of another, not the author, publishers, medical doctor or anyone involved with this book shall be liable to any person or entity with respect of any use, misuse, interpretation or misinterpretation of the information or alleged damage caused by the information contained in or omitted from this book.

Acknowledgments

A heartfelt expression of my deepest gratitude is given to...

Brian, my husband: Although I met you years after I had suffered and recovered from panic attacks and although, when we met, I was a single parent with two young children, you have steadfastly stood by my side throughout – also, thank you for drawing the illustrations in this book.

Mandy, my daughter: For your loyalty, encouragement, selflessness and, of course, your love – for never complaining when others needed me – and for putting the plight of others before yourself; even during the times when, in hindsight, you desperately needed me.

Warren, my son: For never once turning your head from me when I suffered panic attacks but throughout giving me lots of hugs, kisses, love and most importantly hope; for without that hope I would have possibly been lost.

Dr. Carmel Casserley M.B., B.Ch, FF Hom. my medical adviser: For just 'being there' – for teaching, guiding, reassuring and encouraging me – for being my mentor, inspiration and example of true goodness – for showing us all the spirit of a true doctor – and for taking the time to verify all the medical information in this book.

Avril Finch, my ex tutor: For your kindness and patience, for recognising my writing ability and disregarding my dyslexia. A truly inspiring teacher.

Anne Greenhalgh, my 'Girl Friday:' For all the humour, time and patience you have contributed to the making of this book.

All my previous brave-hearted clients, my true teachers: For turning to me when you were in need – for teaching me so much about the diversity of panic attacks – and for allowing me the privilege to now pass all that I have learned from you to others.

To you, dear reader: For choosing this book – for 'staying with it' when, at times, you will feel like giving up – and for all the positive contributions you will make to life, once you are totally free of panic attacks.

Integrity

The author

Lorraine Mason has been involved with panic attacks for almost 50 years... Initially, in 1966, at the age of 21, she developed panic attacks and suffered dreadfully with them for a number of years. A few years after she had recovered from panic attacks, Lorraine began to offer help to those who were suffering the condition as she had. After a few years of helping sufferers and studying the deeper elements of panic attacks, her own approach to recovery began to form. More years passed and, in time, as she continuously adapted and assessed her approach and techniques of help, she realised that, when applying her own personally devised 'five-step' approach, all sufferers were gaining tremendous benefit with most gaining total recovery. For almost 30 years, Lorraine has applied her gentle and totally safe 'five-step' programme to help countless panic attack sufferers gain total and permanent freedom from panic attacks. In addition, by 2005, due to the impossible task of helping every sufferer who sought her help, Lorraine had transferred her 'five-step' programme to book form; in which her vast knowledge and empathic manner is available for the benefit and freedom of every single panic attack sufferer.

The verification of all medical information

All the medical information within this book was verified by Dr. Carmel Casserley MB., BCh, FF Hom.

In 1958 Dr Casserley qualified in medicine (MB., BCh) at University College Dublin. This was followed by a 32 year career in the National Health Service, Great Britain...

- 1958-1962: served in Public Health in Birmingham and Manchester.
- 1962-1980: served as full-time General Practitioner in Wigan, Lancashire.
- 1980-1981: took a sabbatical within the NHS to study homeopathic medicine at the Royal London Homeopathic Hospital, qualifying in 1981, (MF Hom,) later followed by a fellowship (FF Hom).
- 1990: retired from the NHS to run a private practise in St Annes-on-Sea, Lancashire.
- 2002: retired from private practise yet continued to contribute to this book.

A few extracts from letters/emails received

"Hi Lorraine, as you know, in 1991, out of nowhere, the terror of panic attacks suddenly struck me, and for eighteen long and torturous months, day and night, fear and terror became my life, if I could call it life, never knowing when the next one would strike. Then I found you. I could never repay the patience and love, care and compassion you gave me, only to write and tell you that now, five years on, and not having had a panic attack since, I am living a life that I once could only dream of and you were my dream-maker. From the depths of my soul, I thank you."   E/June 1998

———

"In all the years I have had M.E. and panic attacks and all the books I have read, this is the best, most helpful yet. Reading this book, I feel believed, sane and less afraid. Already, I feel stronger."   S/Feb 2007

———

"I have had panic attacks for 30yrs. I told my brother, he has not spoke to me since. Through your book I can now go in lifts which I would never do before."   A/Dec 2006

———

"Dear Lorraine, there are so many things that I would really like to say. It takes a very special person with an overwhelming desire to help her fellow man, who is able to use the in-depth knowledge gained from her own personal experience, to give courage, strength and to guide those in absolute fear and utter distress, through the winding, twisting paths of fear and the forest of hell, into pastures of understanding, fulfilment, peace and joy. You are such a person and you did all this for me. /...my letter could no way compare with the love, dedication and warmth from one human to another."

M/May 2002

———

"Seventeen years I have tried to cope. /...your book gives out a lot of help and understanding. Looking out into my garden I now feel there is hope for me. I feel so lucky to have your help come my way. /...only you understand the pain of it all. With love to you Lorraine. God Bless you and thank you."

V/May 2007

———

"I have suffered these attacks on and off for 10 yrs, more on than off. I had to give up my job in the - - - - - - Service after 25 yrs. /...when I first started to read it I really cried, I am not sure whether that was relief that I saw someone had gone through everything I had gone through. /...I am now up to Step 3, what to do and what not to do in panic attacks, yesterday I wanted to go to the Post Office in the local Co-op, and do a bit of shopping, this is when I run round before the panic comes, but it invariably does. I could not believe how I got round there without a full blown panic, I managed really well, and was very proud of myself, so thank you Lorraine, from the bottom of my heart."

A/May 2006

————

"I should explain first that it is my girlfriend who suffers from panic attacks which she has suffered from for the last seven years and I am reading your book on her advice so I can try to understand what she goes through on a day-to-day basis. It started pretty much how you said you started in your book. She had the same feelings as you and didn't have a clue what it was or why it was happening. She was 17 at the time and had to give up college and was only able to go out the house with her Mum, and that was usually only involved going out in the car. /...my girlfriend is one of the most amazing people I have ever met and it is amazing that she manages to get out of bed in the morning. She has really struggled and has even had thoughts about ending it all... /...before there seemed to be no hope.... /..thank you for your great book."

A/2005

————

"...great book, read so many, this is by far the best."   G /Jan 2007

————

"...a really wonderful book, wonderful, a real eye-opener on panic attacks. I never would have believed that something so simple could have caused my beloved wife so many years of such terrible suffering."   B/Mar 011

————

"A fascinating new book that is set to help hundreds of people overcome this debilitating problem."   Angela Kelly – Bolton Evening News (2005)

————

"How to deal with a panic attack effectively is precisely explained, as is a stress busting routine and the concept of achieving mind rest. Yes, the last mile will probably feel like the longest but the help and guidance in this section is detailed enough to prepare you for a more healthy approach to life. It is clear Lorraine is dedicated to sharing her vast knowledge of panic attacks and how to deal with them. I was fortunate enough to be able to talk to Lorraine about her work and how passionately she feels about helping others. Her book is comprehensive in all respects, including the medical information which has been varied as accurate by Dr Carmel Casserley."

Nancy's Book Review – No Panic (Jan 2007)

————

Contents

Courage does not always roar...
it is often the quiet voice at the end of the
day saying..."I will not give up."
Mary Anne Radmacher (amended)

Panic Attacks
My Personal Experience

The panic began...

Hello! In 1966, at the age of 21, after a combination of getting married, moving house twice, becoming pregnant, realising my new husband was having an affair and having my first baby, all within thirteen months, I had my first experience with panic attacks. I was shopping at the time in my local market when suddenly, and for seemingly no reason, I felt dizzy, my heart started to race, a tremendous wave of fear swept through me, the building itself seemed to close in on me and a need to escape from all the people, noise, hustle and bustle overwhelmed me to the degree where I quickly made my way out of the building.

Once I was outside, the 'funny turn' began to ease but as the experience had happened unexpectedly and seemingly without cause, it left me feeling so unnerved that I immediately caught the bus back home. When home, although relieved to be there, I still felt very unnerved at not knowing what on earth had happened. Nevertheless, as the hours and days passed without a further recurrence, I began to suspect the whole thing had been a lot of fuss about nothing.

About 10 days after the 'funny turn,' whilst sitting in church, and again for seemingly no reason, my heart began to race, my body trembled, I felt faint, claustrophobic, frightened and in need of escape. The very thought of fainting in front of the congregation added to my concerns, so I quickly made my escape outside. Yet, that time, because a 'funny turn' had then happened twice, I began to suspect that I was not imagining things but something 'very real' must be wrong with me.

Over the following few weeks, the 'turns' gradually intensified in both frequency and severity, to where they were no longer merely waves of fear but waves of actual terror. I only had to be in a crowd of people, on a bus, in a lift or queuing in a shop when suddenly, and seemingly for no reason, my heart would race and pound so much I honestly feared it would burst, my body would shake, my legs would buckle, my head would swirl, my mind was frenzied and as the certainty of imminent death screamed inside my head to where it overpowered me, every fibre and sinew throughout my whole body and mind literally forced me to run.

And even though I developed the habit of always sitting or standing near a doorway or exit for a quick escape, the waves of terror increased daily to where, eventually, they were hitting me anywhere and everywhere.

By this time, my disastrous marriage had broken down and my parents had lovingly taken both my son and myself back home to live with them. But whilst I obviously felt very relieved at having help with my son and for being free from my marital situation, my fear over what was happening to me was taking over. As every time an 'attack' struck, all I felt able to do was frenziedly scream to my Mum, "Oh God, it's here again. I'm going mad, I know I'm going mad, I can't stand this anymore. Please help me." Which, understandably, convinced me even further that either something dire was physically happening to me or insanity was imminent.

As the weeks passed, driven by their concern, my parents would try to encourage me to go with them in the family car. But time and time again, as I prepared to go out and indeed whilst out, the same fears flooded my mind, "What if I have an attack whilst outside? Where can I run? Who can I run to? Who will come to my aid? What if I have a heart attack, where will the nearest hospital be?" Consequently by the time we had travelled 200 yards away from home, the fear would have risen-up inside me to such an overwhelming level that, in absolute desperation, I would literally beg to be taken back home.

Exhaustion set in
Up to that point, rightly or wrongly, every single day I had gritted my teeth, gathered my courage and literally forced myself out the door to walk the 30 yards to the local corner shop, genuinely believing that by forcing myself through this tortuous ritual I was somehow hanging on to my sanity. And although, on a few occasions, I did manage to reach the shop and fumble out a few words, ever more frequently fear would rise within me to such an overwhelming level that I was forced to run back home empty-handed and in a state of absolute frenzy. So as the weeks passed, as the journey to the corner shop became ever more torturous and as it all became too much for me, in the desperate attempt to save myself further suffering, I stopped forcing myself outdoors but rather, I stayed indoors, at home, where I felt some degree of sanctuary.

Nervous breakdown ensued
Things were becoming dire and as the months passed, due to our then family doctor being 'of the old school' and out of touch with mind issues, mixed with my own lack of understanding of what was happening to me,

fear, exhaustion, pain and terror became entrenched into every aspect of my life. And although, on the outside, I still looked normal, on the inside I was physically, mentally and emotionally falling apart...

Physically: I was totally exhausted, my whole body throbbed with a grinding-like pulsation, aches and pains shot through my body from one limb to another, my throat felt so tight I genuinely thought I was slowly choking to death, random yet acute knife-like stabbing pains, in the area around my heart, were so severe they took my breath away, my heart was continuously banging, palpitating, jumping, missing beats then thudding and the constant aching pains in the middle of my chest were so strong, I truly feared I had developed a serious heart condition. Indeed the pains in my chest were so strong that, in the hope of finding reassurance, I constantly sat with a finger over my pulse but, needless to say, reassurance never came.

Mentally: My mind was driven to exhaustion/breakdown, for I was then living in the thick, black, foggy places of the mind that brought terror to my very core. Whilst I could physically see and hear my family and the world around me, I was seemingly lost, out of reach, trapped inside my head, as if I was looking out at everything through a glass or plastic shield or as if I was living in another dimension to them. Weird and very frightening thoughts engulfed me, with subject matter laughable to other people but which, to me, seemed very real, plausible, frighteningly imminent and of such intensity that I simply could not understand how everyone was just going about their normal daily life when, as far as I believed, horrors of all kinds were about to happen.

Eventually, as horrific thoughts of doom, gloom, madness and death consumed my mind, all rational thought was lost to me. I couldn't watch television, listen to the radio, read a newspaper or talk to friends for fear I might see, hear or read bad news or come upon descriptions of horrific illnesses with symptoms similar to mine. And when I did inadvertently come upon negativity of some kind, my mind would then tightly grip onto it, turn it upside down, inside out, twist and distort it until another terror was found; serving only to drag me down ever further into my seeming madness. I couldn't bathe or go to the toilet alone for fear of having a heart attack, brain haemorrhage or any sort of attack whilst not being in the position to run. I couldn't look out the window without feeling like a caged animal screaming for freedom. I absolutely dreaded going to bed alone as when lying there hour after torturous hour, sleep didn't come easily. And when I did sleep my dreams were sometimes filled with the most frightening nightmares and even when my sleep was not filled with horrors, I would still wake some nights totally exhausted and completely engulfed in a full blown wave of terror, forcing me to frenziedly jump out of bed and run around the bedroom crying hysterically, "Someone please help me."

Emotionally: I remember one morning just as if it were yesterday, standing in my Mum's kitchen, feeling so very frightened of what might lie ahead yet being totally helpless to do anything about it and thinking, "So this is what it feels like to be insane, this must be insanity because nothing else could be so weird and frightening. I wonder if they'll take me away? Oh God, what's going to happen to me? What's going to happen to my little boy?"

One year turned into two of my suffering 'fear attacks' (not realising they were something called panic attacks) and whilst I believed there was nothing else I could do, nowhere else I could go, no one else I could turn to for help, and with all my hopes, dreams and health fading fast, I reached the point of thinking about death: – "I just can't do this anymore! – It would be so easy to just take an overdose and put an end to all this suffering. – But how can I abandon my beautiful son, what would happen to him if I were not around to protect him? – Yet what use am I to him like this, after all, if I were dead a relative would surely adopt him and give him a wonderful life. – But I'm his mum; he needs me! – Maybe, but I just can't go through this torture anymore."

I saw a speck of light

'The darkest hour is just before dawn,' so the proverb says. And one evening (about 1968/9) due to my Dad being late home from work, I happened to see his local evening newspaper still laying on the desk, and despite my absolute fear and dread of hearing or seeing any bad news, by sheer absentmindedness (or as I believe, by the gentle guiding hand of my guardian angel) without realising what I was doing, I just glanced through the paper. And there it was, an article on a book which was describing my symptoms and explaining something called panic attacks. I just could not believe it, and as my eyes flashed over the article, I absolutely knew that, with help from my Mum, I just had to get the book and somehow read it.

By this time, I had been suffering the 'attacks' and their symptoms for well over two years but as no one around me knew what was happening to me and with me being so convinced that I was surely heading for madness, for me to then read the book ('Self Help For Your Nerves' by Dr Clair Weeks) was as though someone had lit the brightest of lights on that, my darkest of nights. And although I found it impossible to put Dr Weeks suggestion of floating into practice (making me fear I was worse than everyone else) and although I was still left suffering panic attacks and symptoms of stress as bad as ever, and although most of my questions, worries and fears were still left unanswered and even though, over the following two years, I still needed to find my own way out of the condition, I nevertheless found the book to be of the greatest value. Indeed, with my hand on my heart, I know that the information within the book actually saved my life. It did so by a) giving me hope, b) showing me that I was not going insane but was suffering with something called panic attacks and c) assuring me that peace was out there somewhere; all I had to do was somehow find it.

I will not elaborate on the many pitfalls, trauma and ongoing fear that I endured over the following two years whilst trying to find my way out of panic attacks. I will promise you though, by following this 5 step programme, your recovery will be a much smoother journey than mine.

At this point, I would like to openly convey my deepest gratitude to Dr. Weeks by saying, "During my darkest days you gave me hope, please accept my most heartfelt, Thank You."

This programme
I suffered panic attacks, including their painful, confusing symptoms, from 1966 to 1970. However, a few years later, once I was feeling 'normal' again, about 1975, and was back to 'life;' working full-time, looking after my young children and renovating the old house that we were all living in. I began to feel the need to completely change the direction of my life. So in 1981, whilst not really knowing what else to do, I attended a local college in the hope of training to become a Social Worker but in my heart it just didn't feel right for me. Following that I attended a counselling training course but again, for some reason, it just didn't feel right for me. Then it hit me. I would try to help panic attack sufferers. So not really knowing how else to go about it, I just spread the word as much as I could through my family, friends and neighbours.

Sure enough, albeit very slowly, sufferers began to contact me and when they did, I would initially explain that I was not a doctor, nurse or health professional of any kind but rather, I was just a person who had suffered panic attacks and found my own way out of them. After that, we would talk, share our experiences, compare my old symptoms to theirs and I would offer relevant know-how from my own recovery and from the budding recovery of the sufferers I was then working with. And sometimes, with me then only being a novice at helping panic attack sufferers, I would recommend they obtain, 'Self Help For Your Nerves.'

Years then passed, over which time the need to help all panic attack sufferers became my life. And sure enough, as I very slowly gained more insight into panic attacks, as I studied the deeper and more complex elements of the condition from the volumes of medical books I was then reading and as I applied my increasing knowledge to the ever growing number of sufferers who were, by then, seeking my help, my confidence grew and my ability to help (without Dr Weeks book) became apparent.

More years passed and by about 1992 a plan of recovery began to grow ever stronger in my mind and by 1995 I had actually devised my 'five-step' programme out of panic attacks. And amazingly, despite the severity of every sufferer's panic attacks and their related stress symptoms, despite the individuality of every sufferer and the length of time they had suffered and despite whatever treatment or therapy they had previously received or endured, every panic attack sufferer who genuinely followed my programme through to completion gained tremendous benefit, with most making a full and permanent recovery.

By 2005, then aged 60, due to the impossible task of working with every sufferer who needed my help, I had put my 'five-step' programme into book form entitled, 'Panic Attacks – Five Steps to Freedom.'

And so, here we are today. After all my experience with panic attacks: – suffering them to where they nearly destroyed me – recovering from them without hospitalisation, drugs, psychiatry or the notorious electric shock treatment – spending years helping, supporting and learning from all my courageous panic attack sufferers – studying volumes of technical, medical information then transferring it into layman's language – devising a 'five step' programme then using it for many years to help panic attack sufferers – converting my 'five step' programme into book form – and now, based on all the letters/emails I receive, seeing most people make a full recovery.

My many years involvement with panic attacks has taught me much which I consider a true honour and privilege to now pass on to you

———

Throughout the time I suffered panic attacks, despite my being adopted, despite my Mum then being in her sixties, frail, disabled and suffering both chronic bronchitis and emphysema, despite her looking after my son, me, my Dad and herself and despite her having no idea of what was happening to me, she tirelessly stood by me, never complaining, never criticising, yet always offering me her unconditional love, help and support in whatever way she could. My Mum died in 1972, even so, I would like to say to her...

Mum, your acts of love and selflessness
are now being carried throughout eternity.
Thank You! – God bless!

When you walk to the edge
of all the light you have and take that
first step into the darkness of the unknown,
know that one of three things will happen...
there will be something soft for you to fall upon
there will be solid ground for you to stand on
or you will be taught how to fly.

Dr Patrick Overton (amended)

Step One

Be comforted... come in from the cold, sit down,
warm yourself and let us see where you are up to.
For now you are with someone who does know
how you are feeling and how to help you

Please read first

General symptoms of stress: a concise list

Anxiety Attacks - Panic Attacks - Phobic Attacks

Your likely path into panic attacks

Befrienders

Re-cap: To take your first step to freedom

Please Read First

If you are suffering severely with panic attacks you could now be so distracted by your aches, pains, fears and terror that the task of reading any book will seem impossible to you. Added to that, you may suspect that even if you do make the monumental effort to read just a few lines of text, you would still need to read it many times before being able to understand it. That said, let me immediately assure you...

Your concerns are perfectly normal and felt by most sufferers. The text throughout this book is very easy to read and the format is easy to follow. The repetition of key points are all in place and no information will frighten you. In fact, once you begin to read, you will probably understand and retain far more than you thought possible. Nevertheless, irrespective of the speed at which you are able to read this book, let it work around you; read it in your own time, at your own pace, don't rush yourself and don't allow others to rush you. There are no prizes for being first. The one and only prize is your full and permanent freedom from not only panic attacks but also the fear of them ever returning. And so, to begin...

7 Key facts

1. Suffering panic attacks is not a sign of insanity!

The condition of panic attacks, when at its worst, is recognized as being one of the most debilitating, distressing and terrifying conditions known. Yet suffering panic attacks, even at their worst, is not a sign of insanity, long-term illness, imminent death or of being a soft, silly, weak person. Suffering panic attacks is, however, the result of experiencing stress, nothing more! And even when the condition of panic attacks is suffered to the point of nervous breakdown, it is still a condition from which every sufferer can completely recover and not require ongoing management or medication. That being so, please realise, panic attacks are far removed and must not be confused with conditions such as schizophrenia, mania, manic depression, clinical depression, delusion, paranoia or any psychotic illness which, even when stabilised, will require ongoing management and most probably medication.

2. You will not die or go insane during a panic attack!

As you will see later in this programme, your body and mind are built to experience frenzied panic. And whilst you might think that no body or mind could ever withstand such strong sensations of terror as those you are experiencing, I assure you, such symptoms are truly commonplace.

As you saw previously, I have been involved with panic attacks for 40+ years, yet despite all those years and despite the millions of people who suffer panic attacks, I don't know one person who has gone insane or died during a panic attack. In fact, as far as I know, a person going insane during a panic attack is unheard of. And a person dying during a panic attack, unless also suffering with an underlying serious life-threatening medical condition, such as chronic heart disease, emphysema or similar, is also completely unheard of.

So to whatever degree you are suffering panic attacks, you will not go insane during one. If you are not suffering with a serious life-threatening medical illness you will not die during one. And even if you are suffering panic attacks and a life-threatening medical condition, the possibility of you dying during a panic attack is really quite remote.

3. A great many people suffer panic attacks

Many panic attack sufferers go to extreme lengths trying to keep their 'attacks' a secret, as a consequence, no one really knows the true number of people who suffer them. The 'National Phobic Society' and 'No Panic' say that 1 in 3 of us will suffer a panic attack at some point in our live and of those that do, 1 in 20 will suffer severely with them. However, realising that the term panic attacks is often used (and misused) for not only true panic attacks but also for many other panic related conditions. The figures that I am inclined to use are... throughout the western world, 1 in 3 people will, at sometime in their life, suffer with a panic related disorder, 1 in 7 will suffer actual panic attacks and of those who do, 1 in 20 will suffer them to the point of debilitation. That's a lot of people!

4. Know that you really are an incredible person

Although we will discuss this whole subject later in the programme, by which time you will know how to deal with your panic attacks. At this point just realise what an incredible person you are...

You are now suffering panic attacks and perhaps also chronic anxiety, extreme symptoms of stress, utter weariness and debilitation. You might now be feeling weak, a burden, a nervous wreck, at the end of your tether and no use to anyone. You might now be trying to fight your panic attacks by drinking, drugs, staying in your bed all day, medication, sex, aggression or by whatever means gets you through each day. So weakness does not come into it in any way, shape or form. How can it when, courageously, you are now choosing not to give-in to one of life's most terrifying and torturous battles but rather, you are choosing to fight your way through it the very best you can, in the only way you know how?

Furthermore, as you have possibly been fighting panic attacks for some time. You have already shown yourself to be an incredible person gifted with an awe-inspiring strength of spirit and a degree of grit, courage and heart that belongs only to those who possess the strongest spirit of all; making you a tremendous human being and the epitome of mankind at its very best. Whether or not you have used those gifts to their best potential is a different matter, but we will discuss that later.

5. This is not just a book but a programme
To calm actual terror you need to be **extremely** precise in your actions. This book will explain those actions; what they are, how they work, when to put them into practise and how to put them into practise. Having said that, this is the beginning of your recovery and, like many people, your approach to recovery might well be filled with the impatience to finish. Therefore, at this point, I must explain: My work is to help you make a full and permanent recovery from panic attacks; that means, to be free of not only panic attacks but also free of the fear of them ever returning. So during this book you will not find a 'quick fix' out of panic attacks, you will, however, be guided through each step very slowly indeed.

When recovering from panic attacks, via this programme, you will go through five stages, these are your 'Five Steps to Freedom.' The following will give you a brief indication of what to expect…

Step One: be comforted
This step will invite you to come in from the cold: – it offers a few initial words of reassurance and comfort to all sufferers; whether they are suffering mildly or severely – it lists over 100 natural and normal physical, mental and emotional symptoms that any stress sufferer can expect to experience – it explains the similarities and differences between anxiety attacks, panic attacks and phobic attacks – it covers your own likely descent into panic attacks – it explains that despite your wish to keep your panic attacks a secret, a trouble shared is often a trouble halved – it gives advice

to all befriender's on how they can initially help you – and it gives a brief re-cap covering your first step to freedom.

This step will prepare the ground for your recovery and whilst its benefits might not be immediately apparent, it is crucial towards you making a full and permanent recovery.

Step Two: understand yourself

This step is the foundation of recovery: – it takes you to a point of understanding the fundamental elements of what is happening to you, for it was your misunderstanding of those elements that caused you to suffer panic attacks in the first place – it explains why all humans experience arousal to the point of panic – it shows how arousal is made within the body – it describes arousal in action to the point of frenzied panic – it shows, in detail, the physical, emotional and mental effects of prolonged arousal – and it gives a brief re-cap covering your second step to freedom.

This step will lay the foundation of your recovery, it is the strength, the element that everything else rests on and without its understanding any 'so-called' recovery will certainly crumble sooner or later.

Step Three: enlighten yourself

Your 'plan of action' begins on this step: – it explains exactly what you are doing wrong when a panic attack strikes; thereby fuelling it – it explains precisely what you need to do when a panic attack strikes; thereby calming it – it offers an extremely effective stress-buster-routine – it shows, to those suffering nervous exhaustion or breakdown, how to gain 'mind rest' – and it gives a brief re-cap covering your third step to freedom.

This step will lay the first brick of your recovery; very rewarding.

Step Four: empower yourself

Whilst, for some people, recovery from panic attacks can be very quick, for most people it takes a little while, so whilst you are working on your recovery, this step will certainly help you: – it asks you to repeat what you learned in step three – it explains re-balancing and it forewarns you of the potential boulders of recovery from panic attacks – it explains how your recovery is likely to be similar to a roller-coaster ride of good-days/ bad-days and it offers tried and tested ways of getting through those days – it offers an insight into the golden moments of recovery – it covers your possible feelings of guilt/shame for suffering a 'mind' problem and it explains why such feelings do not belong to you – it explains why the current trends in treatment so often fail panic attack sufferers – for those who need it, it offers help with medication withdrawal; as suggested by the British Medical Association and also the Royal Pharmaceutical Society of Great Britain – and it gives a re-cap covering your fourth step to freedom.

This step will build both your confidence and ability. And whilst you might find it hard work, you will also find it tremendously empowering.

Step Five: free yourself
In this step you will claim your life back from panic attacks: – it invites you to search out those places and situations where, up to now, you have avoided due to panic attacks – it asks you to evaluate and adapt your stress-buster routine – it reminds you to give yourself time to heal – it explains how freedom from panic attacks can be the beginning, the starting place, the open door to 'life' and the opportunity to become the person you were really born to be; for your freedom will only be freedom if you embrace it, otherwise you are still holding yourself in bondage – and it gives a brief re-cap covering your fifth step to freedom.

This step will add the final touches to your recovery, for then you will be standing on very solid and well-protected ground.

So you see. The information within this book is not just on general stress or even on panic attacks but rather, it is a programme out of panic attacks. And like all other programmes, if you try to short cut it (by just flicking through the pages or beginning at the back of the book and reading the last chapter, then making your conclusions from that) you will jump to the totally wrong conclusion and overlook the one piece of information that is absolutely necessary for your personal recovery and you will certainly break the sequence of recovery, in which case, recovery will be lost.

6. "You can't tell me anything I don't already know!"
If you are well-read on medical matters but have reached the point of believing there is nothing left for you to learn on the subject of panic attacks then I ask you to consider the following two points...
1. Whilst this book is simplistic in the extreme, don't make the classic mistake of thinking that things of value only ever come wrapped in fancy, highbrow packaging, as often, it is the simplest things in life that eventually prove to be the most valuable. Make no mistake, the text in this book may be simple but the programme within is

the safest and most successful way out of panic attacks that I have ever encountered.

2. "Are you now 100% free of both panic attacks and all fear related to them?" If not, I suspect that somehow you have inadvertently gathered technical information that was not wholly relevant to panic attacks, yet the basic information that is relevant, you either overlooked, dismissed or disregarded, believing it too simplistic to be of relevance to the recovery from panic attacks.

7. To suffer panic attacks is to be lost inside a maze; nothing more
To suffer panic attacks, particularly if severely, feels similar to being lost inside a maze: – claustrophobic tunnels of fear – impenetrable walls of terror – potholes of pain – long dark days of despair – odd shafts of light highlighting rare moments of hope, only for the light to swiftly disappear, leaving you scrambling in the dark more frightened than ever – and exit signs that read 'all symptoms of stress this way' but following them only entices you deeper into panic attacks and leaves you even more lost, confused and desolate than ever.

Every element of life must be viewed from the correct perspective otherwise the perception of it will become distorted. So when you initially experienced your first 'attacks,' due to you not knowing where they had come from, why they had struck and how you could avoid them in the future, you developed fear towards them. Once fear got hold, it confused your mind, clouded your view and distorted your perception to where you then became too distracted by pain, too caught up in worry, too engulfed with symptoms, too distracted by fear, too overwhelmed with terror and too confused with the whole condition to work out how to free yourself.

So whilst no book can ever be 'all things to all people' I say to you, with absolute confidence that, based on my many years experience with panic attacks, as you gradually move through this programme, you will come to understand where you are within the maze of panic attacks, why you developed them, how you developed them, what you need to do to free yourself of them and how to do it correctly. In so doing, you will then no longer view panic attacks from the erroneous position of being lost within them but rather, from the elevated position of being above them, looking down on them. Then being in such an advantaged position you will clearly see the whole maze, recognise your own position within it and slowly walk out; freeing yourself from the maze of panic attacks forever.

As a stress sufferer, you need to know what symptoms to expect

To suffer panic attacks is often to suffer in secret but when a sufferer cannot or will not discuss their symptoms with another person then whose words of comfort and reassurance do they cling to, whose symptoms do they compare their own to and by whose yardstick do they measure the severity of their condition? For when a person suffers alone and their symptoms don't fit neatly into how they think they should be, they can then mistakenly jump to the wrong conclusion.

The following section lists over 100 of the most common symptoms of stress that panic attack sufferers experience. Read it and be comforted!

───────────────

General Symptoms Of Stress - A Concise List

Below you will find a list of behavioural, physical, mental and emotional symptoms caused directly by stress. Nothing in the list will frighten you, in fact, when you go through the list you will possibly, even probably say through your smiles and/or tears similar to, "How do you know I'm experiencing that, I've never dared tell anyone, not even my doctor or family, for fear they will think I'm going crazy?" Or "I feel so relieved at seeing my aches and pains wrote down, it actually validates that my suffering is real." Or "I told them I'm not imagining or exaggerating how ill I feel. Just wait until I show them this list. Now they'll have to believe me." Or "You know, I think my aches and pains could be stress after all." Or "So I'm not going mad. Oh thank God." Or "I find great comfort in reading the list, not at seeing my own symptoms wrote down but at seeing all the symptoms I don't have."

The number of symptoms described as being stress related are as many as there are people who suffer stress. But when all the symptoms are grouped with others of a similar nature they number about 150.

The number of symptoms that any panic attack sufferer can expect to experience range from about 10 to 50 but, as with any generality, some people experience less than 10 whilst others experience more than 50, I give you the average because I know the intensity of your concerns.

The following list consists of about 100 of the most common symptoms that any panic attack sufferer can expect to experience. If you happen to relate to every symptom, don't feel disheartened, don't fear it's going to take you forever to be free and please don't think you must be worse than everyone else; your not. Some panic attack sufferers will relate to virtually every single symptom, to one degree or another, yet they may recover much easier and quicker than many who are only experiencing just one or two symptoms. So please realise, the number of symptoms you are experiencing is no measure at all as to how easily or quickly you will recover.

When reading the list below, if your symptoms are not listed, don't immediately jump to the conclusion that your symptoms must therefore be a sign of a serious illness. I repeat, the only reason I have chosen to list the symptoms below is because they are, by far, the most common.

Behavioural Symptoms of Stress

- expressing frenzied terror
- inappropriate behaviour, often extreme
- bursting into tears at no obvious cause
- obsessive behaviour
- food, alcohol and/or drug abuse
- living continuously at 'fast forward,' eating, talking, moving etc
- general restlessness and feeling unable to sit still
- living slowly, i.e. eating, talking, moving
- withdrawn, introverted, head /eyes always looking down

Physical Symptoms of Stress

Head
- general headache
- a feeling as if the top of the head is about to burst open
- a feeling of great pressure at the back of the head
- feeling as if a knife or fist is burrowing into the head
- feeling as if an ever tightening band of metal is around the head
- shooting pains in one or various parts of the head
- noises in the head when being between sleep and awake

Eyes
- eyes aching
- strange tricks of vision, particularly in the corner vision
- objects and people seem hazy and/or far away
- sensitivity to light; i.e. when outdoors, in offices and shops, when looking at a television or a computer screen

Ears
- sounds seem muffled
- sounds seem too loud, as if they will burst the eardrums

Mouth
- sweet, sour, salty taste or a complete loss of taste
- mouth, lips and/or tongue feels dry, stiff, numb and/or too big
- difficulty forming words and/or saying words

Throat
- the sensation of choking
- the sensation of being unable to swallow
- the sensation as if one has a lump in the throat
- the sensation as if the muscles on one/both sides of the throat are tightening

Chest
- pains in various parts of the chest
- sore breastbone
- a feeling of being unable to take a deep breath
- frequently sighing and/or yawning
- breathlessness

Heart
- sharp stabbing pain (like a knife) around the heart area
- sensations as if the heart is sore, loose, racing, banging, sinking and/or missing beats
- palpitations

Stomach
- feeling sick and/or vomiting
- pains in stomach
- bloated feeling and/or a brick-like-feeling in the stomach
- a sensation of butterflies in the stomach
- stomach churning
- indigestion, heart-burn
- excessive wind; up or down
- overeating
- a complete loss of appetite

Bladder and Bowel
- a frequent desire to pass water
- diarrhoea
- irritable bowel

Sexual organs
- miscarriage and/or premature labour
- impotence and/or premature ejaculation
- low libido

Limbs
- 'jelly legs'
- muscular pain in one or numerous limbs
- throbbing, aching limbs
- pins and needles in hands and/or feet
- cold limbs

Skin
- excessive sweating: palms, under arms, whole body
- skin feels cold and/or clammy
- a sensation of ants or hot/cold water running underneath or on the surface of the skin

General
- dizziness and/or fainting
- weight gain or loss
- fatigue/exhaustion
- raised blood pressure

Mental Symptoms of Stress
- experiencing 'out of place' frenzied terror
- always worrying about something
- racing and/or flashing negative thoughts
- irrational, frightening thoughts
- obsessive and/or compulsive thoughts
- depressive thoughts
- memory loss/forgetfulness
- indecisiveness
- lack of concentration
- inability to think clearly and/or in-depth

Emotional Symptoms of Stress
- de-personalised:
  - feeling detached from oneself or floating above oneself
  - as though one has disintegrated into a million pieces
- feeling unreal:
  - as if detached from 'life' and/or as if living in a glass bubble
  - as if living in another dimension to the rest of the world
  - as if looking out onto the world through a glass or plastic partition

- as if the whole world cannot see one at all
- an overwhelming sense of isolation
- feeling exposed and open to the whole world:
  - as though everyone can see ones innermost thoughts and feelings
- an overwhelming need to be at home and stay there
- impending doom
- a loss of interest and/or a feeling of complete emptiness
- engulfed in sadness, utter weariness and hopelessness
- depressive and/or suicidal
- an overwhelming feeling of wanting to run away, hide and escape from the world and everyone in the world
- constantly crying
- feeling permanently irritated, angry, arguing, screaming, banging, throwing things and/or erupting at the slightest thing
- emotional emptiness
- as though ones brain is made of cotton wool or sponge
- as though ones thoughts are about to shoot right out of ones head
- an overwhelming dread of bad news, as if you just can't take anymore
- a sense of claustrophobia to the night itself
- an aversion to being touched
- craving for warm, loving words, hugs, caresses
- sleeplessness

Feeling so very alone
To suffer the physical elements of panic attacks is difficult enough. To suffer the mental elements is often worse still. But to suffer the emotional elements of panic attacks can be one of the loneliest places on earth.

Many years ago, during my first meeting with one lady, in her attempt to 'get through' to her husband just how alone and desperate she was feeling, she suddenly jumped up and screamed out at him, "Don't you realise, I'm so near to going over the edge that to be free of this fear and terror I'd gladly have both my legs cut off at the hip. In fact I'm so desperate, I'd gladly ask for the knife and do the job myself; right here and now." Fully realizing how serious the lady was, I said, "I know you would." But then, before I could say anything else, her husband jumped up and shouted at me, "Now you see what she's like? She's such a drama queen. I keep telling her to go on the stage, she'd make us a fortune."

Over the years, when trying to explain just how alone and frightened they feel, countless panic attack sufferers have describe, in their own words but each being so similar to: It feels like I am totally alone in a vast ocean, the night is black, the water is icy cold and the strong current is carrying me ever further out to sea. And whilst initially, I screamed out for help, not one of my 'loved ones' gave time to help me. Yes, of course my 'loved ones' knew I was in very deep water, they saw me frantically waving, they heard my screams, they even said I should get help. But because every one of them was so self-focused, they each put their blinkers on and became so blind, they didn't even see that I was actually drowning; and possibly going under, never to rise again.

The loneliness of panic attacks can be so dreadfully debilitating that many sufferers say they genuinely wish they were suffering with any condition other than panic attacks, even a terminal illness. They say at least they would then have the opportunity to meet other sufferers, find comradeship, support and feel that other people do genuinely understand how very frightened and desperate they are feeling.

Get yourself checked out thoroughly

The above listed symptoms of stress are the normal, natural symptoms that any stress sufferer can expect to experience. Nevertheless, if you are experiencing any symptoms, whether on the list or not, I now need to give you the following statutory advice...

1. Go to your medical doctor and request a full medical examination plus all related tests.
2. When your medical examination results show no irregularities, if you are not fully reassured then ask about the possibility of a second opinion.
3. When your medical examination results from the second doctor come back and show no irregularities, if you are still not fully reassured then ask to see a specialist.
4. Once the results from all your medical examinations and tests confirm no irregularities then ask yourself one question, "Am I stressed?" If yes, then expect symptoms to one degree or another. And although your symptoms might be very distressing, painful, debilitating, extremely weird and very frightening, there is every probability they are indeed the normal, natural symptoms of high stress, nothing more! As such, despite their severity, they can be controlled, reduced and totally eliminated. And even if your symptoms are not listed above but have nevertheless been diagnosed as stress related. There is still every probability that your symptoms are indeed due to stress, as such, they also can be controlled, reduced and totally eliminated.

This might surprise you

Even at this early stage, it's worth mentioning that the nature and severity of your symptoms (or indeed of any symptom caused by any illness or condition) is **not** the cause of your panic attacks! After all, many people experience the most debilitating illnesses and suffer extreme symptoms of chest pain, palpitations, breathlessness, head pain, dizziness, feeling faint and so on, without being thrown into panic. So for you to experience such symptoms **and** be thrown into panic then your condition must have an additional element. That is, along with your symptoms, you are also experiencing the additional state of 'heightened responses,' which registers whatever symptoms you do have then over responds to them, throwing you into panic and terror. That being so, whatever the nature and severity of your symptoms, whilst they might be distressing and trigger off your panic attacks, they are not the root cause of your panic attacks. Your panic attacks are due to nothing more than your mind is now over responding to whatever symptoms you are experiencing.

And yes, hyperventilation (and also many other conditions) do cause symptoms and yes, one or two of those conditions might be causing your symptoms. Even so, **no symptom**, from any condition or illness has the power, within itself, to cause panic attacks.

Please understand, only when 'heightened responses' are added to symptoms will a person experience panic attacks.

If you don't understand 'heightened responses' don't worry, I cover the whole subject later in the programme. At this point, I simply want those who do understand to be aware of the fact and, hopefully, be comforted. **You don't need to wait until all your symptoms have gone before you can be free of panic attacks.**

Your correct panic related diagnosis

During the course of a lifetime, most people will experience some of the sensations mentioned above but that does not make them a stress sufferer. Likewise, at one time or another, most people will experience frenzied panic but that does not make them a panic attack sufferer. So before we go any further, we must firstly establish whether your 'attacks' are anxiety attacks, panic attacks or phobic attacks. For whilst anyone can recover from any one of those conditions, we really do need to establish from which condition or conditions you are suffering; as often, knowing the difference will prove to be vital. The following section will help you to identify from which condition or conditions you are suffering.

Anxiety Attacks - Panic Attacks - Phobic Attacks

Anxiety attacks, panic attacks and phobic attacks are not three different names for the same condition but each is a totally different condition, stemming from a completely different thought process. Yet sadly, when a person is experiencing bouts of frenzied panic and seeks help, only rarely are their thoughts investigated enough to determine which of the three conditions they are suffering. Therefore, as this is one area of panic attacks that is very often misunderstood, even the term 'panic attacks' is often bantered around and used (or misused) for a multitude of reasons other than actual panic attacks. I now offer my own distinction between the three conditions because, to the true panic attack sufferer, knowing the difference can be extremely useful and occasionally crucial.

As you read the following section you will see that whilst there are many obvious differences between the three conditions, there are also many similarities; which is why so many sufferers are given the wrong diagnosis. That being so, to help you identify from which condition or conditions you are suffering, I have given each of the three conditions a checklist with ten key points. So read each checklist, tick each key point relevant to you then, once you have covered all three conditions, whichever has the most ticks is the indication of which condition you are suffering. Also, when reading the following information, if it seems too repetitive, just take a break. This whole chapter is only nine pages long, and although it is crucial that you understand the information, if you need to take a break after each paragraph, then do so. No problem at all.

Anxiety attacks

☐ 1. The attacks **do** seem to strike me suddenly, with no obvious cause or trigger.

☐ 2. During an attack I **am** primarily frightened by the mental, physical and emotional symptoms; and the more severe the symptoms become, I become even more frightened by them.

☐ 3. During an attack, the reason why my symptoms frighten me is because I do **not** know what triggers the attacks, or how severe my symptoms will become or how long my symptoms will last.

☐ 4. After an attack, I **do** believe that the attack and my symptoms during the attack are only a by-product of me being stressed.

☐ 5. After an attack, the reason why I do **not** worry over my symptoms is because I know just what is happening to me and why it is happening; namely because I am stressed.

☐ 6. Throughout the day my thoughts are **not** primarily focused on matters relating to the attacks.

☐ 7. There are **no** specific places or situations where I feel so susceptible to the attacks that, as a consequence, I deliberately avoid.

☐ 8. I do **not** 'live in continuous fear' of being struck down again by either the attacks or the symptoms that come with the attacks.

☐ 9. I do **not** fear that, sooner or later, the attacks and the symptoms that come with the attacks will cause me to experience something dire; such as a heart attack, a stroke or madness.

☐ 10. I have **not** organised my life, in any way, around avoiding certain places and/or situations that I feel might trigger an attack.

General Summary...
Initially, this person was under mental, emotional and/or physical stress. And whilst their mind and body were able to carry a limited degree of stress without any obvious symptoms. Sooner or later, the degree of stress became too much for their mind and body, as a consequence, their whole bodily system erupted with physical, mental and emotional symptoms of stress. The symptoms understandably frightened them.

Soon after the first attack, once the severe symptoms had eased, this person thought similar to, "I'm OK it's only stress," as a consequence, they did not attach fear to either the attack or their symptoms during the attack.

Since the first attack, even if one, two or more attacks have occurred, this person's mental approach has not change. After every attack they still think similar to, "I'm OK it's only stress," consequently they do not attach fear to either the attack or their symptoms during the attack. Therefore as this person can attribute the attacks to their experiencing stress, they do not 'live in continuous fear' of the attacks. As such, this person is still at the point of experiencing 'anxiety attacks.'

Panic attacks

☐ 1. The attacks **do** seem to strike me suddenly, with no obvious cause or trigger.

☐ 2. During an attack, I certainly **am** primarily frightened by my mental, physical and emotional symptoms; and the more severe they become then I become even more frightened by them.

☐ 3. During an attack, the reasons why my symptoms frighten me is because I do **not** know what triggers the attacks, or how severe my symptoms will become or how long my symptoms will last.

☐ 4. After an attack, I do **not** believe that the attack and my symptoms during the attack are only a by-product of me being stressed.

☐ 5. After an attack, the reason why I **do** worry over my symptoms is because I do **not** know what is happening to me nor why it happens.

☐ 6. For those suffering mildly/moderately: Throughout the day my thoughts are **not** primarily focused on matters relating to the attacks however, throughout the day my thoughts do tend to wander onto such matters.

   For those suffering severely: My **only** thoughts throughout every day and night are of the attacks and my symptoms during the attacks, i.e. – "What will I do when the next attack strikes?" – "Where can I run to." – "Who can I run to." – Who will be able to help me." "How am I going to get through the day/night without exploding or cracking up."

☐ 7. For those suffering mildly/moderately: There **are** specific places and situations where I feel so susceptible to the attacks that, as a consequence, I deliberately avoid, i.e. lifts, motorways, crowded places.

   For those suffering severely: There **are** places and situations, virtually everywhere, everything and everyone, to which I feel so susceptible to the attacks that, as a consequence, I deliberately avoid.

☐ 8. For those suffering mildly/moderately: I do **not** 'live in continuous fear' of being struck down again by the attacks and the symptoms that come with the attacks. I **do,** however, continuously feel some degree of anxiety, concern and restriction by it all.

   For those suffering severely: I **do** 'live in continuous fear' of being struck down again by the attacks and the symptoms that come with the attacks.

☐ 9. For every sufferer of panic attacks: I certainly **do** fear that, sooner or later, particularly if forced out of my comfort zone, these attacks and the symptoms that come with the attacks will cause me to experience something dire; such as a heart attack, a stroke or madness.

☐ 10. I **have** organised my life in some way (often in every way) around avoiding certain places and/or situations that I feel might trigger an attack.

Summary...
Similar to anxiety attacks...
Initially this person was under mental, emotional and/or physical stress. And whilst their mind and body were able to carry a limited degree of stress without any obvious symptoms. Sooner or later, the degree of stress became too much for their mind and body, as a consequence, their whole bodily system erupted with physical, mental and emotional symptoms of stress. The symptoms understandably frightened them.

Unlike anxiety attacks...
After the first attack: Once the symptoms of stress had eased, this person did **not** think similar to, "I'm OK it's only stress" because, to their mind and misguided thinking, stress alone could not have caused such strange, strong and disturbing symptoms. And, because this person did **not** know what had happened to them but knew that, whatever it was, had certainly disturbed them, it left them feeling quite unnerved and perhaps concern about the possibility of another attack striking.

Since the first attack. Whether this person has not experienced another attack since or, in fact, whether they are now experiencing many attacks throughout the day and night. As they suspect the attacks are caused by something unknown, uncontrollable, terrifying and possibly very serious, they are now so fearful of experiencing an attack that, second-by-second, **they now 'live in continuous fear'** of another attack striking. As such, this person is experiencing 'panic attacks.'

Anxiety attacks or panic attacks
Initially the person experienced an anxiety attack. After one or a number of anxiety attacks, if the person realised the attacks and their symptoms during the attacks were only stress related and therefore they did not attach fear to them, then the attacks remained anxiety attacks. However, after one or a number of anxiety attacks, if the person did not realise their attacks and their symptoms during the attacks were stress related

but rather, the person attached fear to them and indeed began to 'live in continuous fear' of them then the attacks became 'panic attacks.'

- Anxiety attacks:**Individual** waves of frenzied panic, which the sufferer knows are only due to stress.
- Panic attacks: **A self-perpetuating condition** of seemingly uncontrollable waves of frenzied panic, of which, to the sufferer, there seems no obvious cause, means of stopping or prevention.

Phobic attacks; including Agoraphobia and Social Phobia

This person will experience panic as a **direct result** of them experiencing an inappropriately high degree of fear towards a **specific, identifiable stimulus**. And whether the stimulus is a person, place, object, animal, action, situation or sensation (other than the sensations attached to fear) it is irrelevant, for example...

If a person has an inappropriately high degree of fear towards spiders (arachnophobia) but is then confronted by one and, as a direct result of that confrontation, they experience a wave of panic...they experienced a 'phobic attack.'

If a person has an inappropriately high degree of fear towards people (social phobia) but is then confronted by a crowd of people and, as a direct result of that confrontation, they experience a wave of panic...they experienced a 'phobic attack.'

If a person has an inappropriately high degree of fear towards direct sunlight (heliophobia) but is then forced outside into the sunlight and, as a direct result of that situation, they experience a wave of panic...they experienced a 'phobic attack.'

To help you compare the ten elements of 'phobic attacks' to those of both 'panic attacks' and 'anxiety attacks' I will use as a example, the person who has a phobia to sunlight...

☐ 1. The attacks do **not** strike me suddenly, with no obvious cause or trigger. I know the cause and trigger is because I am in a specific, fearful, identifiable, situation, that being, when outside, I fear the sunlight will hurt me.

☐ 2. During an attack, I am **not** primarily frightened by my mental, emotional and physical symptoms; and the more severe my symptoms become, even though I am frightened by them, they are still not my primary concern. My primary concern is the sunlight.

☐ 3. During an attack, the reason why my symptoms do **not** primarily frighten me is because I **do** know what is happening to me, why it is happening, what exactly triggers my symptoms, how severe my symptoms will become and how long my symptoms will last, i.e. until I go inside out of the sunlight.

☐ 4. After an attack I **do** believe that the attacks and my symptoms during the attacks are only a by-product of me being so frightened.

5. After an attack, the reason why I do **not** worry over my symptoms is

☐ because I **do** know what's happening to me and why it is happening; namely, because of my inappropriate, high degree of fear towards a specific, identifiable stimulus; **sunlight**.

6. My general thoughts throughout the day are **not** primarily focused

☐ on matters relating to the attacks but rather, as I have a phobia to sunlight, my thoughts throughout the day are, to some degree, focused on my fear of going into the sunlight.

7. There **are** specific places and/or situations where I feel so susceptible

☐ to the attacks that, as a direct consequence, I deliberately avoid, i.e. the **outdoors**.

☐ 8. I do **not** 'live in fear' of being struck down again by either the attacks or the symptoms that come with the attacks but rather, as I have a phobia to sunlight, I **do** fear going into the sunlight.

☐ 9. I do **not** fear that, sooner or later, the attacks and the symptoms that come with the attacks will cause me to experience something dire; such as a heart attack, a stroke or madness.

☐ 10. I **have** organised my life around avoiding going outdoors because I know it will trigger off an attack.

Panic attacks or agoraphobia

At this point many clients say to me, "I thought all panic attack sufferers experience panic everywhere; inside and outside. Therefore if a person only experiences panic outside, they must be agoraphobic."

The Oxford Dictionary defines agoraphobia as, AGORA: forum, public-place, public-square or market place. PHOBIA: morbid dread.

By that definition, anyone would conclude that every person who experiences a morbid dread of public places, public squares, market places or of any outside public place, are automatically agoraphobic. Not so!

As with any condition, not all sufferers experience the same symptoms, to the same degree, in the same set of circumstances. And whilst most panic attack sufferers do panic both inside and outside their home, many others do not: – some panic attack sufferers never panic at all, as long as their whole life is structured around avoiding them – some only panic when they feel trapped and restricted; usually whilst on buses, in lifts, in traffic, on airplanes, in supermarkets, on motorways, in a group of people, answering the door, on the phone, in the bath; the list is endless – some only panic when they feel aches, pains, twinges or bodily sensations to which they have associated with panic attacks – some only panic when they associate a person, place or thing to a previous panic attack – some never panic through the day but wake every night in full blown panic – and some only ever panic when outside...

Of those who do only ever panic when outside, there are again many variations: – some panic every time they are outside – others only when they are outside alone – others only when the outside is well populated – others only when they are outside and away from a wall or away from some other means of support – others only when they are at a certain landmark such as a particular gate, shop, building or house – and others only when they have reached a certain number of steps away from home or when home is out of sight (this list is also endless).

So whilst I do acknowledge those people who are agoraphobic, in its true sense and therefore have a morbid dread of external elements such as sunlight, rain, air and people because they believe those actual elements will hurt them. Panic attack sufferers do not have that same morbid dread. Panic attack sufferers experience a morbid dread of going outside because, when outside, they are then more likely to experience a wave of seemingly uncontrollable frenzied panic **of which, to them, there seems no obvious cause means of stopping or prevention.** Panic attack sufferers experience a morbid dread of going outside because they know they are more likely to experience a panic attack whilst outside: – whilst caught up in traffic – whilst trapped in a shop – whilst on the street but too far from home to make a quick dash to safety – whilst outside on an empty, deserted street with no one to run to for help – and whilst in a crowd of people, all laughing, gossiping, staring and blocking the way should a quick dash to safety be necessary.

Do you see? Although it is now commonplace to assume that when a person has a morbid dread of going/being outside they are automatically agoraphobic or suffering social phobia . The assumption is wrong! Indeed there are now possibly millions of people all thinking they are phobic and receiving phobia therapy when, in fact, they are not phobic at all but panic attack sufferers.

- Phobic attacks: Waves of frenzied panic, which the sufferer knows is directly due to their inappropriately high degree of fear towards a specific identifiable, fearful stimulus...**the fearful stimulus can be anything except the sensations attached to fear itself.**

The phobic person knows the cause of their attack and whilst they might live in fear of experiencing or being confronted by the thing they fear, they do not 'live in fear' of the attacks or their symptoms during the attacks. That is because the phobic person knows they have total control over the attacks, they know the cause of the attacks, they know how to stop the attacks and they know how to prevent other attacks from striking in the future.

• Panic attacks: **A self-perpetuating condition** of seemingly uncontrollable waves of frenzied panic, of which, to the sufferer, there seems no obvious cause, means of stopping or prevention.

The natural fear response to danger

The three conditions mentioned above are inappropriate fear responses to given situations. There is, of course, a fourth fear response that is not at all inappropriate but rather, it is completely appropriate. That is, the natural fear response to actual danger. For example...

If a person walking down the street is attacked by a wild dog and, as a **direct result** of that situation, they experience a wave of panic. As the panic was caused by an appropriately high degree of fear in such a highly dangerous situation, they experienced a natural fear response to danger.

If a non-swimmer is thrown into very deep water and, as a **direct result** of that situation, they experience a wave of panic. As the panic was caused by an appropriately high degree of fear in a highly dangerous situation, they experienced a natural fear response to danger.

As the two waves of panic mentioned above are completely different from anxiety attacks, panic attacks or phobic attacks, in as much as they are the appropriate responses to a real danger situation, it is not really necessary to elaborate further on them.

After reading the above...

• If you identify yourself as suffering with 'panic attacks' then continue to follow this programme; for it was purposely devised for you.
• If you identify yourself as suffering with 'anxiety attacks' then continue to read this book for it will help you to understand stress, the effects of stress, how to calm yourself during a period of stress and how to protect yourself from ever suffering panic attacks in the future.
• If you identify yourself as suffering with 'phobic attacks' then, again, continue to read this book for it will help you to understand stress, the

effects of stress, how to calm yourself during a period of stress and how to protect yourself in the future. In addition, please consult your doctor as soon as possible to discuss your symptoms further where, hopefully, you will be referred to an appropriate therapist.

• If you do not identify with any of the above conditions then please, go to your medical doctor to discuss your condition further.

To move forward, you need to look back – once

If you now recognise yourself as suffering panic attacks, then I absolutely promise you, recovery really is there to be found. However, as suffering panic attacks is such a lonely and isolating experience, we must now look back and bring into the light your journey from your first attack up to the present-day. If you don't take this opportunity to look back, your long-term recovery from panic attacks could be hindered.

When you read the following section, I hope you identify yourself many times, by doing so, both your conscious and subconscious mind will more readily release all your inner feelings of isolation.

———————————

Your Likely Path Into
Panic Attacks

Your panic began...

Stability, balance, harmony, familiarity, tradition and knowing what to expect, are all the cornerstones of 'life,' from where we can then choose to add the excitement of impulsiveness, unpredictability and irregularity. However some time ago, you experienced a period of mental, emotional and/or physical instability and disharmony severe enough to put your bodily system under stress. And whilst your body might have initially carried the stress without too much effort, eventually the stress became too much and you then experienced the related symptoms of stress, which were unexpected and unfamiliar to you, and which caused you concern.

Now, there are as many causes of stress as there are people who suffer it, so for me to attempt to pinpoint the exact cause of your particular stress is impossible. However experience dictates that your initial stress was likely to have been...

- a mental, emotional and/or physical **strain**
- a mental, emotional and/or physical **shock**
- a **hormonal imbalance**
- a chemical or **drug related** condition

Strain

General: – raising a young family – a bereavement – living through a violent or broken relationship – being either the guilty or innocent party in betrayal – having a disruptive family member – carrying the burden of a secret – noisy neighbours – moving house – losing or falling out with a friend – guilt – becoming overly excited (happy or sad) – an unexpected event (happy or sad) – or going through any major life changing event.

Financial: – mounting debts – making a bad investment – needing to live within a very strict, low budget – the strains of Christmas – paying or not receiving child maintenance payments – tax or benefit problems, etc.

Career: – having an overlarge work load – working to deadlines – working too long hours – no mental freedom – having a difficult work colleague or management – a change of career – boredom – redundancy or retirement and so on.

Health related: – worrying over your own or someone else's health – being over tired – experiencing a sudden mental, emotional or physical symptom – being pre or post natal – having too high or low blood pressure or blood sugar – dieting – enduring either a chronic or acute illness, pain, infection or disability – having a surgical operation.

Shock
Such as: – an accident – a burglary – finding a bodily lump – the sudden need of a medical operation – the sudden death of a loved one – or any sudden event that could shock your mental, emotional or physical system.

Hormonal imbalance
Adolescence: considered to be between 11 years and 16 years.
Pre-natal: from conception to giving birth.
Post-natal: considered to be from giving birth to 18 months afterwards.
Menopausal: generally considered to be between 40 to 55 years but can be much sooner or later. Ovary removal can also cause the menopause.

Chemical or drug related
Such as: – drug dependency – side effects from a substance – introducing or withdrawing from any type of tranquillising or stimulating element, i.e. alcohol, cigarettes, prescription or illegal drugs, certain caffeine loaded drinks and so on.

The 'duration' of your initial stress could have been a few intense days, a number of weeks, many months or it could have slowly built over a few years. But whatever the duration of your initial stress, it built to where your symptoms of stress developed significantly and your first attack struck.

The 'time' when your first attack struck might have been, as you would expect, during a period of very high stress. Or (like the soldier who battles bravely through a war situation but, on returning to the safety of home he/she then suffers with Post Traumatic Stress Syndrome) your symptoms may have struck up to a year after your period of stress had eased. If so, the symptoms might have come as a real shock to you, especially if your life was then comparatively peaceful.

The 'location' of your first attack might have been anywhere: – at work – on the street – in a supermarket – on a motorway – in your home

– in your bed – on holiday or just afterwards – or anywhere and at any time, day or night.

Your 'symptoms' during your first attack might have been any one or numerous of those mentioned previously: – nausea – blurred vision – tight throat/choking sensation – racing/banging/jumping/fluttering heart – stomach churning – breathlessness – tingling limbs – numbness – stiff limbs – profuse bodily sweating – body shakes – buckling legs – pain in head, chest, in one particular limb or throughout your whole body – dizziness and/or feeling faint – hot flushes – a feeling of claustrophobia or agoraphobia – feeling unreal and/or detached from life – and/or having an overwhelming sense of panic, doom or danger.

And the 'severity' of your symptoms would have been obvious on some level: – so mild, you completely dismissed them – strong enough to have caused you concern – so strong you rushed to your doctor/hospital truly believing you were about to die – or so severe you put yourself to bed and have stayed there ever since.

As time passed...
Once your first attack had eased, you might not have had another one since but you have lived in the fear of it happening again. Or within hours, days or weeks of the first attack a second one struck, causing you to take the matter much more seriously than before. Even so, if you are a typical panic attack sufferer, you would have done your best to dismiss your concerns believing you could fight them off. But as the days and weeks passed and the attacks became more frequent and severe, your thoughts would have increasingly become drawn towards every element of the attacks, causing you to worry all the more.

As time passed, if you were lucky enough to have had a loving, caring, supportive relative or friend then you are likely to have confided in them, telling them of your confusion and fear. And if their words of reassurance were able to distract your mind from worrying then you might have averted much suffering. However, if you did not have anyone to confide in then you probably went to great lengths to hide the fact from people that you were having a 'mind problem,' especially if you thought that, should your condition become common knowledge then everyone would surely think you were going crazy, which could have put your social standing, domestic status and employment at great risk.

If panic attacks affected you slightly then you might have continued your life fairly normally, albeit with the help of a 'pocket crutch,' perhaps in the form of a couple of tranquillisers, a sip of water, 'a nip of the hard stuff,' smelling salts, chewy sweets, a picture, your baby's rattle or similar. And whether you actually used your pocket crutch many times or not at all, it would have been your constant emotional support through your days and nights. Indeed just knowing your pocket crutch was there and believing it would help you if needed, might have been enough to have eased your mind, reduced your anxiety, taken pressure off you and lessened your likelihood to panic.

As the days and weeks passed, if your pocket crutch happened to let you down once or twice, causing you to question its effectiveness, or if the attacks themselves became more frequent or severe. Then, sooner or later, in an attempt to avoid doing anything that could trigger an attack, you might have devised a 'plan of avoidance' of every place, thing, situation and body function that you suspected might have been a trigger. In which case, you then dramatically arranged your whole life to where you never exerted yourself and no longer lived your normal life: you no longer – went outside – to work – on motorways – on busy roads – on airplanes – in lifts – in open or confined spaces – climbed stairs – walked fast – made love – played with your children – worked hard or fast – or even laughed heartily.

If you were in the domestic and financial position to succumb to the temptation of 'avoidance' then, although you might have managed to keep the attacks to a minimum, you possibly and inadvertently made yourself a prisoner to them.

Of course, if you were not in the position to devise a plan of avoidance, so you had no other choice but to daily force yourself to live a 'normal' life then, in all probability, the attacks intensified in both frequency and severity to where, sooner or later, they were striking you anywhere and at any time.

And so, whether you were able to avoid 'life' or whether you were not, if the attacks continued, although you would have courageously fought them with all your might, eventually they would have got hold of you to where you found yourself living in continuous high fear, broken only by waves of sheer terror, and all the while you believing the next attack would surely kill you or send you insane.

As the reign of panic attacks continued, sooner or later, your mind and body would have begun to feel the tremendous strain of living in such a highly distressed state. Consequently, along with your symptoms of terror, you probably developed other very confusing and frightening mental, physical and emotional aches, pains, discomforts, disorders and weird thoughts, which almost certainly convinced you, even more, that your symptoms were not merely symptoms of stress but evidence that you were then suffering with something more sinister: – a brain tumour or a brain haemorrhage – heart disease or an imminent heart attack – cancer – blindness – neurosis – insanity – dementia – depression – Parkinson's disease – allergies – or a condition so deep-seated or rare, it could neither be found or identified. And, of course, once loaded with such worries you were then likely to have deteriorated quickly, lost all hope and began to experience the sense of loneliness and isolation that, although quite normal for panic attack sufferers, is far beyond the comprehension of most people.

Your doctor, therapy, medication

Somewhere along your path into panic attacks, whether sooner or later, despite your possible embarrassment and need for privacy, you probably sought professional help; which was most likely your medical doctor...

And so, on initially visiting your doctor, you might have been offered medication but if so, my expectation for it helping you is not hopeful:– some doctors see the panic attack sufferer very distressed and diagnose depression – some doctors see the panic attack sufferer very stressed and diagnose anything from anxiety to mania – some doctors see the panic attacks sufferer with physical complaints and diagnose physical illness – and some doctors see the panic attack sufferer as a hypochondriac. And as every doctor will prescribe medication to suit his/her own diagnosis, the likely medication prescribed to you could have been anything.

As the weeks passed, if your visits to your doctor became much more frequent, then he/she probably offered you treatment or therapy but again, my expectation for it helping you is not hopeful because the treatment or therapy offered to panic attack sufferers can also be variable: – general de-sensitisation therapy – flooding therapy – three day home or hospital supervised sleep – stronger or different medication to that prescribed previously – being admitted into hospital for observation – attending a therapeutic day centre – home visits by a psychiatric nurse – deep seated psychological counselling – "Try going away for a holiday" – or "Come back in three months time and we'll see if you feel any better."

After months of seeking help from your doctor and/or therapists, if all their suggestions of help had failed you, especially if the panic attacks and your symptoms of stress were becoming all-consuming. Whereas during the early days of visiting your doctor, you hoped that no real illness would be found, you were then likely to have hoped and prayed one would. At least then you would have had a diagnosis that you could have identify with. But sadly, it is likely that no illness was found which, in turn, forced you to continue on your path of panic attacks alone. And even if your previous treatment, therapy or medication brought you a degree of relief, your overall stress level reduced and you found a degree of calm. Was it enough? Probably not! (This subject is discussed more in Step Four.)

Finally, I will add here that, as you continued on your path of panic attacks, although you were likely to have returned to your medical doctor many times, that didn't make you a soft or neurotic person, in fact quite the opposite. It did indicate, however, that you are an exceptionally brave person who was simply trying to determine: – the real cause of your suffering – what exactly you were up against – what help and information was available to you – and how you could help yourself. Yes my friend, you are very courageous indeed. (This subject also is discussed more in Step Four.)

Recurring bouts of panic attacks

You might be a person who previously experienced months or years of panic attacks and then, by whatever means, you found freedom. Then, after weeks, months or years of freedom, you again felt yourself being dragged back into panic attacks. In fact over the years, you might have experienced many bouts of panic attacks, initially being dragged into them, suffering them, finding freedom from them and again being dragged back into them. Each bout lasting weeks, months or years, your symptoms being exactly as before or completely different and the reason why they previously went was either known to you or, to your surprise, they simply disappeared on their own.

So, here you are, and whatever the cause of your previous attacks, whatever your symptoms were, however long you suffered them, whatever caused their disappearance, however long you were free and whatever the reason for their return, you are again suffering them and, yet again, looking for your way back to freedom.

It's so easy to become lost in it all

After all your treatments, therapies and medication, if you are still not totally free of panic attacks and your financial and/or domestic position still allows you, then you are now probably looking into every form of conventional and complimentary practise you can afford. And in doing so, you are still able to cling on to some level of hope. On the other hand, if you are in neither the financial or domestic position to keep on looking into other forms of help, particularly if you are desperately trying to cope alone, without any form of help whatsoever then, sadly, you must now be feeling so very desolate.

Befrienders

Over the years, I have worked with some sufferers who were desperately trying to cope with panic attacks and symptoms of stress without any form of kindness, help or support at all. I have also worked with some sufferers who did have a family but sadly, were anything but loving. Indeed, over the years, and actually in my presence, a number of 'so called' loved ones have unashamedly displayed their frustration at the inconvenience of it all, making the sufferer feel very lonely indeed. And I have worked with some sufferers whose family and/or friends were great, wonderful; steadfastly standing by them, supporting them, holding hands and displaying abundant, unconditional love and loyalty. Yet even then, despite the love, loyalty and support given by true family and friends, unless they genuinely understood panic attacks, then the friends and family felt absolutely helpless, and at their wits end, not knowing how to help.

And so, whether you are trying to cope alone, or whether you have family who are becoming a little frustrated with you or whether your family are still loving and supportive to you. Please read the following chapter: – it will remind you that a trouble shared can often be a trouble halved – it will offer a few suggestions on how you might approach finding a befriender – and it will give your befriender a few suggestions on how, in the short-term, they can help you.

Befrienders

When 'life' gets too much for us, to then have someone to turn to is very important, as the human spirit is always strengthened by love, care and kindness. Therefore do you have a loving friend, family member or counsellor? If not, this might be the time to consider finding one, even if only until you are no longer experiencing panic attacks.

And if your response to that request is to say, "Definitely not, my thoughts are so frightening I can never tell anyone. My fears are so weird I am far too embarrassed to tell a single person for fear they will think me crazy or I am much too ill to be bothered with all that." I really do understand your concern. Even so, although you might now be feeling ill, embarrassed and perhaps a little ashamed for suffering panic attacks and although you might have worked very hard to keep them a secret. It is because your symptoms might be extreme, your thoughts might be weird and frightening, you might be feeling ill, exhausted and your perspective might now be out of focus and distorted…that you need a befriender.

And realise, the objective of a befriender is not for you to tell them your thoughts and fears then they, in turn, force their own opinions onto you. Absolutely not! They are there for you; happy to support you, to give you time, to listen without judgement, to offer their shoulder to lean and cry on, to lift your spirit, to empathise with your pain, to be amazed at your courage, to feel saddened when you fall and to feel joy when you succeed.

When choosing your befriender

When choosing your befriender you need to be very careful: **don't** ask: – a friend or family member just because they are nearest at hand – a doctor or priest, just because they are of a caring profession – an intellectual, just because they are intelligent – a self-opinionated person, just because they seem to know everything – or a person who always seems in a hurry; as no time for themselves suggests no time for you.

The person **to** ask is someone special: – wholly trustworthy – sensitive and empathic to your fears and vulnerabilities – capable of listening to you without judgement – with whom you feel totally comfortable and at ease – who will have time for you whenever you need it and for as long as you need it – and is gifted with common sense.

If you don't know such a person or if you feel that your fears are so extreme and bizarre you could never voice them face to face with anyone, therefore you would rather talk to someone who does not know you, or is totally detached from you or to whom you don't have to give your name. Then consider contacting one of the well-known organisations such as MIND or No Panic. And whilst the Samaritans are not necessarily experts in dealing with severe symptoms of stress, they are, without doubt, a most caring, compassionate, empathic and confidential organisation.

1st meeting

Before meeting your chosen person, think for a moment: What if, before you developed panic attacks, a friend suddenly blurted out to you that she thought she was going insane or that she believed she had cancer but no one believed her? How would you have felt? I think having such a thing said to you might have been quite daunting.

So when you are sure in your choice of person, go slowly. During your first meeting just explain that you need to talk to them about something which is both important to you and of which you ask to be held in the strictest confidence. Next, arrange a time and place which is private and conducive to you both. There is nothing more off-putting as when trying to describe one's most private worries and fears with young children running about, or babies crying, dogs barking or a family member of your befriender is sitting in the same room watching television.

2nd meeting

During this meeting, don't overwhelm your chosen person by blurting out everything you wish them to know all in one long verbal outburst, as that too can be very daunting. In-depth discussions are better left until later on. At this meeting just explain that you have recently been under stress from which you are currently experiencing symptoms that they might find a little difficult to understand. Ask them to read this book and then to consider if they feel able to support you through recovery. Arrange to meet then again as soon as possible then leave the matter there.

3rd meeting

Having approached the matter slowly, hopefully your chosen person will not feel overwhelmed and will gladly become your befriender. If so, use this meeting to arrange the times and places where you will both meet in the future. If you are suffering severely and feel too ill to read this book yourself then tell your befriender and arrange times for them to either read this book with you or to you but never have them read this book instead of you, leaving them to explain their interpretation to you.

If your chosen person should feel they cannot help you then try not to feel too hurt. It is, after all, a big responsibility and you don't really know what problems they might have in their life. So obviously tell them you hold no ill feeling, then sadly you will need to choose someone else.

Subsequent meetings

If your befriender is to fully understand your worries and fears you will need to be completely open and honest with them. Therefore during your subsequent meetings, perhaps as you go through this book with them, explain how you are feeling as explicitly as you can, telling them all your frightening thoughts, worries and fears.

Once you start to voice your symptoms and fears, there are a few things to be aware of…

- Your befriender might have many questions to ask you, if so, try not to shy away from giving a full response. Likewise, if you have any questions, ask them. If you have any queries, raise them. If you have any doubts, voice them. And don't forget, it is not your befriender's task to give you their opinions, it is their task to help you to follow my advice. Never forget, **they** are there to help **you**.

- If along with panic attacks you are also suffering with seemingly weird symptoms of stress, then, when speaking to your befriender, try not to feel hurt or angry if they gasp with amazement, smile or try to hide a giggle. Remember, your thoughts and possibly your perspective on life, might be distorted and seem quite bizarre to someone else. So just continue to explain your thoughts and fears the best you can, in the knowledge that despite your befriender being taken by surprise, they really do wish to help and support you.

- When speaking to your befriender you might become overwhelmingly tired to where you have to abandon the meeting until another day. If so, that is perfectly normal, your overtiredness is simply due to your relief at finally having someone to talk to and emotionally lean on.

- The very fact of voicing your symptoms might actually energize you to a point where you feel both totally exhilarated and inclined to talk for hours. If so, bear in mind that, due to the nature and intensity of the meeting, your befriender might be feeling completely exhausted.

- Your befriender might feel somewhat overwhelmed to where they feel the need for professional reassurance and support. If so, although you might prefer to cling onto your privacy, I genuinely feel, in this instance and to benefit you both, you do need to agree with your befriender, whilst, of course, giving your opinion as to which adviser you prefer them to go to, i.e. your doctor, MIND, No Panic, the Samaritans or a trusted member of your family who might not have had the time to be your befriender but is very happy to help you nonetheless.

16 points of advice to all befrienders

To help a person through panic attacks, particularly if their suffering is severe, can be exhausting, challenging, yet deeply rewarding. In fact, during my last meetings with both client and befriender, many befrienders say how the whole experience had proven to be one of the most rewarding experiences of their life, from which their quality of life was made all the richer for the experience.

When the sufferer is experiencing an actual panic attack...
but only during steps one, two and three
1.   Hold direct eye contact with the sufferer throughout until the panic has eased, thereby reassuring them that you really are 'with' them.
2.   Breathe with them whilst taking them through the slow count of – in, two, three – out, two, three, four.
3.   Every two to three breaths give 5–10 second reassurance then return to breathing with them.
4.   During the attack, the sufferer will feel compelled to move quickly, but quick movement will stimulate their state of panic and create even more symptoms. So try to encourage stillness or, at least, slow movement, ask them to sit down, lean against something or stand still.
5.   From Step Four, leave the sufferer to deal with their panic attacks on their own, as then they will know how.

Generally
6.   Read this whole book as soon as possible, then read it again with or to the sufferer.

Regarding the sufferer...
7.   If they are acting strangely, don't constantly watch them, as that will put pressure on them to act 'normally' or feel as if they are trapped inside a goldfish bowl with all their problems on full view.

8. If they are feeling worthless, helpless, useless, vulnerable, insecure, a nuisance, an irritation and/or a burden...reassure them as much as you can and try not to let them see the 'inconvenience' of it all, as that will only reinforce their negative feelings of guilt to where they feel the need to continuously apologise to you.

9. If their thoughts are extreme and, to them, even the smallest problem seems a matter of life or death...then take from their shoulders as many problems as you can, even if the problems seem insignificant to you. And throughout, offer them reassurance by way of short, factual and truthful explanations.

10. If they are unable to involve themselves in any financial and domestic matters they will now be feeling somewhat useless, of no value and unlovable...so constantly offer them reassurances that you are not with them out of duty but out of care for them.

11. If their emotions seem erratic: – one moment their life feels tolerable then the next it does not – one moment they feel confident and even hopeful of recovery then the next they don't – one moment their fears feel bearable then the next they don't – one moment they know you really love them then the next they don't – and one moment they arrange to do something, go somewhere or meet someone then the next moment, or even at the last minute, they cancel the whole thing. Try not to feel angry with them. Believe me, such actions are hurting them far more than it is inconveniencing you.

12. If they are very frightened to venture outside but really wish to try then, during Steps One, Two, Three and, if absolutely necessary, at the beginning of Step Four of this programme, when outside with them, distraction is, by far, the best action to take. So talk to them and point out interesting things that they are inclined to miss. But if they wish to be quiet and free to focus their mind onto this programme then give them the mental space to do so. And if they wish to be left alone for a little while then make an arrangement to meet them moments later at a specific time and place and please **stick to it, to the second.**

13. Try to empathise, be kind and offer lots of praise (believe me it is deserved) also try not to sound patronising or show pity; to show care is not to display pity and pity is rarely appreciated.

14. If you are a close relative or spouse of the sufferer, you might now be shouldering much responsibility. Your workload might be heavy, your life might be difficult, your future might be uncertain and your life might seem to be falling apart. As a result, your exasperation towards the whole situation may sometimes manifest as anger towards

your loved one which, in turn, will obviously put you both under an even greater strain. Therefore throughout this difficult period for you both, whilst still recognising that your loved one is not malingering but is an exceptionally courageous person, look after yourself. Know that you are doing the very best you can. Accept that you need time for yourself; to breathe, think, 'live' and 'be normal.' Understand that to get through this period, you must prioritise your life by putting simplicity, love, care, gentleness, understanding and all your needs before your wants.

15. If you go out to work, please realise, to the sufferer, the four walls of home can often be their prison, where time spent alone is filled with hours, days, weeks, months and years of dire loneliness and fear. So if your loved one begs you to stay at home with them, know they are feeling extremely vulnerable, overwhelmed and greatly in need of reassurance. In which case, ask for and be willing to accept help: – arrange for someone to take your place as a companion when you are at work, perhaps they could – stay in your home to be on hand should your loved one need reassurance and support – accompany your loved one to the shops or for a walk – or simply be on hand for your loved one to either phone or run to if their anxiety gets too much for them. But in whatever way you do it, put both yourself and your loved one at the centre of your universe. After all, there is no point having money, keeping your boss happy, living in denial and 'keeping a brave face on things' if your loved one is actually drowning.

16. An unexpected kiss, cuddle, flower from the garden, cup of tea, either a verbal or written poem, five minutes of quality time, a gentle caring word, an apology when you were not in the wrong or even a smile when a frown is easier, all costs nothing but says so much.

Re-cap:
To Take Your First Step
To Freedom...

1. If you are experiencing any symptoms, whether or not they are on my list...

   a) Go to your medical doctor and request a full medical examination, including all related tests.

   b) When your results come back and show no irregularities, if you are not fully reassured then ask about the possibility of a second opinion.

   c) When your results from the second doctor come back and show no irregularities, if you are still unsure then ask to see a specialist.

   d) Once your medical examination, the related tests, both your doctors and the specialist confirm that your symptoms are nothing other than stress related then, rather than continuing to worry, ask yourself one question, "Am I stressed?" If so, your stress will have a cause and effect and, to one degree or another, you will have stress related symptoms. And whilst your stress related symptoms might be very distressing, excruciatingly painful, totally debilitating, extremely weird and very frightening, they are merely the normal, natural symptoms of high stress; nothing more. And being symptoms of stress, despite their severity, they can be controlled, reduced and totally eliminated. And even if your symptoms are not on my list but have nevertheless been diagnosed as stress related, there is still every probability they are indeed symptoms of stress and as such, they also can be controlled, reduced and totally eliminated.

2. Ensure that you understand the differences between anxiety attacks, panic attacks and phobic attacks.

3. Be assured from my coverage of, 'Your Likely Path Into Panic Attacks,' that millions of people have walked this path before you, including myself, and fully recovered.

4. Whilst being totally honest with yourself, determine whether or not you need a befriender. If so, find one as soon as possible.

5. Whether you have read this step yourself or someone has read it with you or to you, do not have your befriender reading it and then giving their interpretation of it to you.

6. If you had any difficulty understanding any part of this step then please read the relevant section or sections again and perhaps a further time. However, after your third attempt, if you still have difficulty understanding any part of it or if you don't identify with it, then I urge you to discuss the matter further with both your doctor and befriender.

7. If you have not yet read, understood and thought about the contents in this step then you have not yet taken it.

8. Once you have read, understood and thought about the information in this step then move onto Step Two.
    Step Two is the foundation of recovery: – it covers the six basic elements of arousal – it explains how arousal creates panic attacks – it details how arousal creates physical symptoms of stress – and for those suffering nervous exhaustion or breakdown, it explains the potentially weird and very frightening prolonged mental symptoms of stress.

Step Two

Understand yourself... and thereby understand
the fundamentals of what's happening to you

Arousal in the making

Arousal creating Panic Attacks

Arousal creating Prolonged Physical Symptoms of Stress

Arousal creating Prolonged Mental Symptoms of Stress

To take your second step to freedom

Arousal In The Making

Understanding this chapter is so crucial to recovery from panic attacks that I have purposely structured each page and the text on each page in such a way that it is very easy to read and understand. Having said that, when you first begin to read the following information you will probably think, "What on earth has this to do with me?" Even so, keep reading anyway because, I absolutely assure you, it has everything to do with you and panic attacks.

The fundamental objective of all forms of life is survival; survival of the self, therefore the species. As a consequence, life, however basic (from a fly to an elephant, from a blade of grass to a tree and from sea plankton to mankind) has its own inbuilt survival responses. And whenever each life-form senses a threat to its well-being then its own inbuilt survival responses automatically become stimulated: cats arch their back and their fur stands on end to make them look bigger and more threatening, hedgehogs roll into spiky balls for defence and 'man' has the ability to perform extraordinary feats of resilience and strength. Indeed records show that during life-or-death danger, in 'his' attempt to save life, 'man' has scaled incredibly high walls, jumped wide ravines, lifted heavy vehicles and even after an accident involving an amputation, 'man' has walked or crawled over a mile carrying his own amputated limb. We now need to look at how 'man' is able to perform such incredible feats of strength...

The six basic elements in the chain of 'high' arousal

Please see Fig 1: When we 'sense' an imminent threat to our life → a subconscious flash thought of danger automatically alerts the brain and triggers off arousal → immediately, the primitive part of the brain takes over → the stimulating part of the nervous system becomes dominant thereby stimulating all organs and body functions involved in saving life, i.e. lungs, heart, muscles, skin, adrenal glands → the adrenal glands produce and secrete more adrenalin directly into the bloodstream, adding its own massive power to further stimulate all organs involved in saving life → the whole bodily system is now stimulated and ready for action → and the whole process can take as little as 15 hundredths of one second.

Fig 1

WHEN WE SENSE AN IMMINENT THREAT TO OUR LIFE

1 - A *subconscious* flash thought of imminent danger alerts the brain

2 - *Immediately* the primitive part of of the brain takes over

3 - The stimulating part of the nervous system becomes dominant

4 - Adrenal glands produce and secrete more adrenalin

5 - The whole bodily system becomes stimulated and and ready for action

6 - All taking as little as 15 hundredths of one second

A little deeper

We now need to look a little deeper into each of the 6 basic elements of high arousal. And I know that, due to your symptoms and panic attacks, you can hardly think straight. But be reassured: – I have purposefully made all the information in this section exceptionally easy to read and understand – most of the elements are only one or two pages long – no piece of information will frighten you – when reading through each element, take your time – and after each element take a break to allow the information to register in both your conscious and subconscious mind. And so, lets begin…

1. A subconscious flash thought of danger automatically alerts the brain

It is absolutely impossible for any person to experience fear (including the terror of panic attacks) without them first having a negative thought. And I know you will think, "Well I must be an exception to that rule because my panic attacks strike without any thought at all. One moment I am not in panic then the next moment I am in full-blown frenzied panic." You are wrong! Just continue to read and you will see.

Imagine, as you now sit reading this book, a friend of yours (let's call him Tom) quietly creeps up behind you then, without warning, crashes two cymbals together. What would be your immediate response? I think it fair to assume that you would jump, cry out, your heart would beat faster, your mind would feel dazed, your body would tremble slightly and, in general, you would feel quite shaken for a few seconds.

But think about it. What really happened? One moment you were quietly reading then the next moment you were experiencing real mental and physical sensations of arousal. Why? You were not hit. You were not hurt. You were not even touched at all. So **what** had the power to suddenly create such real mental and physical sensations of fear? I will tell you precisely what it was. You had a thought! You will not remember the thought, you will not even remember having had a thought at all. It all happened so quickly. But you did! You had a **subconscious flash thought of imminent danger** which automatically alerted your brain, triggered off the chain of arousal and threw you from peace to panic.

RE-CAP: Thought
No conscious thought is required to trigger off arousal, as just one subconscious flash thought of imminent danger is enough in itself.

THE CHAIN OF HIGH AROUSAL, UP TO NOW
When we 'sense' an imminent threat to our life → **a subconscious flash thought of danger automatically alerts the brain and triggers arousal.**

2. Immediately the primitive part of the brain takes over

Once a subconscious flash thought of imminent danger automatically alerts the brain, a certain part of the brain then comes into play. The simplest way to illustrate the relevance between that part of the brain and panic attacks is to explain it as follows...

Primitive man

When man first walked the earth, by current standards he had little intelligence, vocabulary, tools or weapons. So whenever he faced danger (whether from ferocious beasts of prey, other men trying to loot, pillage or kill him or even when the force of nature was striking at him) the only protection available to him was his own inbuilt survival responses. Having said that, the survival responses. of primitive man would have been useless if they had made him feel timid, sleepy, calm, peaceful and relaxed. Therefore the inbuilt **emotional** survival response of 'primitive man' was for him to **feel** the emotions of **anger** or **fear**.

Anger is obviously aggressive; it encourages feelings of irritation, rage, antagonism and warrior-like. As a result, anger was the automatic survival response of primitive man to those situations where he felt he could overcome the threat. **Fear** is submissive; it encourages feelings of anxiety, trepidation, intimidation and dread. As a result, fear was the automatic survival response of primitive man to those situations where he felt he could be overwhelmed.

The feelings of anger and fear were the emotional 'first line' protectors of primitive man. However, when he faced danger and his only chance of survival was either to fight and overcome the threat or runaway and escape it, him just feeling anger or fear would have been completely useless, because **then** he needed the **physical strength** to run away or stand and fight.

Therefore whenever primitive man 'sensed' an imminent threat to his life, along with feeling anger or fear, his automatic, inbuilt, survival responses would make extra energy.

Anger and fear are opposite emotions therefore one might assume that the automatic inbuilt energy making mechanism of primitive man would have worked opposite for anger than it would for fear or that anger would have made a different type of energy to that of fear. Not so! Again look at the lifestyle of primitive man.

53

To survive, primitive man needed to hunt for food. But life being as it was, whenever he hunted, within a split second, he often became the hunted; the stalker became the stalked. And during such moments of high danger, his survival would have been impossible if he had then to make split second, clear-cut decisions determining whether he was the hunter or the hunted or whether he felt angry or afraid.

Therefore, to aid survival, whenever primitive man 'sensed' an imminent threat to his life, his feelings of **both** anger and fear would independently and automatically trigger and sustain the one same raw primitive energy.

And note, the word is 'sensed.' The body and brain of primitive man did not require detailed facts of a given situation before they responded and triggered arousal, as the time spent acquiring such detailed information would have taken time that he might not have had. For primitive man, the speed at which his survival responses kicked-in was absolutely crucial! No time for conscious thought! No time to ponder over all the given facts of a potentially dangerous situation! Absolutely not! In fact, the mind of primitive man was kicked into full-blown arousal on only split-second, splintered, partial information. The brain of primitive man only had to sense potential danger and the might of his whole arousal responses would become automatically and immediately triggered **without the need for conscious thought**.

Modern day man
'We' (modern day man) are very different to primitive man. Our brain has the ability to rationalise far beyond that of primitive man. 'We' are cultured, civilised and intellectual. The safety of our life does not depend solely on our physical ability to run or fight and comparatively speaking, we have evolved into quite mature, cultured, civilised, intellectual, rational beings. Having said that, don't feel too superior, for it must be said that 'we' and primitive man are not two separate species, as deep within our modern, intellectual brain are still the workings, emotions and instincts of primitive man.

Primitive man saving the life of modern-day man
When we are going about our daily life and sense an imminent threat, the primitive part of our brain is triggered and **immediately becomes dominant over the thinking part,** instantly we feel extreme anger or fear, our body makes the extra energy and we become mentally and physically equipped for danger...

54

Imagine you are about to cross over a road, you look both ways to ensure your safety then proceed to cross. However when about halfway across the road, you suddenly hear the thunderous noise of an engine and a screeching of wheels. Instinctively you turn and, seeing a vehicle almost on top of you, within a split second, you find yourself on the pavement, shaken but safe.

Question: In such a life-threatening situation, which part of your brain saved you? Was it the modern intellectual part? Did you rationally think, "This wagon is going to hit me, so in an attempt to save my life, I will calmly and logically consider all my options. Should I jump to the right or to the left? Should I take off my nice new coat or keep it on but risk getting it dirty? Should I put my parcel down on the ground in case it gets broken or hold on to it in case it gets stolen?" Of course not, as such calm and rational thinking whilst in actual life-or-death danger would distract your mind from the urgent task of saving your life.

So although the 'modern' part of our brain has the ability to produce rational, intellectual thought, making it one of our greatest assets and vital for 'modern day' life. Whenever a life threatening situation is upon us, we then don't need rational, intellectual thought but rather, we do need the **raw power** of primitive energy to help us fight or run from dangers way.

In short, whenever we sense a threat to our life (or to the life of a loved one) we then don't need the rational, intellectual, modern part of our brain but we certainly do need the extra energy making primitive part.

RE-CAP: The primitive element
The fundamental aim of all forms of life is survival. To aid survival, all life has inbuilt **automatic** survival responses. Whenever 'primitive man' faced an imminent threat to life, he immediately felt either anger or fear; each independently making and sustaining raw primitive energy. 'We' (modern day man) have evolved from primitive man and although calm, intellectual, rational thought is one of our greatest assets. When faced with a threat, especially if it is a matter of life or death, we then need the **raw power** of primitive man to help us either fight or run from dangers way.

THE CHAIN OF HIGH AROUSAL: UP TO NOW
When we 'sense' an imminent threat to our life → a subconscious flash thought of danger automatically alerts the brain and triggers off arousal → **immediately, the primitive part of our brain takes over.**

3. The stimulating part of the nervous system becomes dominant

The nervous system is a finely balanced mechanism, which continuously works to maintain the whole bodily balance.

Please see Fig 2: As you see, the nervous system is divided into two basic sections; the voluntary and the involuntary.

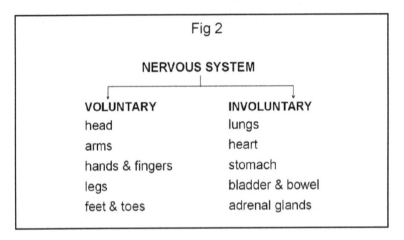

Fig 2

NERVOUS SYSTEM

VOLUNTARY	INVOLUNTARY
head	lungs
arms	heart
hands & fingers	stomach
legs	bladder & bowel
feet & toes	adrenal glands

The **voluntary** section of the nervous system is responsible for all movement over which we have direct control. So when we consciously nod our head, move our fingers, bend our knees or wiggle our toes we do so at will, via the voluntary section of our nervous system.

The **involuntary** section of the nervous system (sometimes called the autonomic) controls the life-support system which, along with many other organs and functions, consists of the lungs, heart, stomach, bladder/bowel and adrenals, and does so automatically, without the need for conscious thought.

Please see Fig 3: As you see, the involuntary section of the nervous system is itself divided into two parts: the **parasympathetic** and the **sympathetic**. These two parts control the **speed** at which the involuntary nervous system works...hence; they control the **speed** of our heartbeat, breathing, digestion, skin temperature, bladder and bowel function and adrenalin production.

When we feel calm, both the parasympathetic and sympathetic work in balance. But when we feel angry or afraid, the sympathetic then becomes uppermost (in control), causing the stimulation of all organs and body functions involved in saving life. The greater the anger/fear, all the faster the sympathetic stimulates the life-support organs.

- As the **parasympathetic** holds the life-support organs at bay, I call it the **parasympathetic peacemaker**.
- As the **sympathetic** stimulates the life-support organs, I call it the **sympathetic stimulator**.

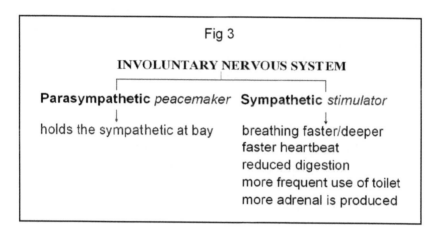

RE-CAP: The nervous system
The nervous system can be divided into two sections, the **voluntary** and the **involuntary**.

The involuntary section itself can be divided into two parts: the parasympathetic peacemaker and the sympathetic stimulator.

When we feel calm, both the parasympathetic and sympathetic work in balance. But when we feel angry or afraid, the sympathetic then becomes uppermost, encouraging the stimulation of all organs and body functions involved in saving life. The greater the anger or fear, all the more the sympathetic stimulates the life-support organs and bodily functions.

THE CHAIN OF HIGH AROUSAL: UP TO NOW
When we 'sense' an imminent threat to our life → a subconscious flash thought of danger automatically alerts the brain and triggers off arousal → immediately, the primitive part of our brain takes over → instantly, **the parasympathetic peacemaker relaxes its hold allowing the sympathetic stimulator to become dominant, thereby stimulating all organs and body functions involved in saving life; lungs, heart, skin, adrenals and so on.**

4. Adrenal glands produce and secrete
even more adrenalin into the body

Every thought creates a chemical reaction within the body and when thoughts are of either anger or fear, along with sympathetic stimulation, another stimulating force then comes into play. **Adrenalin!** Adrenalin is a hormone (chemical) it is an ever present, white or pale brown, odourless, liquid substance. Within the body it is produced by the adrenal glands from which it is then secreted directly into the bloodstream. Outside the body it is produced synthetically then, when necessary, administered into the body. Adrenalin is a powerful stimulant, so powerful that during cardiac arrest, when administered, it can actually stimulate a cardiac response. That is the massive stimulating power of adrenalin!

Please see Fig 4: The organs noted are some of the main organs involved in life support...and **all are stimulated by adrenalin!** Look just above the kidneys and see the adrenal glands, see how they also are stimulated by adrenalin. Do you see? **Adrenalin stimulates the adrenal glands into producing more adrenalin.** ... The more adrenalin in your bloodstream, all the more it will kick your adrenal glands into producing more.

RE-CAP: Adrenalin

Adrenalin is a **very** powerful stimulant. Whilst a small amount is ever present within the body, when increased, it then kicks the named organs into working harder and faster; including the adrenal glands. The adrenal glands then produce more adrenalin, which itself kicks the named organs even harder and faster; including the adrenals. The adrenals then produce even more adrenalin...and on and on and on it goes.

THE CHAIN OF HIGH AROUSAL: UP TO NOW

When we 'sense' an imminent threat to our life → a subconscious flash thought of danger automatically alerts the brain and triggers off arousal → immediately, the primitive part of our brain takes over → instantly, the parasympathetic peacemaker relaxes its hold allowing the sympathetic stimulator to become dominant, thereby stimulating all organs and body functions involved in saving life; including the adrenal glands → **the adrenal glands produce and secrete more adrenalin into the bloodstream, adding its own massive power to even further stimulate all the organs and body functions involved in saving life; including the adrenal glands.**

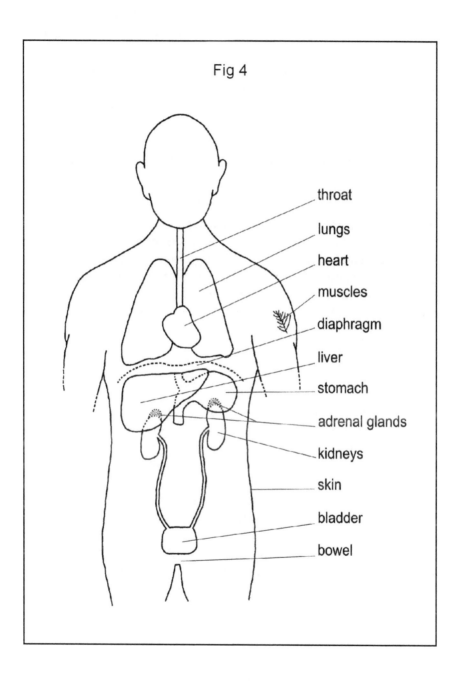

Fig 4

throat

lungs

heart

muscles

diaphragm

liver

stomach

adrenal glands

kidneys

skin

bladder

bowel

5. The whole bodily system
becomes stimulated and ready for action

When we sense a threat to our well-being, whether real or imagined, the body produces extra energy. To do that the organs involved in saving life need to work harder. To do that certain organs of the body need extra oxygen. Oxygen is carried by blood. So when we sense a threat to our well-being there is an **increased** blood flow to those parts of the body and brain that are involved in saving life and a **reduction** to those parts that are not. And whilst this whole 'speeding up' process is totally natural, the resulting mental, emotional and physical effects can be terrifying.

Emotional

When we sense a threat and become aroused, the primitive part of our brain becomes stimulated and we experience an **increase** of raw, primitive, animal-like tendencies. Therefore during periods of high arousal, we can quickly reach a point where the slightest word, glance, misunderstanding or disagreement will cause extreme feelings of anger or fear to where we become totally submissive and tearful or extremely argumentative and aggressive. Indeed an element of arousal that must be understood is the speed and intensity to which emotions of anger and fear can be felt.

Mental

When we **don't** sense a threat to our well-being we feel relaxed and at peace, the primitive part of our brain is not stimulated and the modern part of our brain is fully able to produce and receive calm, controlled, rational thought. So as we do not feel any degree of either anger or fear, we are quite able to go about our normal everyday tasks of life.

When we sense a **slight threat** to our well-being (whether real or imagined) we feel anxious, nervous, agitated and 'not quite with it,' the primitive part of our brain becomes slightly stimulated and the modern part of our brain becomes somewhat restricted; therefore we are slightly less able to produce and receive calm, controlled, rational thought. As a result, despite feeling 'not quite with it,' we are still able to go about our normal everyday tasks of life.

When we sense a **great threat** to our well-being (whether real or imagined) we feel frightened, the primitive part of our brain becomes significantly stimulated and the modern part of our brain becomes notably restricted; therefore we have difficulty producing calm, controlled, rational thought. As a result, we find it very difficult to go about our normal everyday tasks of modern life.

When we sense **actual life-or-death danger** (whether real or imagined) we feel terror struck and out of control, the primitive part of our brain becomes **highly stimulated** and the modern part of our brain becomes **severely restricted,** therefore we are unable to produce calm, controlled, rational thought. As a result, if we are then asked to add 2+2, whilst our mouths would open and words might come out, no controlled logic, rational thought would be possible. Causing us to hysterically reply similar to, "2+2, YES. 2+2 – OK, OK, JUST GIVE ME A MINUTE – 2+2 RIGHT – I'M OK, I'M OK, JUST GIVE ME A MINUTE – 2+2 RIGHT!" In short, we lose virtually all our mental control, making it impossible to go about our normal everyday tasks of modern life.

Physical
Dilation — made wider or more open
Contraction — made smaller or tighter

Blood supply...
is decreased to organs and body functions not involved in saving life and increased to those that are, causing...
a throbbing and a quickening sensation in various parts of body

Head...
blood runs faster through larger arteries thereby aiding the co-ordination of saving life, causing...
throbbing sensations
a feeling of dizziness, faint, light-headedness

Eyes...
light is encouraged into the eye to aid sight, causing...
a retraction of the upper lids
the pupils to dilate (made bigger)
the retina to become more sensitive to light
enhanced middle vision (between five and ten metres)
impaired near and distant vision

Ears and Hearing...
enhanced hearing, causing...
sensitivity to sound

Face...
increased blood flow to facial muscles, causing...
flushing and blushing

Mouth...
inhibition of mouth secretion, causing...
a dry mouth

Throat...
muscular contraction and lack of mouth secretion, causing...
throat to tighten and/or a feeling of being unable to swallow

Neck and shoulders...
muscular contraction, causing...
a tightening and knotting sensation
soreness, aching, tender to touch

Chest...
muscular contraction, to protect vital internal organs, causing...
tightening
soreness, painful, tender to touch

Breathing...
to encourage more oxygenated air into the bloodstream and more carbon deoxygenated air out, there occurs a faster movement of air in and out of the lungs, resulting in breathing becoming faster and deeper, causing...
over-breathing
hyperventilation

Heart...
pumping faster and stronger in response to the body's need for extra oxygenated blood, causing...
heartbeat to become faster and stronger

Stomach...
muscle contraction, digestive system slowed and a decreased production of digestive enzymes; 'we don't feel hungry in fight or flight,' causing...
stomach churns, cramps and fluttering

Liver...
releases stored up glucose, causing...
a raised blood sugar level: thus more energy is produced

Adrenals...
produces and secretes adrenalin directly into bloodstream, causing...
a raised adrenalin level: thus extra stimulation

Uterus...
in pregnancy contraction is stimulated, causing...
a propensity for miscarriage and premature birth

Male sex organs...
closure of sphincters, causing...
premature ejaculation

Urinary...
relaxation of muscular wall, causing...
a release of urine

Bowel...
muscular contraction, causing...
a release of stools

Skeletal...
limbs become irritable, causing...
body shakes, trembling, tingling and throbbing

Skin and Hair follicles...
assist with body heat regulation, causing...
a tightness of skin, an erection of body hair and/or body sweats

RE-CAP: Arousal responses
When we sense a threat to our well-being; whether real or imagined, the body needs to either fight or take flight, as such it needs to make **extra** energy. To produce extra energy, the organs involved in saving life need to work harder. To work harder certain parts of the body need **extra** oxygen. Oxygen is carried by blood. Therefore when we sense a threat to our well-being, there is an **increased** blood flow to those parts of the body and brain that are involved in saving life and a **reduction** to those parts that are not.

And whilst this whole 'speeding up' process is a natural transition, the resulting mental, emotional and physical effects can be disturbing and absolutely terrifying...

THE CHAIN OF HIGH AROUSAL: UP TO NOW

When we 'sense' an imminent threat to our life → a subconscious flash thought of danger automatically alerts the brain and triggers arousal → immediately, the primitive part of our brain takes over → instantly the parasympathetic peacemaker relaxes its hold allowing the sympathetic stimulator to become dominant, thereby stimulating all organs and body functions involved in saving life; including the adrenal glands → the adrenal glands produce and secrete more adrenalin directly into the bloodstream, adding their own massive power to even further stimulate all organs and body functions involved in saving life → **the whole bodily system is now stimulated and ready for action**.

6. All taking as little as 15 hundredths of one second

You have now seen 5 basic elements in the chain of high arousal but once arousal is in operation, its duration can then become an issue in itself. And as you are now learning how to calm frenzied terror, one point you need to be aware of is that frenzied terror can be divided into two parts...

Part 1. First Flash Response

When we sense an imminent threat to our life, this first stage **kicks-off** the whole process of fear/arousal stimulation, with the aim to literally throw us out of danger. This stage will pass through: – a thought of danger – primitive arousal – nervous system stimulation – additional adrenalin stimulation – emotional/mental/physical sensations – to frenzied terror – in as little as 15 hundredths of one second...and will last for only a split-second.

When we sense an imminent threat to our life, this first stage will work very fast and below the level of consciousness, therefore it is usually over before we consciously know what's happened.

Part 2. Sustained Response

Once we have sensed an imminent threat to our life and the 'first flash response' has passed, this second stage then comes into play and **sustains** the whole process of fear/arousal stimulation, with the intention to help us throughout any **ongoing** ordeal. This stage **sustains** arousal through:

– a thought of danger – primitive arousal – nervous system stimulation – additional adrenalin stimulation – emotional/mental/physical sensations – to frenzied terror – **and can last indefinitely.**

During this stage it is possible to work on a conscious level, therefore it is possible to determine the duration of the state of arousal.

The key points being...

• Recovery from panic attacks is never found by trying to work on the panic attack during the 'first flash response' because, a) the thought that triggered the attack was probably below the level of consciousness and b) once begun, the 'first flash response' will automatically run its course. Recovery from panic attacks is, however, found by learning how to take control of the thoughts either **before** the 'first flash response' begins or **during** the 'sustained response;' as controlling the thoughts during either of those stages controls the panic attack.

• As the thought process involved with high arousal can work so fast, deep and below the level of consciousness, we could easily think that the extreme sensations 'come out of the blue' and 'just appear from nowhere,' which itself could easily worry us, frighten us and quickly shock our consciousness.

RE-CAP: Time span involved in arousal

Arousal can be divided into two stages...

1. **First Flash Response,** which works on a subconscious level and can go from peace to frenzied panic in just 15 hundredths of one second but lasts for only a split-second.

2. **Sustained Response,** which lasts for as long as we feel frightened, it can last indefinitely, be brought to a conscious level and calmed.

THE WHOLE CHAIN OF HIGH AROUSAL

When we 'sense' an imminent threat to our life → a subconscious flash thought of danger automatically alerts the brain and triggers off arousal → immediately, the primitive part of our brain takes over → the parasympathetic peacemaker relaxes its hold allowing the sympathetic stimulator to become dominant, thereby stimulating all organs and body functions involved in saving life, including the adrenal glands → the adrenal glands produce and secrete more adrenalin directly into the bloodstream, adding its own massive power to even further stimulate all organs and bodily functions involved in saving life → the whole bodily system is now stimulated and ready for action → **and all that can take as little as 15 hundredths of one second.**

Arousal: friend or foe?

ental objective of arousal is, of course, to be a protector. During of imminent danger, despite us experiencing the extreme emotional, mental and physical sensations of arousal, we are not normally shocked or frightened by them because a) we then **expect** such extreme sensations to occur in such extreme circumstances and b) we are far too **distracted** and **preoccupied** saving our life.

Think about it! If you were being chased by a ferocious lion, would you really be angry or frightened by your heart pounding and palpitating, or by your body shaking and sweating or by your inability to think calm, controlled, logical, rational thought? I think not! For in such a dire situation, your only concern would be on escaping from the lion. And moments later, once you had escaped, although you would still feel shaken, dazed and have strong sensations of arousal, you would not be concerned by the sensations but rather, you would feel very relieved and grateful for having had the strength to free yourself. ... So in this instance, arousal and its resulting sensations, was a good friend to you.

The bodyguard

A more positive approach towards your arousal responses might be to think of them as being your own personal, protective, inbuilt bodyguard. So when you feel calm and relaxed your bodyguard, being on 'stand-by,' quietly watches over you. When you believe you are under a slight threat your bodyguard becomes aroused, 'on-guard' and puts slight pressure on you to remove yourself from the situation. When you believe you are in actual life-or-death danger, your bodyguard then jumps forward and with both the strength of a wild bull and the speed of a trained athlete, it physically fights or throws you out of dangers way. And once the danger has passed and your bodyguard believes you are safe, it then goes back to watching over you. ... So yet again, arousal, including its resulting sensations, is a good friend to you.

A foe

There are a number of occasions when arousal is not your friend, indeed arousal can prove to be an absolutely terrifying enemy...

- When we are faced with an **actual** threat to our well-being from which we want to fight or run but cannot, i.e. lack of money, redundancy, bereavement, a damaging relationship, ill health and so on. ... As we will then experience the resulting prolonged mental, physical and emotional sensations of arousal then, sooner or later, those sensations of arousal will begin to worry or frighten us.

- When we are **not** faced with a threat to either our well-being or our life but we think we are: we think we have a serious health complaint, we think our partner is unfaithful, we think our children are in permanent danger and so on. ... As we will still experience the resulting mental, physical and emotional sensations of arousal then, in time, those sensations of arousal (symptoms of stress) will start to worry us.
- When we are **not** faced with a real, actual life-or-death situation but we think we are, as during a panic attack, we will still experience the resulting extreme mental, physical and emotional sensations of arousal but without expecting them, without being distracted from them and **without** being preoccupied trying to save our life. As a consequence, our thoughts will then be free to focus onto the severe sensations whereupon the severe sensations will then terrify us.

This might surprise you
There are not three different types of arousal: one for real danger, another for imagined danger and yet another for stress. There is only one type of arousal. And whether arousal is due to a real threat, a perceived threat or stress, it is absolutely irrelevant. Arousal is arousal, whatever the cause!

Do you see?
If, due to nothing more than a mistake, you give your bodyguard the message that you are under a threat. Your bodyguard, not realising you are mistaken, will carry out its task of protecting you; to whatever degree it deems necessary, even to frenzied panic. Added to that, if your bodyguard itself becomes a little over sensitive, over protective and over zealous, you will then need to work on three individual elements. Firstly, you will need to acquire the correct information, secondly, you will need to pass on the correct information to your bodyguard and thirdly you will need to help your bodyguard to calm. All of which you will do as you journey through the following steps.

The automatic mechanism that enables 'man' to create inbuilt surges of raw, primitive energy, is known by various terms, the most common are: The fight or flight response – Primitive arousal – The survival responses.

Arousal Creating Panic Attacks

As explained previously, there is only one type of arousal. And whether arousal is due to a real life-or-death threat, or a perceived threat, or life's general stresses or panic attacks it is irrelevant. Arousal is arousal, worry is worry, fear is fear and terror is terror, whatever the cause!

And so, during a panic attack, although your mental, emotional and physical sensations are extreme and absolutely terrifying, they are the very same mental, emotional and physical sensations of high arousal that every single person who has ever lived on this planet has experienced and will continue to experience. You doubt me?

The Jungle

Imagine you are not suffering stress, panic attacks or anything but rather, all your thoughts, feelings and sensations are of love, peace and joy.

Now imagine a jungle. Not a pleasant woodland with magnificent trees, pretty flowers and beautiful singing birds but a dark, dense, dangerous place where behind every leaf there lurks potential danger: hostile natives, wild animals, venomous snakes and poisonous spiders, plus maggots, grubs and worms, all waiting to have their fill from your last remains.

Also imagine yourself inside a cabin in this jungle. So directly outside of where you are right now are not houses, fields, traffic or the sea but the jungle; not a mile away, not even 20 feet away but so close that even the roots, branches and leaves are entwined into the very fabric of the cabin. Now imagine that you are alone in this cabin, the nearest person being a few miles away and in fifteen minutes time you have to begin a journey through the jungle to make contact with this person.

Trepidation

As the moments pass, waiting to begin your perilous journey through my jungle, even though, on a conscious level, you know you are perfectly safe at the moment whilst inside the cabin. Your subconscious mind, being designed for survival and fully aware that you are about to face danger, is already automatically triggering off arousal; stimulating the primitive, rousing your bodyguard and doing whatever it can to prepare you and protect your life. So whilst waiting to begin your journey through my jungle, how might you now be feeling, mentally and physically?

Mentally

It is fair to say you are likely to be feeling anxious. Your mind will be working out, analysing and anticipating every possible eventuality. One-moment thoughts of protection will flash through your mind, "What might be my safest route? What might be my quickest route? If danger strikes, what will I do then? If I get hurt, where will I go, who will come to my aid?" The next moment, thoughts of encouragement and reassurance will flash through your mind, "Come on now, you can do this, you really can do this. Just stay calm and take a deep breath: in-2-3 out 2-3.

So during this period of waiting to go out into the jungle, although you know you are safe at the moment, you will not be feeling calm, peaceful and relaxed, nor will you be finding it easy to sit quietly, listen to the radio or even read a book. You might go through the motions of listening to the radio or looking at a book but, as your mind becomes ever more occupied with thoughts of protection, encouragement and reassurance then worry, anxiety and fear will be taking over. And realise, throughout this whole period, your mind is **not** neurotically worrying over senseless trivia but rather, your mind is a good mind, working exactly as it should in such a situation, it is simply protecting you by showing justifiable concern and by changing its focus from the here and now onto anticipating every possible eventuality. Your mind, knowing that to be forewarned is to be forearmed, is a wondrous mind, designed for survival!

Physically

It is fair to say that you are likely to be feeling a little uncomfortable. Your heart rate and breathing will have quickened, you might be pacing the floor, unable to settle, your stomach might be churning and you might need to visit the toilet more frequently than usual. In fact, you will be experiencing any number of the sensations of arousal. Of course, at this early stage, your sensations will still be manageable but as each moment passes and your impending journey becomes nearer, your state of arousal will be getting ever stronger. And again, in this situation, your body is **not** ill, neurotic or malingering but rather, it is working exactly how it should in such a situation. Your body is now protecting you by preparing you for battle; it is warming up, limbering up and getting itself into gear. Your body is a wondrous body, designed for survival and working exactly as you would want it to in that given situation.

Fear
Let us now assume that time has passed and you are about to begin your journey through my jungle…Tentatively you step towards the door. Pausing to take a deep breath, you try to muster up whatever strength and courage you have left, in the hope they will somehow get you through your impending ordeal. Now, taking your last step towards the door, with your mind racing, your heart pounding, your breathing quickening and your body trembling, you take one last deep breath, you reach for the door handle and gripping it tightly, you turn it, open the door and see outside. Fear now explodes inside you and your mind screams, "Run back inside and try again tomorrow," but you know you cannot. You know that somehow, someway you must force yourself through the door and face whatever dangers lie ahead. So you begin…one step, then another, then another and then another.

High fear and terror
You have now been trekking through my jungle for quite some time, all the while knowing that every step taken could be your last, every blink of an eye could cost your life and every thought in your mind is of how to survive. And in all this you are totally alone, no one to give you aid should you fall, no one to hear your fear should you scream and no one to run for help should you need it. Slowly, very slowly you tread, your brain is now buzzing, your thoughts are racing, your throat is tightening, your stomach is knotting, your breathing is rapid, your heart is pounding, your muscles are throbbing, your legs are buckling, your body's shaking, your eyes are searching and your hearing is picking up the slightest sound. Suddenly the bushes rustle! "What's that?" **Terror** now sweeps through you and you find yourself running in desperation for life itself: your racing mind can't think a rational thought, the jungle engulfs you yet you notice nothing, the screeching wildlife deafen you yet you hear nothing, your eyes wide open notice nothing, you bang and cut yourself on the undergrowth yet feel no pain, your heart feels about to burst yet you give it no thought, your breath's hot and burning your throat yet you gulp the air even harder, your body drips with sweat, your feet feel on fire, every limb, organ, fibre and sinew of your body and mind now feel charged with electricity and shaking violently, yet still you keep on running… **Stop!**

That is exactly what's happening to you right now! Of course not literally! You are not literally living in high fear believing, at any moment, a wild ferocious beast, poisonous spider or venomous snake will suddenly strike you down, hurt you or kill you. And you are not literally living in high fear believing, at any moment, you are about to be overcome by ants, grubs, worms, slugs and maggots. No my friend, you are not literally living in high fear in my jungle. But you **are** literally living in high fear in a jungle, a very real jungle, with its own horrors, fears and beliefs of imminent danger and death. For you are now living in the jungle of panic attacks! You are now living in high fear/terror believing, at any second, a wild ferocious panic attack will suddenly appear from nowhere, strike you down, hurt you, kill you or send you insane. You are now living in high fear believing, at any second, your heart will burst, your mind will break, your legs will buckle, your body will collapse, your throat will choke you, your eyes will blind you, your pains are cancerous, your headaches are tumours, your thoughts are madness and your prognosis is certain death.

Do you see? Whether you are living in high fear in **my** jungle with its wild, ferocious beasts or living in high fear in **your** jungle with its wild, ferocious panic attacks, you are still living in high fear believing, at any second, you could be struck down, hurt, killed or driven insane. And it's of no consequence which jungle you happen to be in, what horrors you happen to fear or what extreme sensations you happen to experience. A jungle is still a jungle! Fear is still fear. And primitive arousal is still primitive arousal, it's only the location that's different. You have simply exchanged one jungle for another, one cause of fear for another. But fear is fear whatever the cause, and your body's response to it is exactly the same.

And if you are now thinking, "All that sounds very well but I don't need to encounter a wild ferocious beast to throw me into frenzied panic. My panic comes on suddenly, from nowhere and for no reason." Cast your mind back to when you were in my jungle. Do you remember the incident that threw you from high fear into frenzied terror? I will remind you. It was a rustle in the bushes. But suppose I told you, the bushes rustled simply because a little bird was nesting there. So as the bushes offered you no danger and the bird offered you no danger, what threw you, so quickly, from high fear into frenzy terror?

The answer is of course…whilst you were in my jungle, you knew you were in great danger but because you did not know, from one second to the next, when the danger would strike, what it would be or from which direction it would come from. Your primitive survival mechanism, then believing it was protecting you, kept you in such continuous high arousal that it was not necessary for you to stand face to face with danger, it was not necessary for you to see, hear, smell, touch or taste danger, it was not even necessary for danger to be present at all. As then, your whole mind and body was so highly aroused, so stimulated, so charged with nervous energy and so sensitised to the slightest of movements or sounds, it then only took the slightest of movement, making the slightest of sound, to throw you that little bit further into 'full blown lifesaving arousal.'

To summarise

You are, at present, experiencing panic attacks and possibly extreme symptoms of stress. As a result, you are now living in high fear, believing, **at any second**, a wild, ferocious panic attack or symptom is likely to strike you down, hurt you, kill you or send you insane. But because you never know when it will strike, what will trigger it off or where it will come from. Your primitive survival mechanism is now in the continuous **extreme** state of 'on-guard,' looking out for the next panic attack over your shoulder, around every corner, up every street, on the motorway, in church, at work, in the supermarket, in your neighbourhood, in your home, in your bed, inside your own body, inside your own mind and everywhere that is connected to you. That being so, you now don't need to stand face to face with life-or-death danger. You don't need to see, hear, smell, touch or taste danger in any way. You don't even need to be near danger at all. Because now, you only need the slightest of words, the slightest of sounds, the slightest of breezes, the slightest of body sensations, the slightest of thoughts or the slightest of anything to throw you that bit further into frenzied terror.

Please realise

As your survival responses are now so heightened and only ever one whisker away from frenzied terror, whatever thought you have before a panic attack, even if it's something as simple as "Oh dear, it's raining" or "Oh no, next doors cat is in my garden again," that one simple thought is enough in itself to throw you that little bit further into frenzied panic. And once the frenzied panic has eased, it's pointless then trying to identify the actual thought that triggered it off because that thought was probably subconscious anyway and therefore would have come and gone long before your conscious mind had chance to register it.

RE-CAP: Arousal creating panic attacks

You are, at present, living in such high fear of panic attacks and your other symptoms of stress that the primitive part of your mind is permanently 'battle ready.' And because the primitive mind does not wait to acquire all the facts of a situation but rather, it jumps to split second conclusions based on partial, splintered information. You now only need the slightest sound, the slightest breeze, the slightest body sensation, the slightest word, the slightest thought or the slightest of anything to instantly throw you into full-blown, frenzied panic.

YOUR CHAIN OF HIGH AROUSAL

Initially, you were experiencing, or had recently experienced, a period of stress significantly higher than normal which, in-turn, was stimulating your arousal responses. Then one day you sensed 'something,' perhaps a little bird made you jump → a subconscious flash thought of danger then automatically alerted your brain → immediately, the primitive part of your brain took over → your parasympathetic peacemaker relaxed its hold allowing your sympathetic stimulator to become dominant, thereby stimulating all organs and body functions involved in saving your life; including your adrenal glands → your adrenals produced and secreted more adrenalin directly into your bloodstream, adding its own massive power to even further stimulate all organs involved in saving your life → you experienced high mental and physical sensations of arousal → your mind, not having to save your life, focused onto your sensations → the sensations frightened you → more adrenalin was pumped into your bloodstream → faster, ever faster your primitive arousal responses raced → your sensations were now being taken to their extreme → you were experiencing the full sensations of frenzied terror whilst consciously focusing onto them, which absolutely terrified you → higher and higher your sensations went → and the whole process could have taken as little as 15 hundredths of one second but would have lasted for as long as you felt fearful. The whole experience frightened you, serving to add even more stress to your already overstressed state...

Do you see? You are currently suffering panic attacks for no other reason than your mind has become tricked by your primitive arousal sensations into thinking that your primitive arousal sensations are a threat...**making it all a simple case of mistaken identity.**

When the sensations of arousal become the foe

If you are not experiencing any mental or physical symptom of stress during your everyday life, other than during your actual panic attacks, then, for now, go to the page headed, 'Re-cap: To Take Your Second Step To Freedom,' which begins on page 129. I will invite you to read the following two chapters later in the programme.

Excluding the times when you are in an actual panic attack. If you are experiencing any physical and/or mental symptom of stress then you do need to read the following two chapters; 'Arousal Creating Prolonged Physical Symptoms of Stress,' which begins on the following page and Arousal Creating Prolonged Mental Symptoms of Stress,' which begins on page 104. And note: the order in which you choose to read the two two chapters is completely irrelevant.

Arousal Creating Prolonged
Physical Symptoms of Stress

Remember... symptoms of stress are only sensations of arousal

When we experience arousal, irrespective of whether it is mild or severe, the exact same muscles, organs and body functions are involved. So although I have referred to the following body parts and functions previously, I need to do so again but this time in more detail...
Muscle – Head – Sight – Smell – Hearing – Taste – Throat – Neck and Shoulders – Chest – Heart – Stomach – Hypoglycaemia – Physical exhaustion – Blood pressure – Body temperature – Secondary illness.

Muscle

Symptoms
• general bodily aches, pains, twinges and discomforts

Cause
Every muscle in the body consists of numerous muscle fibres. Muscle fibres work by being either contracted or relaxed. The strength of each muscle is determined by the amount of muscle fibres contracting in it at the same time.

When only a little exertion is required then bundles of muscle fibres within each muscle contract in series, thus preventing the muscle from becoming fatigued. However, when extreme or prolonged exertion is experienced (such as when running a marathon or during a period of high or prolonged stress) whereupon tremendous demands are placed on the body muscles, then virtually every muscle fibre within each muscle contracts, with the result that the muscle involved becomes fatigued and, as a consequence, develops aches and pains.

Head

Symptoms
• general headache
• feeling as if the top of the head is about to burst open
• a feeling of great pressure at the back of the head

- feeling as if a knife or fist is burrowing into the forehead
- feeling as if an ever tightening band of steel is around the head
- shooting pains in one or various parts of the head
- a thick dull pain in one or various parts of the head
- noises in the head when resting, similar to symbols crashing, a gun firing, a whip cracking, a piercing whistle or a rumbling sound.

Cause

Please see Fig 5: The cranium (or skull) is the bony part of the head that protects all the brain and is formed by a number of bones including the frontal, parietal, temporal, occipital and sphenoid bones. The occipital, parietal, temporal and sphenoid bones have immovable joints and, in part, contributes to symptoms involving the head.

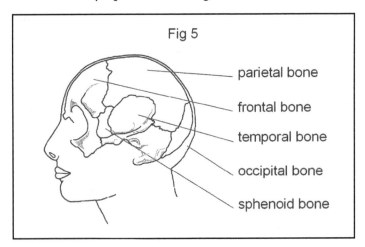

Fig 5

parietal bone

frontal bone

temporal bone

occipital bone

sphenoid bone

Please see Fig 6: Surrounding the cranium are numerous muscles including the occipitofrontalis and the temporalis. The front part of the occipitofrontalis (anterior) extends across the frontal bone, covering the forehead. The back part of the occipitofrontalis (posterior) extends across the occipital bone at the back of the head. Both parts are joined together by the middle part (aponeurosis), which is a flat tendon that stretches over the dome of the cranium. The temporalis muscle is positioned at the side of the head, extending from behind the ear, passing behind the cheekbone, to be inserted in the part of the upper jaw that gives attachment to muscles and ligaments. When stress is experienced, the muscles of the scalp, being similar to all other muscles of the body, respond by contracting. However the occipital, parietal, temporal and sphenoid bones have immovable joints. So when the muscles of the scalp tighten, albeit slightly, the tension then caused by the tightened muscles around the immoveable joints will often cause head pain.

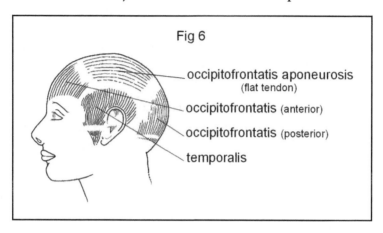

Fig 6

occipitofrontatis aponeurosis (flat tendon)

occipitofrontatis (anterior)

occipitofrontatis (posterior)

temporalis

The body is designed for survival. And because the brain is so integral to life, the protective bones of the cranium are extremely strong. Therefore when stress is experienced, although the resulting muscle contraction (tension) can cause excruciating pain (often to the point where the sufferer believes the pain must surely be symptomatic of a brain tumour or imminent brain haemorrhage or stroke) the muscle contraction itself is only comparatively slight, causing no short-term or long-term damage whatsoever.

Migraine

Whilst stress related headache is thought to be of a muscular origin, stress related migraine is thought to be due to the stress hormones adrenalin and noradrenalin affecting the blood vessels in the head by encouraging their constriction and dilation. And to repeat, although stress related migraine can be exceptionally painful, often forcing the sufferer to sit in a darkened room, rocking backward and forward or lying crouched, with their head in their hands. The stress related migraine does not automatically indicate an abnormality of the brain, nor is any short or long-term damage done.

Note: For headaches also see, Senses, Blood pressure and Neck tension.

Noises in head when resting

When a stress sufferer is in the period between being asleep and awake they will often hear noises similar to those mentioned in the list above. The noises can be so loud that the person involved will suddenly wake up with a jolt, sit up and even get up thinking the noise must surely be an indication that something in the brain is bursting or snapping. However although such head noises can be very loud and startling, they can also be the indication that tense muscles are relaxing and sleep is near. Therefore to any stress sufferer, such head noise need not be feared but rather, they might be looked upon as a welcome friend.

The Senses in general

Due to each of the five senses being directly involved in saving life, when a person experiences either acute or prolonged stress, their senses of sight, smell, touch, taste and hearing are all likely to be affected, causing many seemingly strange and awfully frightening sensations. However once the stress and senses have again calmed there is absolutely no short-term or long-term damage done.

Sense of smell

Symptoms
- sense of smell distorted, i.e. things not smelling as one remembers
- sense of smell lost or heightened

Cause
The primary function of the nose is to take in and prepare air for the lungs. The roof of the nose is lined with mucous membrane, which is also served by the olfactory nerves. When we inhale air, it is initially warmed by the inner surface of the nose, it is then moistened by mucus and, as the impurities in the air stick to the mucus, it is filtered. So when we inhale in an odorous environment, as all odorous materials give off chemical particles which are carried in the air, the chemical particles are carried, via air, into the nose. Once in the nose and moistened by mucus, the particles stimulate the nerve endings of the olfactory section which, in turn, send their impulse message via the olfactory nerve to the cerebrum where the sensations of the smell are perceived.

When a person is under stress, they tend to sniff, swallow and breathe through their nose more vigorously and more frequently than normal. But the sense of smell is a finely balanced mechanism; a) the body only has to produce too much or too little mucus to alter the strength of the odours reaching the olfactory nerves, b) the olfactory section and in particular the olfactory nerves only have to be affected slightly for their messages to be distorted and c) the brain itself only has to be affected slightly by stress to misinterpret the messages received and thus distort the whole perception of smell.

Smell also has a big effect on the appetite. Hence, when ones sense of smell is lost or distorted, the inclination to eat will often be affected or lost.

Sight

Symptoms
- strange tricks of vision
- objects seem to shimmer as if covered by a heat haze
- objects seem to be in shadow
- objects seem to jump when caught in ones side vision
- objects seem to move nearer or further away, when in vision
- blood-shot eyes and/or other sensations of eyestrain
- the need to frequently blink, rub eyes or squint
- eyes sensitive to light (photophobia)
- a seeming rapid deterioration of eyesight
- dizziness and/or headaches

Cause
The workings of the eye are so complex I will not even begin to try to cover them in any depth. Yet because so many panic attack sufferers worry so much over their eyesight, some level of factual information is required.

Please see Fig 7: Whilst the following information only covers the more basic elements of the eye that are, in part, affected by stress, most sufferers find the information enough to be reassured.

Six external eye muscles control eye movement and are attached at one end to the walls of the orbital cavity and at the other to the sclera. The sclera, being the white part of the eye, is the firm membrane that holds the shape of the eye. The cornea is the extension of the sclera, it is transparent and covers the front of the eye. The choroid lining, being attached to the retina, lines most of the inner surface of the sclera. The ciliary body, being the continuum of the choroid, consists of non-striated muscle fibres and is attached to the suspensory ligaments. The iris is the coloured part of the eye and consists of pigment cells and two layers of muscle fibres; one circular and one radiating. The pupil, being the black part of the eye, and positioned in the centre of the iris, is simply a hole, varying in size depending on the amount of light on it.

The retina, being highly responsive to light rays, is an extremely delicate structure consisting of nerve cell bodies, their fibres and a photo sensitive pigmented layer of cells called rods and cones. The lens, being a bi-convex, elastic, transparent body works by bending the light rays entering the eye and focusing them onto the retina; the convexity of thickness of the lens determines the refractory power. The suspensory ligaments, being positioned on each side of the lens, determine the convexity and thickness of the lens; depending on whether or not they themselves are being pulled by the ciliary muscle. The optic nerve is an outgrowth of the brain itself. External stimuli register in the cerebrum (brain). The individual vision from each eye is registered at the same time thus creating one perception; binocular vision.

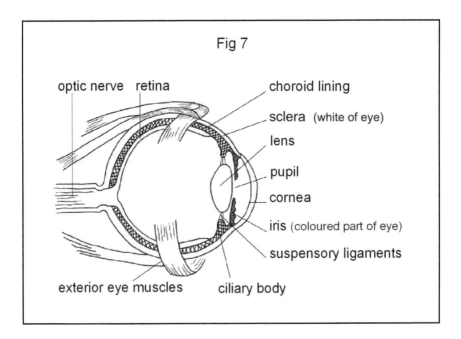

Fig 7

optic nerve   retina

choroid lining

sclera (white of eye)

lens

pupil

cornea

iris (coloured part of eye)

suspensory ligaments

exterior eye muscles   ciliary body

Light enters the eye through the cornea and pupil. The cornea helps to bend the light rays to focus them on the retina. The iris then comes into play by immediately adjusting the size of the pupil: in bright light the circular muscle fibres of the iris contract thereby constricting the pupil (making it smaller) and in dim light the radiating muscle fibres of the iris contracts thereby dilating the pupil (making it bigger). The ciliary body, working by constriction and relaxation, determines to what degree the suspensory ligaments are pulled, thereby determining the thickness or convexity of the lens: the nearer the object the thicker the lens. The lens then focuses the light on the retina in the form of upside down images. The highly sensitive retina, with its photosensitive pigmented layer of rods and cones now becomes involved in the conversion of light rays into nerve impulses, thus making sense of the light and colours entering the eye. The choroid lining then absorbs the light and gathered information to then pass through the vital point where the nerve fibres of the retina converge to form the optic nerve. Finally, the optic nerve then carries all the information, which reaches the occipital lobe of the cerebrum.

Whilst the direction of eye movement is under **voluntary** control, the coordination of eye movement is under **involuntary** control. As a result, during a period of high or prolonged stress, when the levels of muscular contraction and involuntary/sympathetic stimulation are extremely high throughout the whole body, particularly within the senses, a dramatic change will occur within the eyes themselves, causing a dramatic yet temporary disturbance to the delicate balance of sight.

So if your eyesight seems bizarre and/or deteriorating at such a rate that you can't trust what you see to be an accurate portrayal of life. Don't fear that blindness is surely imminent, or that something within your eyes or something in your brain itself is malfunctioning. I assure you, a distortion of vision really does go hand in hand with stress; with no short or long term damage done.

Hearing

Symptoms
- ringing/whistling/buzzing sound in ears or head (Tinnitus)
- hearing over-sensitive to sound (Hyperacuisis)
- sounds seem muffled as if being filtered through cotton wool
- partial deafness, headaches, dizziness and/or nausea

Cause
Outer ear – collects sound
Middle ear – transmits vibrations to the inner ear
Inner ear – changes the vibration into nerve impulses

Please see Fig 8: The outer ear consists of both the outer ear itself and the ear canal. The latter is a tube about 2.5 centimetres long that passes inwards from the external ear to the eardrum. Then, separating the ear canal from the middle ear is the eardrum, which is a thin sheet of skin that vibrates when sound waves strike it; just like when the skin on a drum is struck. The middle ear, which connects to the nasal tube, is a cavity filled with air. Within it are fibrous tissue, fine ligaments and three tiny bones called the hammer, anvil and stirrup. The inner ear, which can be described in two parts, consists of a) the bony labyrinth, which is the larger part and consists of the vestibule, cochlea and the three semicircular canals and b) the membranous labyrinth, which fits into the bony labyrinth; similar to a tube within a tube. Between these two parts of the ear is a layer of fluid

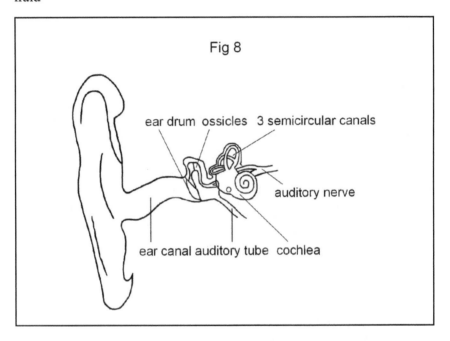

Fig 8

Air enters the ear through both the ear canal and nasal tube. Sound vibrations enter the ear through the ear canal. Once sound vibrations enter the ear they strike the eardrum. The presence of air (then at equal atmospheric pressure on both sides of the eardrum) enables the eardrum to vibrate. The three tiny bones within the middle ear pass the sound vibrations from the eardrum to the inner ear. The vibrations of the fluid, the cells and their nerve fibres in the inner ear are changed into nerve impulses. The nerve impulses then pass through many processes to finally reach the hearing area in the cerebrum.

Ringing/whistling/buzzing sound in ears or head (Tinnitus)
Whilst Tinnitus can be an internal noise in the head, most people hear it in their ears. It is experienced by up to one person in every ten. And whilst its

onset can be attributed to head trauma or prolonged loud noise or when elderly, tinnitus it is very often caused by stress.

Hearing oversensitive to sound (Hyperacuisis)

When suffering this condition, sounds seem heightened, even to where running water from a tap or a bird whistling or people just talking will sound so piercing to the ears that the person will wince and have to move away from the noise. The onset of this condition can sometimes be caused by stress and once begun, can be made much worse by stress.

Noise related headaches

If your auditory system is now disturbed by stress then, in all probability, you will experience headaches.

Dizziness

This element is slightly different: All movement of the head will stimulate certain nerve endings in the semi-circular canals. And although they have no auditory function themselves, they do provide information about the position of the head in space, thus contributing greatly to the maintenance of balance. The nerve impulses (relating to the semi-circular canals) are then transmitted by the vestibular nerve, ending in the cerebellum. Once in the cerebellum, nerve impulses from the eyes, nose, mouth, muscles and joints are all coordinated, whereupon the position in space is perceived and balance maintained.

Whenever stress is experienced, however, whilst many changes take place within the eyes, nose and mouth, the ears are not affected in quite the same way. In fact, the ears may not even be the cause of the dizziness at all but rather, as the eyes, nose and mouth are so interconnected with the ears, and as the ears are such a finely tuned and balanced mechanism, the whole hearing system can simply be caught up in a knock-on effect.

Taste

Symptoms
- a sweet, sour, bitter, salty or bad taste in the mouth
- a sticky mouth, a dry mouth, a lack of taste or loss of appetite

Cause

Taste buds are found on the tongue and are primarily made up of cells and nerve endings. When we eat, chemical substances in the food stimulate both the cells and nerves then transmit the message of taste to the brain.

When a person is calm, they experience the stimulation and secretion of a high volume of watery saliva with a comparatively low content of body material, such as mineral salts, enzymes and other organic substances. However, when a person is stressed, only a small volume of saliva will then be secreted but containing a high concentration of bodily material which, in turn, overwhelms the taste buds, masks-out or distorts the true taste of food and drink and gives the person a dreadful taste in their mouth. So the distortion or loss of taste experienced by the stress sufferer is primarily due to the lack of watery liquid and the high concentration of organic substances in the mouth.

Taste is not only a great pleasure but it also encourages us to eat and drink. So being a stress sufferer, if you are now experiencing a restriction of saliva, the volume of your mouth substances is high, your food is bland and you are gaining no pleasure whatsoever from eating or drinking. You might easily come to look upon both food and liquid as being a necessary chore that you have to endure to sustain your life. If so, instead of forcing yourself to eat a full meal, try to eat small amounts of food throughout the day.

Throat

Symptoms
- feeling as if an ever-tightening clamp is around ones throat
- the sensation of being unable to swallow
- the sensation of having a lump stuck in ones throat
- a feeling of having pressure on ones Adam's apple
- a throbbing sensation in one s throat

Cause
Please see Fig 9: The sternocleidomastoid muscles, positioned on each side of the neck, extend from the top of the sternum (sterno) and part of the clavical (cleido) ending just behind the ear (mastoid). When a person is experiencing stress, the contraction of these two sternocleidomastoid muscles (along with the other neck muscles) are greatly influenced and, in part, then contribute to the sensations listed: – feeling as if hands are tightening around the throat – being choked – the throat tightening – inability to swallow – feeling of having a lump in the throat – and having pressure on the 'Adam's apple.' I say 'in part' because these sensations are also due to a number of other elements including a) a contraction of numerous muscles around the throat and face, b) having a dry mouth, c)

over swallowing; and thereby causing waves of muscular contraction of the oesophagus and d) a constriction of the larynx muscles.

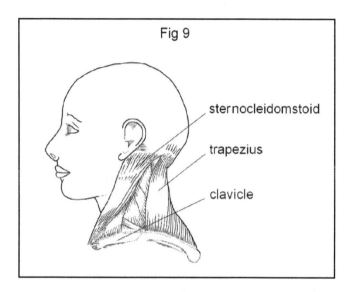

Fig 9

sternocleidomstoid

trapezius

clavicle

Most stress sufferers experience the above symptoms. Time and again this sufferer will go to their doctor **convinced** that something is growing in their throat and getting bigger by the day. Yet time and again their doctor will try to reassure them that no irregularities are present at all.

To feel as if one has a clamp around one's throat squeezing ever tighter, or as if one is being slowly choked to death or that a golf ball is stuck in ones throat, can be so very frightening. Yet when such sensations occur, despite their discomfort, they really can be due to nothing more than muscular contraction. And realise, when anxiety is experienced and the throat muscles contract, **neither the throat nor associated muscles ever tighten to the degree of restricting air flow**. After all, it would be a useless tool for saving life if, whilst the body was escaping danger thanks to muscular contraction, the muscle contraction itself choked the body.

Quick suggestions of help
• Try holding a warm, hot water bottle on the area.
• Chew a sweet, biscuit or piece of bread.

A throbbing sensation in the throat
Veins carry blood to the heart. Arteries carry blood away from the heart. The walls of both the veins and arteries consist of muscles and elastic-like

tissue. The walls of the arteries, in comparison to those of the veins, are much thicker; the medium and smaller sized arteries consist of more muscle than elastic tissue, the larger arteries consist of more elastic tissue than muscle and the largest arteries consist almost entirely of elastic tissue.

During a period of high stress, when the heart is pumping blood faster around the body, the main arteries of the body, including the neck, utilise their strong elastic tissue and slightly expand. And it is only the result of the blood pumping faster through the expanded arteries of the neck that give the sensation of pulsating/throbbing in the neck. Nothing more.

Back, shoulders and neck

Symptoms
• pain and stiffness in one or numerous parts of the area

Cause
Please see Fig 10: The major muscles of the back are extremely powerful: The trapezius muscles, which extend in a diamond-like shape, from the middle of the back (12th thoracic vertebrae) covering the shoulders and extends up the back of the neck to connect to the base of the skull. The sternocleidomastoid muscles extend from the top of the chest (sternum), pass up each side of the neck to the mastoid process, situated just behind the ear at the base of the skull. The latissimus dorsi muscles extend from the lumber and thoracic region, passes upwards and across the back to just under the arm. And the deltoid muscles extend from the clavicles and shoulder blades covering the shoulders and pass downwards, covering one third of the upper arm.

During 'normal' breathing, the inter-costal muscles and diaphragm are enough in themselves to support breathing (discussed in chest). However during 'deep' breathing, the muscles of the neck and shoulders also come into play. So during stress, along with the major muscles of the back, the shoulder muscles and neck muscles can also tighten and occasionally spasm; from which the resulting pain can be excruciating, often feeling as if the whole muscular mechanism of the back, shoulder and neck is locked or frozen. In fact, the person involved will sometimes be unable to turn their head even slightly as the pain is so incredibly debilitating. Also, as the major muscles of the back, shoulders and neck extend upwards, headaches are also likely.

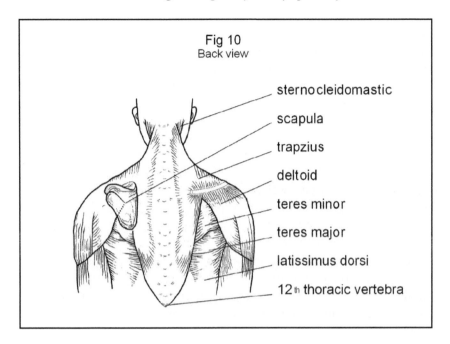

Fig 10
Back view

sternocleidomastic

scapula

trapzius

deltoid

teres minor

teres major

latissimus dorsi

12th thoracic vertebra

Quick suggestions of help
- Very gently massage the muscles and surrounding area but ensure you do not press too hard.
- Try placing a warm hot water bottle on the involved muscles or take a warm bath or shower.
- A body massage can be very useful; particularly if accompanied with aromatherapy oil; of course only if you know you are not allergic to the oils.

Chest (thoracic cavity)

Symptoms
- the top part of the sternum feels very sore and tender, as if the chest wall is bruised, even when not being touched
- inability to take a deep breath and/or breathlessness
- constantly yawning
- over breathing
  - feeling dizzy
  - bodily stiffness/rigidity
- disturbing/frightening heartbeats (see Heart section)

Cause

Within the chest cavity are the oesophagus, heart, lungs and trachea, each served by a multitude of nerves and protected in the thoracic cage. The thoracic cage itself consists of 12 thoracic vertebrae, 12 pairs of ribs, 11 pairs of intercostal muscles, cartilage and ligaments. All thoracic contents are covered by both the breastbone (sternum) and the pectoralis major muscles. And all are influenced, to some degree, by stress.

Sore and tender to touch, as if the chest wall is bruised

Please see Fig 11: The pectoralis major muscles cover the front of the chest and originate from the clavicle and sternum. The clavicles (collarbones) are the long bones that lie between the top of the sternum and shoulder. The sternum is the flattish bone that lies midline down the chest. Attached to the uppermost part of the sternum are the first two pairs of ribs and the clavicles. Attached to the middle (or body) of the sternum are the middle 8 pairs of ribs. Attached to the lower part of the sternum are the lower ribs and under them are the diaphragm and the muscles of the abdominal wall.

In comparison to the deeper internal organs (such as the heart) the sternum and pectoralis major muscles lie nearer to the surface of the chest. So using your fingertips, press over your chest and test if certain areas are sore to the touch. If so (assuming your chest discomfort has already been diagnosed by your doctor as being caused by stress) the likelihood is that your chest pain is, in reality, nothing more than stress.

The symptoms relating to a sore and tender chest, particularly around the sternum, can feel so painful that the sufferer will often genuinely believe they are having a heart attack.

Inability to take a deep breath

Many stress sufferers find themselves in the extremely frightening position of feeling they cannot inhale a sufficient and satisfying deep breath. As a result they find themselves pacing the floor for hours, gasping in as much air as they can but genuinely fearing it isn't sufficient and they will surely die from lack of oxygen.

As you see, the sternum is the central bone in the chest. It is used in co-ordination with many other bones, muscles and body functions. It is 'the kingpin;' the tension bearer. As such, during a period of high or prolonged stress, the sternum, particularly the uppermost part, can come under great pressure, resulting in it becoming tender and sore to the touch. Also, as you can see, the pectoralis major muscles are large and literally cover the whole chest. Therefore during any period of high or prolonged stress, to protect the internal 'life saving' organs within the chest, the tension on the pectoralis major muscles can become so great that, similar to the sternum, they can become sore and tender to touch.

The main reason why many stress sufferers feel as if they are unable to inhale a sufficient and satisfying deep breath is because of the reasons below...

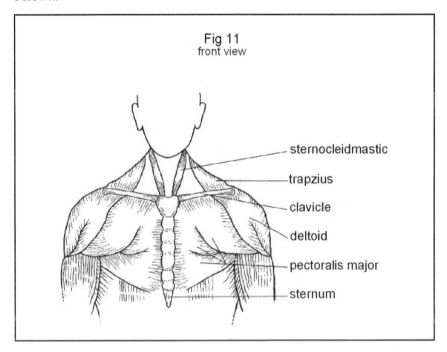

Fig 11
front view

sternocleidmastic

trapzius

clavicle

deltoid

pectoralis major

sternum

The primary organs and muscles involved in breathing are the lungs, the main chest muscles and the diaphragm. The lungs consist of the bronchi, small air passages and air sacks (alveoli) connecting tissue, blood and lymph vessels, nerves.

The main function of the lungs is to ensure that the overall balance of various gases is maintained within the body. Within the chest, each of the intercostals are positioned between two ribs (like a sandwich) and are attached to both the rib above and the rib below; their function is to assist the ribcage to expand and contract. The diaphragm consists of domed-shaped muscles and fibres and is situated between the thoracic and abdominal cavities; thus forming the floor of the thoracic cavity and the roof of the abdominal cavity. Its function is to ensure enlargement of the thoracic cavity; which is achieved when, on inhalation and muscle contraction happens, it is pulled downwards, enlarging the thoracic cavity.

The cycle of breathing: Oxygenated air is inhaled, carbon deoxygenated air is exhaled, then rest. The cycle is repeated about 10-12 times a minute.

The process of breathing: On inhalation, due to nerve impulses (that originate in the respiratory centre and passing to both the diaphragm and the intercostals) both the diaphragm and the intercostals contract at the same time. Then, due to the shape of the ribcage, the chest expands, the lungs inflate and we inhale. Once sufficient breath is inhaled and the correct overall balance of the various gasses is achieved, we exhale.

The control of breathing: For the major part of our life, breathing is controlled by the involuntary nervous system, which ensures that we inhale, exhale and rest appropriately to our needs. For the remaining part of our life, such as when singing or reading aloud, our breathing then comes under our own conscious, voluntary control.

When we feel calm, peaceful and relaxed, our breathing is likely to be silent, comparatively slow, shallow and with no particular effort. When we experience either physical activity or mental anxiety, our breathing then becomes louder, faster, deeper, requiring much more effort and needing much more involvement from the chest muscles and diaphragm. In which case, when we experience a prolonged period of physical activity or mental anxiety, the point can be reached where the chest muscles and diaphragm become tired. And although when tired, the muscles of the chest and diaphragm are still perfectly able to function and perform their tasks adequately, they do find it slightly more difficult to contract to their tightest, making both a full expansion of the chest and a full inhalation of breath slightly more difficult to attain.

During any period of stress, whether acute or prolonged, the chest muscles and diaphragm will always assist chest expansion enough to ensure sufficient air is inhaled and sufficient breath is achieved. Again, it would be a useless system for saving life if, whilst escaping danger, muscle contraction itself starved the body of oxygen preventing it from breathing.

Breathlessness
To repeat myself slightly. When we feel calm, peaceful and relaxed, our breathing is likely to be silent, comparatively slow, shallow and with no particular effort. When we experience either physical activity or mental anxiety our breathing becomes louder, faster, deeper and requiring much

more effort. Therefore, as you are suffering a stress related condition, it is very likely that you are experiencing a breathing issue; whether it is an inability to take a deep breath or breathlessness. And as either of those conditions can be very frightening and distressing, I strongly recommend the breathing exercise, 5. Hold it, in the stress buster, page 174.

Over breathing (Hyperventilation)

This might surprise you: During the latter part of the last century, after many years research into the health effects of over-breathing and the involvement of carbon dioxide (CO_2), the results of the research by the renowned Russian physician Dr Konstantin Pavlovich Buteyko proved that whilst oxygen is certainly 'the breath of life,' carbon dioxide is not an unwanted waste gas but rather, it is a vital element in aiding red blood cells to release oxygen, hence, it actually assists the bodies uptake of oxygen. Carbon dioxide also stimulates the respiratory centre in the brain. Therefore where there is a reduced level of carbon dioxide there will be a reduced uptake of oxygen. In short, as carbon dioxide assists the bodies uptake of oxygen, the body needs carbon dioxide just as it needs oxygen!

During the course of breathing, oxygenated air is inhaled and carbon dioxide is exhaled. The balance within the body of oxygen/carbon dioxide is continuously monitored and maintained by both the respiratory centre in the brain and the respiratory organs and nerves. That being so…

When we are calm and both the speed and rhythm of breathing is at the 'normal' rate, our breathing is slow, shallow and each cycle of breath is about 10-12 times per minute. However, when we are in stress and both the speed and rhythm of breathing is deeper and faster than normal then too much carbon dioxide can be exhaled; upon which not enough carbon dioxide is then left in the system to sufficiently stimulate the respiratory centre in the brain, which, in turn, lessons our bodies uptake of oxygen.

Now, whilst the body can easily cope with slight imbalances of oxygen and carbon dioxide, whenever acute or prolonged anxiety is experienced and over-breathing occurs, the imbalance of oxygen to carbon dioxide can sometimes be too much for the body, causing symptoms such as those mentioned above.

When the above symptoms are experienced they can be so terrifying that some sufferers ring for an ambulance. However in such cases, the attending paramedics should always be informed that the patient is a panic attack sufferer, as this information will help the paramedics to assess whether or not additional oxygen is required. After all, if the panic attack sufferer is hyperventilating and therefore in need of carbon dioxide, to then have additional oxygen administered is not always the best solution.

A quick suggestion of help
- Gather up the open end of a paper bag until it is small enough to allow two fingers through the hole. Then, holding the open end of the paper bag over your mouth and nose, slowly breathe in and out, all the while keeping the bag over your mouth and nose. Repeat until your symptoms have eased.

By breathing this way, not only will you exhale carbon dioxide into the bag but you will also inhale the carbon dioxide that you have just exhaled and thereby redress the balance.

Caution: Do not, under any condition, try this with a plastic bag. Also, any pain or discomfort in the chest area must be checked by a medical doctor.

Heart

Although the heart is positioned within the chest, as it is the cause of so much concern to the sufferer, I have placed it separately here.

Symptoms
- stabbing pain in the heart area
- fast heartbeat
- a feeling of missed and/or jumping heartbeats
- a feeling as if the heart has stopped
- heartbeat thud
- slow heartbeat

Most stress sufferers expect to experience symptoms of stress but when unusual sensations occur around the heart area, the sufferer can then be so frightened, they either sit or lie down with a finger on their pulse believing they are either having or about to have a heart attack. Indeed some stress sufferers believe they are so near to a heart attack they literally put their life on hold, doing only the barest minimum 'just in case.'

And when the sufferers concerns become too much and they call out the doctor whereupon he/she confirms, "Your heart is fine, yes it is a little fast/slow but you are certainly not experiencing a heart attack." Even then, as soon as the doctor has walked out the door, the sufferer will think, "Yes, perhaps when the doctor was here my heart was OK but I'm sure if I was examined now, the doctor would recognise that I really do have a heart problem." So if you are suffering this element, the following will bring you some degree of comfort...

Cause
Stabbing pain in the heart area
The organs of the thoracic cavity are prime targets for stimulation however as every heartbeat itself is a muscular contraction, the muscles around the **outside** of the heart can also carry the added tension of the heart beating faster and stronger.

Therefore, during prolonged anxiety, as the muscles around the heart area carry so much ongoing tension, the build up of muscle tension will occasionally express itself by causing a momentary spasm.

So although stabbing pain in the heart area can be sharp, severe and force the person involved to take a gasp of air and cry out in pain whilst pressing their hands to their heart, the pain itself is due to nothing more than the muscles around the heart and the chest wall expressing tension.

Fast heartbeat
The heartbeat rate of a resting adult can range from 60-80 beats per minute; 74 considered the average. The heartbeat rate of an active adult can be much higher. Indeed the rate of an active healthy heart during exercise can deal with 200+ beats per minute without any evidence of damage.

Whilst a heartbeat consists of one overall beat, within that one beat are many processes, including two movements that sound similar to 'lub/dub;' 'lub' being the first and stronger movement and 'dub' being the second and softer.

The normal heartbeat of a non-stressed person will often go un-noticed. The normal heartbeat of a slightly stressed person will be faster, with the stronger 'lub' movement sometimes being felt. And the normal heartbeat of a highly stressed person will be faster still, with both the 'lub' and 'dub' movements being felt...which can feel as if the heart is beating twice as fast as it really is.

When a person is experiencing stress, particularly if it is prolonged and extreme, they often feel as if their heart is racing at 300 beats per minute. But when their pulse is taken, the heartbeat rate is usually no more than 120 to 150 beats per minute; which itself can be very frightening to the stress sufferer because, to their misguided thinking, with every heartbeat comes the probability of a heart attack.

We are designed for survival. As a result, when we are in life-or-death danger and our heart is pounding and racing, to then free ourselves from the danger we are usually participating in great physical exertion. And that is exactly how it is supposed to be! In fact when we are in life-or-death danger, our heart purposely beats stronger and faster to help our need for physical exertion. Therefore, when we experience a fast heartbeat due to stress, whilst our inclination is to sit and rest with our finger permanently placed on our pulse, in reality, we are then supposed to be involved in physical activity.

So whilst calming oneself is by far the best way to help a stressed heart to slow down, another way is to partake in a few moments of physical activity; that is assuming a) the heart has been confirmed healthy by a medical doctor, b) the physical activity is within the persons comfort zone and c) the activity is non aggressive.

A feeling of missed and/or jumping heartbeats
or as if the heart has momentarily stopped
The timing of the heartbeat is a finely balanced mechanism, influenced by a number of factors including a) the stimulation of the myocardium (the muscle tissue of the heart) and b) the stimulation of the nerves and nerve impulses that pass from the brain to the heart via the autonomic nervous system.

When stress is experienced, the myocardium, the sympathetic nervous system and the nerve impulses that pass from the brain to the heart are all greatly influenced, causing an ongoing build-up of the effects of stress. As a result, and in an attempt to release those built-up effects, either the body or the heart itself will adjust the timing of the heartbeat. So whilst the stress sufferer might feel as if their heart is missing a beat, jumping or even stopping, the sensations experienced are due to nothing more than the heartbeats being spaced irregularly to release the built up effects of the stress. It really is nothing more than that.

Heartbeat-thud
When a person experiences high or prolonged stress, no heartbeat is ever missed but rather, in order to fine-tune the volume of blood in the heart,

the heart itself will occasionally give a stronger beat, which feels as if the heart itself is literally jumping out of the chest. And whilst the stronger heartbeats will feel very strange and can last throughout the day, often for many days, they are, in reality, nothing more than a healthy heart working perfectly normally, as one would hope when under stress.

A too slow heartbeat (Vasovagal Attack)
Remember, the sympathetic nervous system stimulates the internal life support system and the parasympathetic nervous system holds the internal life support system at bay. However when a person is experiencing high or prolonged stress, their parasympathetic nervous system can sometimes overcompensate and hold their sympathetic nervous system too much at bay, causing it to slowdown too much, resulting in the person feeling very dizzy and faint.

Be assured...
If you have any concern regarding your heartbeat be assured, all the above symptoms do go hand-in-hand with stress. And once your nervous system has calmed, your body and heartbeat will return to normal, with no damage being done to the heart.

Also realise, whilst ongoing stress is certainly very damaging, muscle itself is strengthened by exercise. So every time you have experienced a panic attack, your heart muscle has been exercised as if you had been participating in a five, ten or fifteen plus minute run. Therefore once your doctors have examined you, all related tests show no irregularities and your medical advisors have assured you, "Your heart is as strong as a lion." Believe it! The human heart cannot only deal with frenzied panic, it is designed and intended to do so.

Stomach

Symptoms
- butterflies in the stomach
- feeling as if the whole stomach is turning over
- a churning, grinding feeling in the stomach
- stomach cramping, tightening, knotting
- nausea and vomiting

Cause
The alimentary tract is the tube that extends downwards from the mouth and encompasses the pharynx, oesophagus, stomach, small intestine,

large intestine, rectum and anus. And when stress is experienced, the blood vessels that supply the alimentary tract constrict, thereby affecting the involved organs to one degree or another, including the stomach.

The stomach is situated (along with other organs) in the abdominal cavity. The function of the stomach is to chemically breakdown food by way of the secretion and utilization of gastric juices (hydrochloric acid, mucus, mineral salts, enzymes and protein compound) then on muscle contraction (via an action similar to a rippling, churning movement) the food is driven on.

When food enters the mouth a salivary enzyme (ptyalin) starts the digestion of carbohydrates, this is why thorough chewing (mastication) is so important. While this is taking place, the stomach contents (mainly digestive juices) are getting ready to receive the food. Once the food is being digested in the stomach, the next stage (the duodenum) gets ready to receive the food. At this point, bile (gall) is released and the contents are further broken down and mostly emulsified. Now, and only now are the contents in the right state for absorption to take place. Nutrients are delivered, via the bloodstream, to the liver; which is the powerhouse of the body and act as a storage mechanism for proteins, carbohydrates and fats, which are delivered into the bloodstream as required.

The parasympathetic peacemaker **promotes** both stomach muscle contraction and the secretion and utilization of the digestive juices. The sympathetic stimulator **inhibits** both stomach muscle contraction and the secretion and utilization of digestive juices. And this whole alimentary tract process is **greatly** affected by stress.

Butterflies in the stomach/stomach turning over

When stress is experienced and sympathetic stimulation is dominant, due to a reduction of the secretion of gastric juices and a change in emphasis of the stomach muscles, both will contribute greatly to the sensation of butterflies in the stomach and stomach churning.

Stomach cramping/tightening/knotting

Six pairs of muscles form the abdominal wall. In order to protect the organs in the abdominal cavity, four of the broad, flat sheets of muscle of the abdominal wall (the transversus abdominis, the internal oblique, the external oblique, and the rectus abdominis) cover the whole abdomen by occasionally crisscrossing and overlapping. So when stress is experienced, the abdominal muscles tighten; resulting in 'clamp-like,' 'muscle-bound' sensations.

Nausea/vomiting

When stress is experienced, changes take place in the stomach such as a transference of blood from the gut, a reduction of gastric juices and a change of emphasis of the stomach muscles. As a result, the sufferer can feel as if they are on a fairground ride or sailing the high seas in a force ten gale, which causes them to feel 'off their food' and even lose their appetite completely. And even if the sufferer is able to eat a morsel of food, moments later they are invariably sick. This, however, should not be surprising, after all, if you were living in my jungle knowing, at any moment, you could be fighting for your life, the likelihood of you sitting relaxed and enjoying a hearty meal is quite remote, and you certainly would not be eating during actual fight or flight!

A quick suggestion of help

During any period of stress, if, due to stress, nausea and vomiting are experienced, the dilemma can then occur of whether or not to try to eat something. However, whilst some doctors say the stress sufferer should try soup, milky drinks, a biscuit or any light food (as in-between vomiting some nourishment will be absorbed) other doctors say to not introduce food at all. So if you are suffering stress related nausea and/or vomiting, you will need to be guided by both your own judgement and your medical doctor's advice as to which might be the best course of action for you to take, but either way...

- Seek medical advice.
- If you are frequently vomiting, your body will be losing a lot of bodily fluids, and as the body cannot survive long without fluid, you must try to drink plenty of liquid.
- Whilst the body can survive many days without eating, everyone must obviously eat something, at sometime, somehow.

Hypoglycaemia

Symptoms
- bodily weakness/fatigue
- feeling as if the body has turned into jelly
- hot and cold shivers
- clammy
- dizziness, feeling faint
- body trembles and shakes

Cause
The body makes most of its energy from sugar, and during a high or prolonged period of stress (when the body is making an enormous amount of extra energy) the continuous demand for body sugar can become more than the body can supply. Then, due to a shortage of sugar in the blood, a hypoglycaemic attack will occur.

A quick suggestion of help
• suck, eat or drink something sweet

Physical Exhaustion

Symptoms
• bodily aches and/or fatigue
• trembles and shakes
• body weakness; as if your body has turned into jelly
• body feels hot, cold, shivers, clammy
• dizziness, light-headedness and/or feeling faint

Cause
Body energy is produced from a number of sources including glucose, which itself is derived when body fats and sugars are broken down within the body and released into the blood stream.

Arousal can be divided into two stages, 'first flash response,' that lasts for only a split-second and 'sustained response,' that can last indefinitely. The sustained response stage, which is intended to assist the body escape prolonged danger, will kick, kick and kick the internal bodily system into producing more and more energy. But if the body is kicked too much for too long, it will eventually reach exhaustion.

So, you being a panic attack sufferer and consequently experiencing ongoing stress, whether or not you are physically active, the probability of you experiencing physical exhaustion is very real.

Dizziness - Feeling faint

Symptoms
• dizzy, light-headed, feeling faint and/or fainting

Cause
There are numerous reasons why a stress sufferer might feel dizzy, light-headed and faint: - Over breathing - Low or raised blood pressure - Slow heartbeat - Blood pressure - Physical exhaustion - Hypoglycaemia.

To have one's visual world de-stabilised, to reach out for something and miss it, to step onto ground that seems to be moving, to look at the world only for it to seem unsteady, to feel continuously bilious, to have ones legs feel like jelly and to never feel still. What an unnerving experience! No wonder so many panic attack sufferers seek the support of another person, a piece of furniture or a wall.

Prolonged, raised blood pressure

Symptoms
- dizziness
- feeling faint and/or fainting
- fast heart beat
- ringing noise in head and/or ears
- pulsating sensations throughout the body

Cause
The force at which blood flows through the body is a variable element, as age, gender, lifestyle and mood all play their part. Hence, there is no exact level at which blood pressure is thought to be normal for all people, of all ages and in all sets of circumstances. Having said that, there are certain guidelines used by most General Practitioners, which are fundamentally based on the continued **maximum** levels, beyond which might indicate a cause for concern. Those guidelines being: For adults aged up to 25 years: 120/80. For those aged from 25 to 50 years: 140/80-85. And for those aged from 50 to 75 years: 150/85-90.

When in my jungle and high fear is taking place, the heart will work harder than normal, the blood vessels of the body will contract and blood will course through the body at a faster than normal rate, thus causing a 'temporary' rise in blood pressure. That is exactly how and when blood pressure is supposed to occur, 'temporary' rising in response to danger. Then once danger has passed, blood pressure will return to a normal level. Being a panic attack sufferer, therefore every day having to fight your way through life, you having a rise in blood pressure is a very real possibility.

In which case…
- Please seek medical advice as soon as possible. Raised blood pressure, over whatever timescale, must always be investigated by a medical doctor.

- should a suspicion of raised blood pressure occur then readings need to be taken on at least three separate occasions, when you have rested for ten or more minutes, in familiar, quiet and warm surroundings.
- elderly people may have elevated readings due to a number of things including non-compressible vessels (hardened arteries).

Hypertension

This diagnosis is usually given when blood pressure rises above the age related maximum level and stays risen. And although the reason for the prolonged raised blood pressure can be due to a number of things such as being overweight, having a sedentary lifestyle and/or a bad diet, one of the main culprits for anyone having high blood pressure is stress.

A diagnosis of hypertension is not usually warranted in people under 50 years of age unless their blood pressure exceeds 140/90 mmHg on, at least, three separate occasions after they have rested for over ten minutes in familiar, quiet, warm surroundings.

Pulsating sensations throughout the body

This happens for the same reasons given for a throbbing sensation in the throat. Veins carry blood to the heart. Arteries carry blood away from the heart. The walls of the veins and arteries consist of muscle and elastic like tissue. The walls of the arteries, in comparison to those of the veins, are much thicker: the medium and smaller arteries consist of more muscle than elastic tissue, the larger arteries consist of more elastic tissue than muscle and the largest arteries consist almost entirely of elastic tissue.

During a period of high stress, when the heart is pumping blood faster around the body, the main arteries, then utilising their strong elastic tissue, slightly expand, and it is just the result of blood pumping faster through the expanded arteries that gives the sensation of the body pulsating.

Body temperature

Symptoms
- feeling hot and cold and/or clammy (similar to a cold sweat)
- body sweats
- the sensations of ants, worms, running water or similar on skin

Cause

Body temperature is regulated by the temperature regulating centre in the brain and it is maintained by the finally balanced operation between heat production and heat loss. Generally speaking, body temperature remains fairly constant at about 36.8C (98.4F) but when the body is working harder than normal and making extra energy, an outcome of that arousal process is the production of extra body heat. This causes bodily sensations such as feeling too hot and/or clammy.

Body sweats

When a body is experiencing stress, which of course triggers arousal, a by-product from the process is a production of extra body heat. Extra body heat needs to be lost otherwise the body will overheat. Skin is the largest organ of the body therefore it makes sense that most body heat is lost through the skin.

Therefore during stress, the temperature regulation centre relays its response via the sympathetic nerves. The smaller arteries (the arterioles) then dilate, allowing more blood into the capillary network. Heat then transfers from the capillary network to the cooler cells of the outer layers of the skin (the epidermis). Sweat glands (which are distributed all over the body but are particularly numerous in the palms of the hands, soles of feet, axillae and groin) open on the skin surface and, being stimulated by sympathetic stimulation, respond by producing sweat. The sweat, then on the surface of the skin, evaporates.

If you are suffering body sweats, a point of potential comfort to you is that, sweating is the most efficient way in which the body is able to rid itself of toxins. So whilst sweating can be tremendously uncomfortable and sometimes very embarrassing, overall, you should be much healthier for the experience.

The sensation of ants, worms, running water or similar on the skin

The skin is the external protector of the body, so naturally, during a period of stress, the particular elements of the skin that are involved in protecting life will be influenced...

The sensations mentioned here will often feel as if they are on the surface of the skin (the epidermis) but they are not; the surface of the skin has no blood supply. The sensations mentioned above are, however, felt on the next layer down (the dermis).

During a period of stress, sweat glands (stimulated by sympathetic nerve fibres) contract and bundles of muscle fibres, which are attached to hair follicles (also stimulated by sympathetic stimulation) cause the body hairs to stand erect and the skin around the hairs to rise (goosebumps).

Millions of sensory nerve endings (from the nerves that extend from the cerebrum and run through the spinal cord ending in the dermis) being highly sensitive to pain, pressure and temperature, (all stimulated by sympathetic stimulation), gives sensations such as those described above.

Secondary illness

Throughout these pages you have seen how prolonged stress will place enormous demands on the body, often taking from the body what it can not afford. When the body is forced to give so much of itself then, sooner or later, its resources and reserves become depleted, making it vulnerable to conditions not of stress itself but those secondary to stress such as allergies, ulcers, diabetes, numerous or lingering colds and sore throats, asthma, bodily infections, constipation, hormone imbalance, irritable bowel and so on.

Ensure your safety

The above symptoms of stress are the normal, natural symptoms that any stress sufferer can expect to experience. Even so, if you are experiencing any symptoms, whether on the list or not, please ensure your safety by following the advice below...

1. Go to your medical doctor and request a full medical examination and all related tests.
2. When your examination/test results come through and show no irregularities, if you are still not fully reassured then ask about the possibility of a second opinion.
3. When your examination results come back from the second doctor and show no irregularities, if you are still not fully reassured then ask to see a specialist.
4. Once your medical examination, the related tests and both your doctors' and the specialist confirm that your symptoms are nothing other than stress related, then rather than continuing to worry about your symptoms, ask yourself one question, "Am I stressed?" If so, your stressed state will have a cause and effect, as a result, to one degree or another, you will have stress related symptoms. And whilst those stress related symptoms might be distressing, excruciatingly painful, totally debilitating, extremely weird and very frightening, they are merely the normal, natural symptoms of high stress...nothing more! Being such, despite their severity, they

can be controlled, reduced and totally eliminated. And even if your symptoms are not on my list but have nevertheless been diagnosed as stress related, there is every probability that they are indeed stress related and as such, they also can be controlled, reduced and totally eliminated.

Erroneous beliefs

Panic attacks, mind problems, mental illness and insanity are not all one condition. In fact panic attacks and insanity are as far removed from each other as chalk is from cheese. Yes, of course, both panic attacks and insanity involve the mind but so what? Appendicitis and a broken leg both involve the physical body but they also are as far removed as chalk is from cheese. Yet still the myths, erroneous beliefs and 'getting the wrong end of the stick' all continue. So if you are suffering prolonged mental symptoms of stress, particularly if to the point of nervous exhaustion/ breakdown, then the following chapter is for you where, hopefully, you will come to understand what is really happening to you.

Arousal Creating Prolonged
Mental Symptoms of Stress

Firstly, to repeat myself slightly, I absolutely promise you, not one piece of information in this chapter will frighten you. The aim of this chapter is to both lessen your fear of mind problems and show you that, despite your weird, distressing and frightening thoughts, you are categorically **not** going insane.

Also, be assured, in this chapter, I do not detail the brain itself, or the workings of the brain or even where the mind is positioned within the brain. I simply refer to the part of the brain relevant to stress/panic attacks as the mind. And again, I absolutely promise you, nothing in this section will frighten you, in fact, you will gain much peace of mind from it.

Your issue is symptoms of stress; nothing more

Generally speaking, 'mind problems' can be divided into three groups…
1. **Mental Symptoms of Stress**: which includes…
A panic disorder – Anxiety – A lack of mental ability – Flash thoughts – Out of place thoughts – Thought based fearful thoughts – Record thoughts – Content based fearful thoughts – Introspective thoughts – Compulsive thoughts – The veil of mental exhaustion – Catastrophic thoughts – Morning strikes – Disintegration – Nest syndrome – Self assessment – Emotional Deprivation/Hibernation – Overflow – Dreaded darkness – Insomnia – Suicidal thoughts – Loneliness of spirit – Emotional isolation – Nervous breakdown.

Recovery from any of these conditions is dependant on 'mind rest.' And whilst this sufferer will always require information, they will not necessarily require counselling, medication or hospitalisation. Therefore, the long-term freedom from these mind problems need not require ongoing management or medication.

2. **Emotional Trauma**: which includes…
Child abuse – domestic violence – post-traumatic stress – rape – trauma based emotional isolation – bereavement.

Recovery from any of these conditions might not necessarily require either management or medication. However, in most cases, some form of counselling would be beneficial. If counselling is needed, then recovery will rest on the person receiving the appropriate type of counselling and also on them having the correct client/counsellor relationship. In severe cases, however, medication and/or hospitalisation might be needed.

3. **Physiological Dysfunction**: which include...

Delusion – manic depression – mania – hysteria – schizophrenia – paranoia – and all psychotic illness.

The long-term stability of these mind problems will, in most cases, require both ongoing management and medication.

Do you see?

Yes, the workings of the mind are positioned within the brain but, as far as panic attacks and mental symptoms of stress are concerned, these mind problems do not suggest a problem within the brain itself. **I stress**, panic attacks, mental symptoms of stress and insanity are not all one condition, indeed they are as far removed from each other as chalk is from cheese. **Yes** panic attacks, mental symptoms of stress and insanity involve the mind but so what? Appendicitis and a broken leg both involve the physical body but they also are as far removed as chalk is from cheese. So if you are suffering panic attack and mental symptoms of stress, particularly if to the point of nervous breakdown then this chapter is for you where, hopefully, you will come to understand what is really happening to you, as that knowledge will become the bedrock for your recovery.

The mind

The mind at work

Please excuse the blatant oversimplification throughout this section. It is explained in such a way to make an extremely complex issue very easy to understand...

Think of the mind as if it were only able to perform three functions, working similarly to the gears of a car...

Gear 1. **receiving bay:** this function receives all the information from the five senses.

Gear 2. **stores:** this function registers, sorts out, labels and holds all the information. It also does the thinking and worrying.

Gear 3. **order picker:** this function searches out, identifies and brings to the conscious mind all information relevant to the given moment.

Therefore, working similarly to the gears of a car, whilst each individual part of the mind is part of the whole, working for the good of the whole, **only one gear is ever engaged at any one time**. When gear 1 is engaged (receiving information) gears 2 and 3 are resting. When gear 2 is engaged (registering, sorting out, labelling and holding information) gears 1 and 3 are resting. And when gear 3 is engaged (searching, identifying and bringing to the consciousness information relevant to the given situation) gears 1 and 2 are resting. An example of this could be...

Imagine you are not suffering stress but happily walking down a road on a lovely spring morning. As you walk, enjoying the day, you notice the daffodils in flower...you are then **receiving** information (gear 1). Your mind, knowing the information is of interest to you then **stores** it away (gear 2). Later in the day, when you wish to share the information with your family...your mind then **recalls** the information (gear 3) whereupon you then tell your family, "The daffodils are flowering."

So, when you were happily walking down the road on that lovely spring morning, although your whole mind was continuously working, each individual segment of your mind was working then resting, working then resting and so on, **with only one segment engaged at any one time**. And even though each gear of your mind was working and changing countless times every second, no individual gear ever reached the point of being overtaxed, hence, you had **mental balance**.

The mind begins to tire

Now obviously, we all try to live a 'balanced' life but sometimes we have a day when we need to use one or another part of our mind a little more than usual. For example, we might have a day when we need to **receive** too much information; perhaps a teacher/tutor is loading us for hours with information that we need to remember. Or we might have a day when we **think** too much: perhaps when worrying over matters of uncertainty, swaying back and forward from one angle to another but not able to reach a conclusion. Or we might have a day when we **recall** information too much: perhaps when re-checking facts and figures over many hours.

So during such a mentally taxing day, even though it is only for one day, if the mental demands are long enough, intense enough and taxing enough then a degree of **mental tiredness** could begin. And realise, **when the physical body is tired it has a tendency to slowdown but when the mind is tired it has a tendency to speed up**.

Therefore on our mentally taxing day, when on our way home and we see the lovely daffodils in bloom, as our mind is then tired, it will not even register the daffodils. So later that day when a family member says, "The daffodils are flowering," we reply, "Are they, I didn't notice."

And come that same evening, when we retire to bed, even though the particular part of our mind has then been working all day and is therefore tired. We would not then quickly fall asleep but rather, we would find ourselves unable to sleep due to our mind then analysing, postulating and worrying over all the possible outcomes of the day. Over and over our tired mind would go, getting ever more tired, becoming increasingly faster and finding it ever more difficult to slow down, turn off and fall asleep.

Over the following few days, if the overtaxed part of our mind is able to rest then no significant overtaxing would occur. On the other hand, if we do not allow that particular part of our mind to rest but rather, we continue to work it for days or perhaps weeks. Then from that one particular part of our mind being overtaxed, the whole of our mind could then become caught up in a knock-on effect; from which, sooner or later, our mental tiredness would turn into **mental exhaustion.**

Once a mind has reached the point of exhaustion, if still not allowed to rest then, due to the on-going relentlessness of thought, it will very soon become so exhausted that it will begin to lose its strength of balance to where, eventually, it will become unable to disregard negative, irrational, fearful thoughts, leaving the mind weak and defenceless to all negative, irrational, fearful thoughts; **mental breakdown.**

As you see, mental tiredness, mental exhaustion and mental breakdown are, in reality, the same condition, born from, fed and prolonged by stress. The difference being, however, that mental tiredness is placed at one end of the condition, where the mind is still able to function relatively OK. And mental breakdown is placed at the other end of the condition, where the mind can still function but with the greatest difficulty.

Your mind
Being a panic attack sufferer, particularly if your suffering is acute and prolonged, you will now tend to spend most of your time locked inside your head worrying. And as that worrying is not merely for one day or a few days but is over weeks and months, then all that mental strain might have taken your mind to the point of exhaustion and possibly breakdown. In which case, along with the more common mental symptoms of stress such as insomnia, inability to concentrate, introspective thoughts and so on. Your mind might now have lost both its strength of will and its ability

to disregard irrational, negative, fearful thoughts, perhaps to where you now believe that you are going insane.

The following information will help you understand the 'mystique' of what's happening to you. The information on how to free yourself of those thought patterns will come a little later; learn to walk before you run.

Typical thought patterns relating to mental symptoms of stress

Throughout this section, as we will only refer to the thought patterns caused by stress, then whichever of the following thought patterns you are experiencing, your mind can certainly recover from them, even to where it becomes stronger than it has ever been...

A panic disorder – Anxiety – A lack of mental ability – Flash thoughts – Out of place thoughts – Thought based fearful thoughts – Record thoughts – Content based fearful thoughts – Introspective thoughts – Compulsive thoughts – The veil of mental exhaustion – Catastrophic thoughts – Morning strikes – Disintegration – Nest syndrome – Self assessment – Emotional Deprivation/Hibernation – Overflow – Dreaded darkness – Insomnia – Suicidal thoughts – Loneliness of spirit – Emotional isolation – Nervous breakdown.

A lack of mental ability

- inability to think clearly and in depth
- lack of concentration and/or hazy, foggy brain
- indecisiveness and/or memory loss

If you are experiencing this element, your thoughts will be so lost in worry, fear and terror that, to your subconscious mind, any matter other than an genuine life-or-death situation will not be deemed important enough to warrant any degree of thought. So, whilst your mind is just as capable of thinking as any other mind, it has, temporarily, 'cut off' from the seemingly trivial matters of everyday life, as it is now too pre-occupied focusing onto what it believes is the priority.

Flash thoughts

If you are experiencing this element, you will have a tendency to 'flash think:' such as, "I wonder if I locked the back door? – What shall I cook for dinner tomorrow? – Oh no, I didn't wash my jumper. – I'm so tired,

I've got to get some sleep. – I must remember to ring Jim tomorrow. – Did I order an extra bottle of milk? – I wonder if the gas bill will come tomorrow? – Did I lock the back door?"

Out of place thoughts

If you are experiencing this element, you will have a tendency to 'flash think' intermingled with 'out of place' thoughts: such as, – "I wonder if I locked the back door? – What shall I cook for dinner tomorrow? – Oh no I didn't wash my jumper. – I wonder why stars twinkle, I don't know? – I'm so tired, I've got to get some sleep. – I must remember to ring Jim tomorrow. – I wonder if Elvis is still alive – Did I order an extra bottle of milk? – Will the gas bill will come tomorrow, I don't know. – Did I lock the back door?"

Introspective thoughts

To the mind, good health equates to longevity, symptoms equate to ill health and ill health equates to a potential threat to life. So if you have any symptoms, your mind will now be inclined to focus onto them as it would a potential enemy. In which case, if you have not yet reached the point of mental exhaustion, you might still be able to rationalise your symptoms as being nothing more than stress related. But if you are now at the point of mental exhaustion/breakdown and your mind is unable to disregard irrational, negative thought. Then your mind could now be so caught up, introspective (looking inward) examining, diagnosing and worrying about every ache, pain, twinge and negative thought, that it now finds focusing on anything other than your own body very difficult.

Thought based fearful thoughts

If you are experiencing this element, you will have already experienced thoughts that seemed so irrational, extreme, disgusting or disturbing to you that you now feel deeply ashamed, disgusted, hurt and/or afraid **at having such an awful thought in the first place**. For example…

A new mother, totally exhausted and experiencing mental exhaustion, might have thoughts similar to, "I'm so tired, I've got to get some sleep. – If only the baby would stop crying all the time. – Well at least she's asleep now and with luck, she might sleep for half an hour. **Perhaps she might not wake up at all, at least then I'll get some sleep**. – Oh God, I can't believe I just thought that! What a terrible thing to think. – How could I have thought that? – Is that what I'm really hoping for? – Oh listen to me, what kind of mother am I to think such a dreadful, horrible thought? – But is it true, do I really want it to happen? – What if, deep down, I really want it to happen? – Could I really be on the verge of wanting my baby to die? – What if I harm her? – Oh stop it, stop thinking such thoughts. – But might it be true, do I really wish my baby dead? – Am I on the verge of killing my baby? – Oh no!"

If you are experiencing this element then your 'thought based fearful thought' might have gained such importance in your mind that it will now seem as if the thought itself has become engraved into your mind.

Content based fearful thoughts

If you are experiencing this element, your primary concern will not be in you having had a thought but rather, **in the implication of the thought.** For example…

Ellen: When I initially started to work with Ellen, she was about six months pregnant and had been suffering panic attacks and symptoms of stress for over a year. She proceeded to explained that, previously to her becoming pregnant, her boyfriend, Sam (not his real name) had been out of the country and very soon after them meeting each other she became pregnant. However, when she was about three months pregnant, Sam cruelly told her that just before meeting her he had slept with another woman. Ellen was devastated. And over the following few days, as she desperately tried to sort out what to do, the thought suddenly popped into her exhausted mind, "**What if that other woman's egg was carried on Sam's penis and when we made love, that other woman's egg was implanted into me.**"

Suddenly, within that one second, Ellen was struck by the **implication of the thought** and was immediately thrown into both total panic and the heartbreaking position of fearing that she could be carrying the child of her boyfriends previous lover.

Now, from time to time, we all have negative, weird thoughts, especially when tired and, when we do, we simply recognise them as being silly and immediately dismiss them. And to a rested mind, Ellen's thought would be totally ridiculous and dismissed immediately. But as Ellen was then trying to cope with her general life problems, panic attacks, prolonged symptoms of stress and continuously vomiting due to her pregnancy, plus the fact that Sam could be so cruel. Her mind was neither rational nor strong enough to recognise the thought as being ridiculous and immediately dismiss it. Indeed to Ellen's mind, not only was that particular thought feasible but all the other frightening thoughts relating to the **implication** were also feasible and free to imprint themselves onto her exhausted mind.

Record thoughts

Imagine you are at home alone until tomorrow evening, at which point your family will then come home. So, having the time, you decide to play one of your all-time favourite songs. You put your player on continuous play, adjust the volume to high, sit back and enjoy. After a while, and now tired of hearing the same song playing over and over, you go to turn it off but for some reason it won't turn off. Thinking what to do next and not wishing to trouble anyone, you decide to leave it for a little while in the hope it will somehow correct itself.

Over and over the record plays to where it really is annoying you so you decide to ring for help. But when nearing the phone, a floorboard gives-way beneath you, the rug under your feet slides into the hole taking your foot with it, pinning your leg between the broken floorboard. You are not hurt, in fact on realising your predicament you actually smile but after a few moments, once you fully realise your predicament, you decide to shout for help in the hope that a passer-by might hear you. No one hears you so no one comes. Hours then pass, the song keeps playing over and over yet you are completely unable to do anything about it.

More hours pass, and whilst hoping a member of your family will arrive home sooner than expected, you get through each hour the best you can. But as the song continues to play over and over, your ability to 'think straight' is becoming ever more difficult…and still the song continues to play over and over and over, hijacking your thoughts and drawing them ever more into the song itself.

Evening comes, and as your head feels on the brink of bursting, as dread and desperation fill your heart and as you become evermore daunted at the prospect of enduring a long, lonely night alone, mental exhaustion begins to seep in. Night time arrives and almost goes, but just as dawn breaks, out of sheer exhaustion, you fall asleep, only to suddenly wake 10 minutes later hearing the damn song still playing over and over and over. And so it goes. In whatever state your family find you when they arrive home is determined only by the sheer strength of your will.

If you are suffering this element, your thoughts will now have become stuck on one or a small number of issues relating to literally anything or anyone and the one day mentioned above might have turned into weeks or months. And whether or not your particular issue is resolvable, the more you try to rid the thoughts from your mind or try to work them out, all the more they become entrenched into your mind, even to where they might now be the one controlling factor in your life.

Compulsive behaviour

A compulsion is a persuasion of the mind to 'act out.' However, as this whole subject is so complex and impossible to cover here in any depth, I will only cover it in general terms...

To these sufferers, when in certain situations, their degree of doubt in their own judgement or in their belief that a ritual has to be maintained will, to some degree, actually control their daily life. For example...

- When going outdoors and after locking the door, some sufferers feel such indecision as to whether or not they actually locked it, they feel compelled to repeatedly check and double check the door otherwise they are unable to proceed with their outing.
- When waiting to cross over a road, some sufferers feel so unsure in their decision making, they are forced to stand on the pavement indefinitely or until the road is completely clear of traffic.
- After touching something or even when not having touched anything at all, some sufferers feel so convinced that their hands are infected, they feel compelled to repeatedly wash them, even to where their hands bleed.
- Some sufferers feel so unsure that their domestic chores are completed satisfactorily, they find themselves vacuuming the carpet six, seven times a day even to where the pile on the carpet has to be pointing in a certain direction. And whenever this sufferer finds anything out of place, whether it's a small ornament, cushion, a piece of cutlery, scrap of paper, speck of dust or, in fact, anything, they then feel so compelled to make it 'just so,' they find it absolutely impossible to concentrate or think straight until they have corrected it.
- When going outdoors, some sufferers feel such indecision or their fear of tempting fate is so controlling, they are compelled to put their coat on in a particular way, then turn the light switch on and off a certain number of times then lock and unlock the door a certain number of times and so on. Indeed, for these sufferers should their ritual be broken in any way, they then feel totally compelled to start the whole ritual again otherwise, to them, disaster will certainly befall them.

Do you see? The issue here is not in the act itself but rather, that the sufferer feels powerless against the force that drives them to perform the act.

Seemingly no solution

I use the following testimony because it's a good example of 'seemingly no solution.' I have, however, changed the name of the person involved.

David: David was Roman Catholic and one day he became drawn-in and participated in an act that was against everything his religion had taught him. After the event, fully realising what he had done, David felt that by allowing himself to be drawn into such an act and fully participating in it, he had deliberately wronged God. This situation threw David into such torment that he genuinely feared he was forever cast out.

Over the following weeks, as David desperately searched his mind for a solution, he very soon became lost in thought to the point where mental exhaustion took over. David was absolutely desperate, always found in his chair, scribbling and scribbling, forever looking at things from one point of view then another, all in the desperate hope of finding a solution, yet sadly, he becoming mentally ever further lost from life, from his family, from his friends and from himself.

The veil of mental exhaustion

- feeling trapped behind a mental veil that covers one's mind
- a sense of unreality
- feeling as if one is looking out onto the world through a glass, plastic or net curtain
- feeling hazy, as though one is mentally floating
- as though one's thoughts are about to shoot right out of one's head
- as though one is living in a glass or plastic bubble
- as though one's brain is made of cotton wool or sponge
- as if one is living in a different dimension to the rest of the world

Virtually every person who suffers mental exhaustion will experience 'the veil,' and although every sufferer has his/her own way of describing the sensations involved, I consider the most common descriptions of 'the veil' are as those listed above.

Catastrophic thoughts

Catastrophic thinking is an element of primitive arousal therefore, at one time or another, everyone has catastrophic thoughts. For example...

Myself: In 1985, when facing a medical operation (a hysterectomy) I found myself thinking, "What if things go wrong and I don't make it through the operation? My family will be devastated, my husband will find it difficult to cope, my children could be put into care and possibly separated and abused?" And yes, when taken out of context, such thoughts can seem catastrophic. But when taken in context, such thoughts are justifiable. After all, from time to time, operations do go wrong, some people don't make it through and some children are put into care, separated and abused.

When a person is facing an event which literally puts their life or well-being at risk, their protective primitive arousal then steps in by showing justifiable concern, offering cautionary warnings, presenting all the worst scenarios and giving the person the opportunity to make plans A, B and C, 'just in case;' which I did. Then, once the event is over and the person looks at the matter from the position of safety, their protective primitive aroused state will then relax and their mind will refocus back onto 'normal life.'

Being a panic attack sufferer, living each moment believing you are about to face an imminent threat to your life. Catastrophic thoughts will now strike your mind continuously because, to your mind, everything currently in your life is catastrophic; being nothing less than a matter of sheer survival. And if your mind is now exhausted, not only will catastrophic thoughts strike your mind but, once struck, they will tend to be exaggerated and stick. To your mind: – your general aches and pains of stress are now signs of cancer – a knock at the door or the phone ringing is now the police informing you that a loved one has been involved in an accident – your child with stomach ache has appendicitis – a neighbour's curtain twitching is indicative that all the neighbourhood is watching your every movement and criticising you – the postman delivering a brown envelope is bad news – when your partner is late home, he/she is having an affair – a general domestic difference of opinion is a certain divorce – a simple bang on the hand is the world turning against you – and a cloudy day is doom and gloom covering the whole world.

Morning strikes

On waking, you might experience moments of being neither asleep nor awake but just drifting in pure bliss on a semi-conscious cloud of oblivion, no real thoughts, just floating from one half thought to another, nothing real, nothing tangible and nothing clear, simply floating in a semi-conscious dreamland. On the other hand, you might wake only to be immediately struck by the realisation that you are suffering panic attacks, anxiety and perhaps weird, extremely frightening thoughts. And within that split-second of realisation, as if being struck by a bolt of lightning, you feel completely overwhelmed with the horror of it all. In which case, perhaps even before opening your eyes, you feel totally engulfed in fear, pains shoot through your body, thoughts of illness, death and insanity may strike your mind and feelings of utter weariness may engulf you, all dragging you ever further into fear and despair. And as the realisation of your situation grabs hold of you like a vice around your soul, you will possibly beg, **"Please God, not another day of this living hell."**

Disintegration

- having thoughts of great loss and deprivation
- feeling as if you have disintegrated into a million pieces
- feeling empty and/or worthless
- feeling mentally and emotionally numb
- feeling isolated
- feeling as if you are falling apart and can't get a hold on yourself
- feeling as if the whole world can see your innermost thoughts
- feeling invisible
- indecisive and/or experiencing a loss of confidence
- feeling extremely vulnerable to life
- feeling mentally, physically, emotionally and spiritually set apart from everyone and everything

Your individuality, personality, stability, life decisions, likes, dislikes, self validation, self-worth, self-respect, self-confidence and integrity are all built on, strengthened by and held together with the personal and individual building blocks that make up your 'I am'...

I am...

a good mother/father
a good wife/husband
a good friend/listener
a good communicator
dependable
the one who brings calm to any storm
the one gifted with common sense
a good companion
a person of whom my parents can be proud

the provider and protector of my family
the rock on which my family stand
intelligent
artistic

However, due to the savagery of worry, fear and terror connected to panic attacks, over the previous weeks, months and years, whether sooner or later, one by one, the building blocks that made up your 'I am' were stolen from you by the panic attacks, leaving you now feeling...
I am no longer...
a good mother/father/husband
a good friend/listener
a good communicator
dependable
the one who brings calm to any storm
the one gifted with common sense
a good companion
the person my parents are proud of
the provider and protector of my family
the rock on which my family stand
intelligent
artistic

Indeed you may now be feeling as if you have lost so much of who you once were that the real you is now gone and lost forever and the way back to who you once were is surely beyond your reach.

Overflow

- an overwhelming feeling of wanting to scream
- a tendency to bang, smash and/or throw things
- a tendency to argue and/or fight
- constantly crying

If you hold a glass tumbler with a small hole in the base then pour water into the tumbler. As long as the volume of water being poured into the tumbler is comparable to that running out, you can then continuously pour water into the tumbler without it ever overflowing. And even if the volume of water going into the tumbler varies slightly, as long as the variance of water is not too much, the tumbler would still not overflow.

On the other hand, if you should pour more water into the tumbler than that running out then, sooner or later, the tumbler will overflow.

Under normal circumstances, most of us encounter life's difficulties and cope with them relatively well. But sometimes, we can encounter a difficulty that, even to the strongest of us, will prove to be just too much, thereby causing us to overflow with the emotion of either anger or fear.

Along with life's general stresses, you are also suffering panic attacks, worry, fear, terror and symptoms of stress. So your emotional tumbler is probably full to the brim. Added to that, being a panic attack sufferer whose primitive arousal is now at 'battle ready,' when you do 'overflow,' your tendency will be to overflow via either the **frenzied aggression of anger**, which will compel you to hit out, argue, fight and throw things or the **defeated submission of fear**, which will compel you to hysterically cry for hours on end. And even when you are not at actual 'overflow,' you are still likely to – speak with an aggressive tone – verbally snap and argue with everyone – or speak with a submissive tone – give-in to differences of opinion, whether you believe yourself to be right or wrong – and cry at the slightest emotional upset.

Your sensations of 'overflow,' which cause you to feel unable to cope with even one additional drop of negativity, is why you feel reluctant to watch television, read a newspaper, talk to people and so on. You fear, if you do but then see or hear any negativity, your mind will then twist and distort it and throw you even further into turmoil, terror and despair.

Do you see? The reason why you feel so reluctant to speak to people, watch television, read newspapers etc is because, on both a conscious and subconscious level, you are retreating from all the potentially negative elements of life and in doing so, you are doing everything you can to prevent an 'overflow;' which is pure survival at work.

Nest syndrome

- an overwhelming feeling of wanting to hide from the world
- an overwhelming feeling of wanting to run home as fast as you can
- an overwhelming feeling of not wanting to leave the safety of home

When most animals are wounded and at their most vulnerable, their primitive survival responses compel them to seek out and retreat to a place of safety where they can lick their wounds, rest and recuperate. That place being their lair, nest, den, sett, home.

You are suffering panic attacks, pains, discomforts, worries, fears and terrors, from which you are feeling emotionally battered, bruised, beaten and vulnerable. As a result, your primitive survival responses are now heightened, which is driving your mental, physical and emotional instincts onto survival. So, of course, your primary driving force will now compel you to be at home.

And realise, in this context, HOME is not necessarily the place where you happen to live at the moment or where you pay the bills, do the cleaning, cooking, child-rearing, house maintenance and have responsibility. HOME is not necessarily the upmarket, gadget filled, triple glazed, double garage status symbol that stands at the end of a long driveway. HOME is, however, the place where you don't have to pretend to be coping, where you don't have to pretend to be strong and where you don't have to pretend to be in control. HOME is where you **feel** safe, protected, cared for and loved. HOME, in this case, is not necessarily a place but a feeling in your heart.

Once you understand 'nest syndrome' you will then understand why your overriding need for 'home'(to run home, to be at home, to 'go back home to mum,' to retreat to your shed at the bottom of your garden or to return to a place from your past where you felt safe) is not the whim of a soft, spoiled person. Indeed, it is one of the most compelling, overriding, basic and fundamental primitive survival response of mankind.

Deprivation/hibernation

- loss of interest
- a feeling of impending doom
- depressive thoughts
- feelings of deprivation
- just wanting to hide away, hibernate and be alone
- inclined to keep saying to people, "Just leave me alone"
- always feeling sleepy, tired, exhausted, sluggish
- feeling separated and separate from life
- mentally sluggish, as if living in a hazy fog
- emotionally withdrawn, introverted, cold, barren, overcast and grey
- physically sedentary, not moving out of the bed or chair all day, eating sparingly and having a low libido.

Primitive man lived a variable existence. During times of plenty, when strengthened by sustenance, he lived at his most active and outgoing: – mentally alert – having an interest in life – having the physical energy to hunt and gather food – eating heartily – and being highly sexually active. During times of famine, when food was scarce, to conserve energy, he then lived at virtual shut down: – mentally sluggish – sedentary – eating sparingly – physically inactive – and having a low libido.

As you see, primitive man experienced mental, emotional and physical shutdown when the quality of his life deteriorated and he was deprived of the essentials of his life. But being primitive, his essentials were the most basic, such as food, water and shelter. As a result, for primitive man to feel deprived and experience emotional shutdown, the **only** requirements were for food, water and shelter to be in short supply.

'We' are very different to primitive man. Yes we need food, water and shelter to sustain our life but to sustain our quality of life we need more. As a result, we do not have to be denied only the basic elements of life to feel deprived, for we feel deprived if we experience a shortage of the things that make up our 'quality' of life, such as freedom, love, security and peace.

Panic attacks may now be depriving you of everything important to you: peace of mind, physical strength, dignity, freedom, partner, friends, security, stability, social standing, career, hopes, dreams, self-esteem, confidence, self-respect and your 'I am.' If so, you will be experiencing deprivation/hibernation, to one degree or another, perhaps to complete shutdown.

The feeling of emotional deprivation/hibernation, in its mildest form, will affect everyone at some time or another. Look how we are all inclined to withdraw from life on a cold, overcast, grey day, when all we want to do is just laze around the house, doing nothing in particular, dozing in front of the fire, curling up with a good video or book and just hibernating. However when deprivation/hibernation is experienced not merely for a few days but for weeks and months on end (as during panic attacks) then the primitive survival mechanism, believing it to be wintertime, 'kicks in' and, in turn, puts the whole bodily system into virtual shutdown.

The dreaded darkness

Every panic attack sufferer will, to one degree or another, live under the emotional dark and threatening shadow of fear. But for many sufferers, the 'time of day' will influence just how light or dark that shadow is...

Some sufferers welcome the daytime because during the day there are numerous distractions from fear: things to do, people to see, places to go and tasks to perform. For these sufferers, the brightness of the daytime will offer enough light to allow them to see through their own emotional darkness and thereby lift their spirit. On the other hand, some sufferers dread the daytime because during the day they have to go outdoors, speak to people and put themselves into all kinds of situations which, in turn, makes them feel overly vulnerable. Indeed, for some sufferers, just seeing the buzz of life around them only highlights their own disconnection from life, which makes them feel even more isolated.

Some sufferers welcome the night time because within the darkness of the night they are able to hide from the world or they know that sleep is near and through sleep they are able to escape from their worries, fears and terrors. On the other hand, some sufferers dread the night time because during the night there is not the same distraction from fear or they know they are facing a very long, lonely and sleepless night filled with fear, desperation and exhaustion.

There is also another group of sufferers who dread the night, or to be precise, they dread the darkness that comes with the night. These sufferers feel threatened by the night itself, as if the darkness of the night is a black and menacing shroud that wraps itself around them, closing in their mind, locking in their fears with only their own dark and frightening thoughts for company, and with no possible means of escape, adding even more emotional darkness to their already emotionally darkened state.

Insomnia

If you are experiencing a lack of sleep the likely causes are...

- If you were lost inside my jungle (see 'Arousal Creating Panic Attacks,' page 68) and surrounded by great danger, you would not find it easy to simply detach yourself from the danger and go to sleep. But rather, you would stay 'on-guard' all night, perhaps dropping off to sleep for a few moments at a time but then waking at the slightest trigger. So being a panic attack sufferer, living in your own jungle of worry, fear and terror, of course sleep will not come easily, of course, when sleeping, your dreams will be full of horror and of course you will sleep on and off throughout the night, wakening at the slightest sound with a sudden jolt. That is exactly what your body is supposed to do when in fear.
- As you saw previously, when the body is tired it has a tendency to slow down but when the mind is tired it has a tendency to speed up. So any exhausted mind will have some difficultly falling asleep and a mind in breakdown will, most certainly, have difficulty falling asleep.
- Sleep has six stages (or levels) and whilst every person will have their own unique sleep pattern, sleep generally follows a 60-90 minute pattern consisting of peaks and troughs; the peaks being the relatively shallow sleep and the troughs being the deeper sleep.

Many stress sufferers tend to have difficulty sleeping. And whilst some have difficulty falling asleep, others fall asleep and sleep through the deeper sleep only to awaken during the shallow sleep then, after a while, they again fall asleep, only to, yet again, awaken 60-90 minutes later. This broken sleep pattern will continue throughout the night but on wakening, the person will genuinely believe they haven't slept a wink all night. This is a really common experience but nevertheless very distressing.

Self assessment

If you are experiencing this element you will find yourself increasingly thinking about your pains and distress and, by doing so, you fear that you are deliberately inviting them to come on. That is not so.

Whenever we are experiencing pain or distress, in order to protect life, our mind will continuously reassess whether or not our level of pain and distress has eased or intensified. That is part of its purpose. You are currently experiencing pain and distress, as a result, your mind will be repeatedly reassessing your symptoms. As such, self-assessment is not self-inflicted, it is, however, a natural function of your mind.

Loneliness of spirit

Being a panic attack sufferer, particularly if your suffering is severe, you will now be feeling the 'loneliness of spirit' in every aspect of your life, from the moment you wake to when you manage to sleep...

Your 'loneliness of spirit' is surely in: – you being labelled neurotic when, in truth, you are very courageous, just getting through life the best you can – you fearing that you are becoming mentally and physically out of control, yet thinking there is absolutely nothing you can do about it – you knowing that, despite telling doctors, loved ones, family and friends how desperate and frightened you feel, it is totally impossible for them to really understand the true degree of your suffering – and your misguided belief that, one day soon, your fear and symptoms will become so all-engulfing, they will strip you of everything you have, everything you are, everything you love and everything you hope to be.

Your 'loneliness of spirit' might also be in: – you praying for the morning when you no longer wake in the early hours only for your heart to sink in dread at the prospect of having to endure another day of living hell – your mourning for the old you who now seems so far away and possibly lost for ever – and you feeling totally overwhelmed by the world, terrified by panic, weary of life and daunted by the future.

Your 'loneliness of spirit' is possibly in: – your torment and dread of meeting people yet longing for friendship – praying for strength when you are so weary of trying to be strong – being forced to fight when your only wish is for peace – praying for courage when just hanging onto life is the most courageous act of all – struggling to appear normal when your whole world feels insane – trying to hold your family together when your own self feels shattered into a million pieces – and desperately clinging on to life when life, as a panic attack sufferer, can so easily be forfeited.

Your 'loneliness of spirit' is surely in: – your grief at the passing of time and all those lost days, weeks, months and years of simple 'normal' life – the pleasurable life events that could and should have been so memorable but which are now lost and gone forever – your yearning for the day when you are, again, free to enjoy life's simplest of pleasures: going outside, feeling the space, standing in the rain, feeling the sunshine on your body, picking flowers from your garden and arranging them in a vase, going to a football match, following a television programme, taking the children to the park, looking into the eyes of your family without feeling guilt and shame for being the seemingly demented person who has to be 'looked after' – and in every fibre and sinew of 'you' which is now screaming for one blessed moment of peace.

And your 'loneliness of spirit' is probably your isolation: – knowing that when you begin to feel the fear rising, within a split-second, you will be experiencing the most extreme mental and physical sensations of terror whilst having no idea of how to stop them – knowing that despite having a caring, loving, protective family and friends, it is you alone who has to suffer and endure the distressing and terrifying sensations of panic attacks – and knowing that yes you are physically with your friends and family, your eyes might be on them and words might come out your mouth but emotionally you are not with them, you are in a completely different world to them, you are alone, trapped, desperate and suffering. You are in pain, despair, fear and terror. You are in the world of panic attacks.

Suicidal thoughts

- experiencing the feelings mentioned in Deprivation/Hibernation
- feeling completely engulfed with blackness
- feeling utter weariness and hopelessness
- feeling totally isolated and empty
- inclinations and/or attempts of suicide

Every panic attack sufferer who is affected severely will have suicidal thoughts, some consider it and immediately dismiss it, some consider it, plan it and are currently holding it in mind 'just-in-case,' some attempt it and live, some attempt it and perish.

And so, if you are suffering severely: – if full-blown panic attacks are striking you many times a day – if your every moment is now spent in pain, fear, torment and dread – if you are utterly weary of dragging your exhausted body through one torturous day after another – if your suffering seems endless and all hope of recovery seems lost to you – if the continuous battle of trying to hold yourself together and keep your thoughts under control has become too much – and if you have reached the point of not washing, dressing or getting out of bed because it all seems too much effort and 'oh so pointless.' Then in all probability you are experiencing 'suicidal thoughts.'

I will immediately follow that statement by saying, from all my years involvement with panic attacks, I know that the vast majority of those sufferers who do wish to die, do not wish death for deaths sake but rather, they simply yearn to escape the mental, physical and emotional torture of panic attacks, and not knowing how else to escape, they conclude that dying must be their only option.

I will also add here that, in my experience, when a panic attack sufferer has had suicidal thoughts and then recovers from panic attacks to find peace, it is they who invariably prove to be the ones who really appreciate life and, in so doing, go on to live their life to its fullest.

Mental/Nervous breakdown

Stress related mental breakdown and stress related nervous breakdown are not two terms used for two separate conditions but rather, they are two terms used for the same condition. And as most sufferers tend to find the term 'nervous' breakdown much less frightening than 'mental' breakdown, I always try to use the term 'nervous' whenever I can. That now being said, sometimes, to ensure clarity, it is necessary for me to use the term 'mental' breakdown.

When I suffered panic attacks, surprisingly, the question of whether or not I was in nervous breakdown never entered my mind; I simply suspected that I might be going insane. However, one day whilst reading a particular book, and before I fully realised it, the book had told me that I was having a nervous breakdown. What a shock! For whilst I was relieved to know that I was not going insane, I was still not prepared to hear that I was actually in nervous breakdown, particularly as, in the 1960s (similar to those who were suffering insanity) they often 'took people away' who were suffering nervous breakdown and put them into a mental asylum then given electric shock treatment. So, in that one brief moment, to my mind, I was suddenly judged, sentenced and doomed to a life of mental hospitals, electric shock treatments and drug-fed to live a zombifyed existence.

The reason why I tell you this now is because, whilst virtually every person who suffers panic attacks will suspect they are either in or heading for a nervous breakdown, not every sufferer is prepared for the diagnosis when given by their doctor or therapist. For example, when told they are **not** in a nervous breakdown, whilst some sufferers feel incredibly relieved at 'not being that ill,' others feel completely misunderstood. Similarly, when told they **are** in a nervous breakdown, whilst some sufferers feel relieved at finally having their degree of suffering recognised, others feel totally overwhelmed and become very frightened. So bearing this in mind, I have divided the following information into two sections...

Section One is 9 vital pieces of information for everyone to read.

Section Two is positioned alone on page 126. So only read page 126 if you wish to know the general indications of nervous breakdown.

SECTION ONE – FOR EVERYONE TO READ

1. During nervous breakdown there is – no organic breaking of the nerves – no organic breaking of the nervous system – no organic breaking of the mind – no point where any organic damage is done – no point of no return for the brain – no point of no return for the mind – no point of no return for the emotions – and no point of no return for you.

2. The acute mental symptoms of stress we normally experience whilst waiting to visit the dentist or waiting for test results (a lack of concentration, vagueness, oblivious to surroundings, racing thoughts, thoughts of doom and so on) are real. But when we are waiting to visit the dentist or waiting for test results, despite us then experiencing acute mental symptoms of stress, we are not automatically in a nervous breakdown. Therefore, the mere presence of acute mental symptoms of stress is not an automatic indication of nervous breakdown.

3. Some people experience numerous mental symptoms of stress but it is wrong to say they are in breakdown. Yet other people experience only one or two mental symptoms of stress but they are

clearly in breakdown. Therefore, the number of mental symptoms of stress experienced is not an automatic indication of breakdown.

4. When an unstressed person is suffering extreme and overwhelming anger, fear, frustration or jealousy they can temporarily lose control of their rational behaviour. Yet it is incorrect to say that when one is temporarily 'out of control' one is automatically experiencing nervous breakdown. Therefore, to be temporarily mentally 'out of control' does not and is not an automatic indication of nervous breakdown.

5. Most panic attack sufferers feel panicky when they are in certain places or situations, so in order to attain some control, many sufferers adapt their whole life to where they no longer go into such places and situations, thereby avoiding experiencing panic. Yet in such cases, it is totally wrong to assume that the sufferer's apparently strange and extreme behaviour is an automatic indication of nervous breakdown. Therefore, seemingly strange, extreme and even eccentric actions are not an automatic indication of nervous breakdown.

6. You are experiencing panic attacks and mental symptoms of stress, your symptoms might be numerous and extreme, you are often out of control and you may have adapted your lifestyle to where other people think you you are crazy. Yet not one of those elements is, in itself, an automatic indication of breakdown. Even combining them altogether is still not an automatic indication of nervous breakdown. Indeed, at this very moment, there are possibly millions of panic attacks sufferers experiencing numerous symptoms of stress, having temporary periods of being out of control and have adapted their lifestyle to where other people think they are crazy. Yet they are definitely not in nervous breakdown.

7. For many people, the actual moment of breakdown is not a frenzied affair. In fact many people in nervous breakdown are not even sure if it has occurred at all.

8. There are a few people who reach the extreme point where they feel they cannot take any more and their mind dramatically calls stop. Yet whether the 'stop' is manifested in a physical frenzied eruption or a complete mental shut down, their mind does not actually breakdown; it is simply demanding rest.

9. Nervous breakdown need never be the end of the road, for when used to its best advantage, it can be the gift that puts the person 'back on track' and indeed be the making of them.

Read the boxed section below only if you want to know the general indications of nervous breakdown.

SECTION TWO

There is not one universally agreed point at which every doctor will diagnose a patient to be in mental breakdown. The diagnosis of mental breakdown is, most certainly, based on the individual person involved. Having said that, there is a 'general indication' of mental breakdown, which I will now explain...

Up to now, whilst covering mental breakdown, I have deliberately omitted to use one word, and when that one word is added to the above symptoms, then it alone will determine whether or not you are showing the general indications of nervous breakdown...the word being degree.

If you are now experiencing mental symptoms of stress to the degree where, despite having adapted your life around them, you are still mentally unable to cope with your normal everyday tasks of life, then you are displaying the general indications of nervous breakdown. Having said that, I will immediately repeat. For many people, nervous breakdown is the catalyst that proves to be their making; that includes myself.

Remember, every mental symptom of stress mentioned above can be eradicated

Remember, if you are suffering mental tiredness, exhaustion, breakdown or anywhere in-between then your thoughts will not fit neatly under one or two particular thought patterns but rather, your thoughts will be a mixture of many patterns, including some not mentioned previously. Having said that, don't feel discouraged thinking that the mending of your mental symptoms of stress must be a highly complex and complicated procedure. It need not be. Of course, on an individual level, you will need to adapt your recovery to your own ability and requirements but on a general level, your recovery rests solely on your mind gaining sufficient rest.

The calming of your mental symptoms of stress is covered, in part, in the next step. I say 'in part' because, when taken as a whole, the calming of your mental symptoms of stress is, in fact, covered throughout this whole programme.

A few words to your relative, friend or befriender

If you have never experienced panic attacks or acute stress then, with my greatest respect, it is absolutely impossible for you to fully comprehend the degree of fear and despair that the sufferer is experiencing. In which case, you might now be feeling very angry with me for raising the issues of both 'suicidal thoughts' and 'nervous breakdown,' believing that, by my raising the subject, I am putting ideas into the mind of the sufferer. That is not the case at all...

Re: Suicidal thoughts
Every person who is severely affected by panic attacks has already had, and might still be having, suicidal thoughts, whether they voiced them or not. You doubt me?

Being a friend or relative of a person who is suffering severely with panic attacks and symptoms of stress, you have probably heard their cries of despair, you have witnessed their utter desperation, you have seen their absolute hopelessness and you are aware that they are living moment by moment in acute fear and terror. So think of a situation that fills **you** with utter terror, your worst nightmare: perhaps; – you being trapped in a lift or underground whilst suffering claustrophobia – you being held hostage in a filthy, foreign, cockroach infested prison cell where, after witnessing others being brutally and systematically beaten and worse, you believe the brutes are now coming for you – or you being trapped in a pit of rats, cockroaches, bees, spiders or snakes whilst being phobic to them – or you are waiting to parachute out of an airplane whilst suffering vertigo.

Once you have identified your nightmarish scenario, emotionally put yourself trapped there, twenty four hours a day, seven days a week, week in and week out. Then: – as the fear and terror rises within you until panic takes over – as you fight to swallow all your screams of sheer terror whilst trying to put on a brave face – as the sense of failure eats at you when, time and again, you try to free yourself only to fail – as weariness and fatigue sap the life out of you whilst you dig ever deeper into your soul for the grit and strength to endure – and as despair fills your very being at the prospect of never escaping that hell-hole until death itself finally claims you, ask yourself, "Could I **really** take it?"

So realising that anyone can act with bravado when, in reality, they know they are safe, put your hand on your heart and **truly** ask yourseif, "If that was really happening to me, twenty-four hours a day, seven days a week, week in and week out, how would I really cope? How strong would I really be? How much grit would I really find? And how long would I really last; days, weeks, months, years?" Has the thought of suicide crossed your mind yet? If not, how much more could you really take before it does? And what if, right now, you are at that point?

As the relative, friend or befriender of a severely affected panic attack sufferer, please realise: My raising the issue of suicide will not put new ideas into the sufferers mind but rather, it will help your very courageous loved one to realise that, even in their darkest hours, they are not alone, as many of us who have also been there are truly with them in spirit and, in truth, will stay with them until they also are totally and permanently free of panic attacks.

Re: Nervous breakdown

In your quietest moments, have you ever wondered whether or not your befriended is experiencing a nervous breakdown? If so, do you really think they have not thought that also? Of course they have.

Re-cap:
To Take Your Second Step
To Freedom...

1. Understanding this step is absolutely crucial to recovery from panic attacks because once the mind understands what is happening and why it is happening, it will then be much more willing to 'stand down' and release its tight hold.

2. Whether you have read this step yourself or someone has read it with you or to you, **do not**, under any circumstances, have someone read it then they give their interpretation of it to you.

3. If you found certain parts of this step difficult to understand then do please try to read the relevant section or sections again. However, after that, if you still have difficulty understanding it then I do urge you to discuss the matter further with your befriender and medical doctor.

4. Once you have truly read, understood, thought about and followed the information in this step relevant to you then please move onto Step Three...
   Step Three is enlightening: – it explains all that you are doing wrong during a panic attack; thereby fuelling it – it explains what you need to do during a panic attack; thereby calming it – it forewarns you of the potential 'boulders' of recovery and how recovery can so often feel like a roller-coaster ride of good-days/bad-days and it suggests ways of getting through those days – it offers a very effective stress-buster routine – and if you are suffering with mental symptoms of stress, especially if to the point of nervous exhaustion/breakdown, it explains how you can gain some much needed 'mind-rest.'

Step Three

Enlighten yourself… to how you
will achieve recovery

Panic attacks – Wrong

Panic attacks – Right

The roller-coaster ride of good-days/bad-days

The stress-buster

To ease ongoing mental symptoms of stress

Re-cap: To take your third step to freedom…

Panic Attacks – Wrong!

As you saw in my jungle, arousal itself has many levels; from slight irritation and apprehension to pure rage and frenzied terror. In this section we will concentrate solely on the higher levels of arousal such as those you experience during a panic attack...

During a panic attack...you move quickly

During a panic attack...you try to rationalise

During a panic attack...you try to fight your way through it

During a panic attack... you move quickly

When the terror of panic attacks strike, whilst a few sufferers become terror struck and unable to move, the vast majority feel an overwhelming compulsion to do something. But when the terror of the panic attack and the compulsion to do something is added to the sufferer's confusion of not knowing what to do, then utter frenzy is often created: – some sufferers find themselves smashing and hitting whatever or whoever happens to be within reach – others rip off their clothes, or curl up in cupboards, or grip tightly onto something for fear of what they might do if they were to let go – others throw themselves into physical activity, or jump into a bath of cold water (whilst fully dressed) hoping the shock will calm them down – and others find themselves running...

Supermarket shopping is a classic place where panic attack sufferers find themselves running. One moment they are walking around the store then, on feeling their fear rising, they immediately abandon their basket or trolley in the middle of the aisle then race through the supermarket, crashing into trolleys, pushing other customers to one side, banging into the beans and barging through anything that happens to be in their path. Once at the checkout, whilst some sufferers do manage to fumble out a few words to the checkout operator (usually something to do with forgetting to lock a door or turn off the cooker) others run straight out of the store not really caring what anyone thinks.

Once outside the supermarket, whilst some sufferers feel compelled to run around the car park until their panic calms, others desperately seek the sanctuary of their car then sit there shaking and sweating, with their heart pounding and their hands gripping the steering wheel so knuckle-white tightly it would take a crowbar to free them. And even when in the sanctuary of their car, many find it impossible to stay stationary, so off they screech with wild looks on their faces, their bodies hunched over the steering wheel and driving as if they were on a racing track or in a dodgems car on a fairground. This state of 'energised compulsion to do something' mixed with not knowing what to do, can be so overwhelming, I challenge any wild bull to stop a panic attack sufferer in full flight.

Of course the reasons why so many panic attack sufferers feel the compulsion to run is because a) their 'fight or flight' is then in full alert, b) they know that by escaping public view, the pressure of having to look 'normal' will then be off them and c) they know they will minimise any potential embarrassment and ridicule from any onlookers.

Whenever a frightened person moves quickly, their own primitive survival responses assume that danger is near. As a result, their nervous system becomes more stimulated, their body becomes more energized and their mental and physical sensations of arousal become ever more heightened.

Therefore as running or moving quickly in high fear serves only to stimulate arousal...**running or moving quickly during a panic attack is the wrong thing to do.**

During a panic attack...you try to rationalise

During extreme danger, when arousal is at its highest, the modern thinking part of the brain loses virtually all its ability to rationalise. Likewise during a panic attack, when arousal is at its highest, the modern thinking part of the brain then loses virtually all its ability to rationalise. In which case, during a panic attack, when trying to 'think' your way out of it, to stop your mind racing, to calm yourself down, to rid your mind of terrifying thoughts of imminent heart attack, brain haemorrhage, choking, collapsing, snapping into insanity, erupting into a frenzied maniac or dying. **You are then demanding a degree of rational thought from the modern part of your brain which, in such circumstances, it cannot and is not designed to provide.** As a result, it all becomes too much for the modern part of your brain, causing it to overload and lose virtually all its ability for rational thought. And the more you then try to think your way out of the panic attack, all the more you 'lose it,' become even more out of control and spiral into ever more terror.

Therefore, as trying to rationalise during high fear serves only to overload the modern thinking part of the brain and therefore stimulates arousal...**trying to rationalise during a panic attack is the wrong use of brainpower.**

During a panic attack... you try to fight your way through it

When we think of the word 'fight' we imagine pumped-up muscles, flared nostrils, gritted teeth and frenzied men with wild facial expressions, all punching, kicking, stabbing and killing with the sole aim to overpower the enemy. However fighting is not always so blatant and obvious, indeed for literally millions of people, fighting is a very quiet and private affair...

In domestic life

The person riddled with arthritis is fighting every time they struggle to climb the stairs – the exhausted mother is fighting every time she drags herself out of bed to endure yet another day – the terminally ill person is fighting by just hanging onto life for one more day – we are all fighting every time we reassure ourselves, encourage ourselves and tell ourselves with **grit** and **determination**...

"Come on now, you can do this, you really can do this.
Stay calm: keep a grip.
Just take a deep breath: in-2-3 out-2-3.
You can do this, you really can do this!"

In sport

Before any sporting event, in the attempt to lift with more strength, run faster, jump higher, fight with more aggression and achieve greater feats than they would normally, the sports person will deliberately psyche themselves up, bring forth their fighting spirit, stimulate their primitive arousal and energise themselves by reassuring themselves, encouraging themselves and telling themselves with **grit** and **determination**...

"Come on now, you can do this, you really can do this.
Stay calm: keep a grip.
Just take a deep breath: in-2-3 out-2-3.
You can do this, you really can do this!"

Panic attacks

Panic attacks make an illusive foe. You can't get a grip on them, squeeze the life out of them, beat them, stab them, shoot them, drown them, poison them or suffocate them. As a result, during a panic attack, although **it** has the ability to inflict the severest of symptoms onto **you**, **you** feel helpless to **it**, forever at **its** mercy; you never knowing the outcome but always fearing the worst. It feels like you know you are about to be struck but you don't know if by a butterfly or a bus, "Oh God how bad will this one be? How far will it take me? How far can it take me? Is this the one that gives me a heart attack or brain haemorrhage? Is this the one that throws me over the edge into insanity? Is this the one that will take me to the point of no return? Will I survive it but be permanently damaged? Will this be the one that finally kills me?"

So during a panic attack, when experiencing high fear but not being able to physically fight and protect yourself, you find yourself mentally fighting: – fighting to prevent the panic attack from becoming 'full blown' – fighting to control it, contain it, suppress it – fighting to stop your mind racing and keep your thoughts under control – fighting to rid your mind of terrifying thoughts of imminent madness, deformity and death – and fighting by digging deep within yourself, finding more strength then psyching yourself up by reassuring yourself, encouraging yourself and telling yourself with **grit** and **determination**

"Come on now, you can do this, you really can do this.

Stay calm: keep a grip.

Just take a deep breath: in-2-3 out-2-3.

You can do this, you really can do this!"

You have to fight the panic attack: don't let it beat you!

Come on now, you can do this, you really can do this."

Wrong! Wrong! Wrong!

All thoughts of getting a grip, controlling, containing, suppressing, dominance and force are all thoughts of aggression. They are all 'fighting talk' and do not calm arousal but actually stimulate it.

Do you see? Every time a panic attack strikes, you being a person of grit and deep inner strength but not knowing what else to do, you valiantly psyche yourself up and mentally fight it. However by mentally fighting the panic attack you are, in fact, stimulating your primitive arousal, producing and secreting more adrenalin, making more nervous energy, creating more mental and physical sensations of arousal and taking yourself ever further into the spiral of terror.

Therefore, as mentally fighting, **at any time**, serves only to **'psyche up'** the body and mind, thus stimulating both primitive arousal and the fighting spirit... **mentally fighting during a panic attack is absolutely the wrong mental approach.**

When Tom frightened you,
you had a choice

Cast your mind back to Tom (Step Two, page 52) and how no conscious thought is required to trigger off arousal. Another significant point from that incident is that when Tom frightened you, you then had a choice of how to respond. And although you will probably disagree with that statement, you **did** have a choice! Likewise, whether or not you believe it, when a panic attack strikes, just like your choice with Tom, you do have a choice of how to respond. You doubt me? You'll see in the next chapter.

Panic Attacks – Right!

"Come to the edge," he said.
They said, "We are afraid."
"Come to the edge," he said.
They came, he pushed them...
and they flew
Guillaume Apollinaire

To calm a panic attack is to let-go of it. But to let-go of frenzied terror you need to be **exceptionally** precise in your actions. This section will explain those actions: what they are, how they work, when to put them into practise and how to put them into practise. However when reading this section you will probably read something and think, "Lorraine you must be joking, I am far too ill for this to help me." Even so, I ask you to please, read this **entire** chapter before making your judgement.

Let-go

When a panic attack is throwing its worst at you and the hurricane of terror is engulfing you, you then need to take shelter, sanctuary until the storm has passed. The following list is a glimpse into how you will find your shelter, the more detailed information will follow that. And please take your time, as reading this section too quickly could hinder your recovery...

Let-go: using a thoroughly tried and tested practice
Let-go: knowing the body is merely the servant of the mind/brain
Let-go: using your limited brainpower
Let-go: going to the necessary depth
Let-go: using the right words for you
Let-go: voicing your words out loud, if possible
Let-go: whispering your words; if need be
Let-go: in stillness
Let-go: at the correct time
Let-go: and be 'somewhere else'
Let-go: with a desire to recover

Let-go: by using
a thoroughly tried and tested practise

There are two primary ways to let-go. The first is to completely empty the mind of all conscious thought thus allowing spontaneous, intuitive, often spiritual thoughts to simply float freely in and out. But as that technique is impossible during a panic attack we don't even attempt it. The second way to let-go is by distraction. That is, to distract the mind away from negative thoughts by focusing it onto a positive element…and that is possible for **all** panic attack sufferers, without exception, if done in a very precise way. And when letting-go by distraction is adapted to suit the needs and abilities of the panic attack sufferer, it has proved itself to be the gentlest, safest, most powerful and permanent means by which freedom from panic attacks is attained.

The **practise** of letting-go by distraction works by distracting the mind enough, in a very particular way, that will allow the mind moments of freedom.

The **act** of letting-go is practised in many forms throughout the world.

The **subject matter** used to let-go can relate to anyone or anything.

The **duration** can last from minutes to hours.

The **frequency** can be from once a week to numerous times a day.

And whilst the essential elements of the practise are held fast by every participant, the **non-essential elements** can be adapted to suit the personal needs of each individual participant.

Let-go: knowing the body is merely
the servant of the mind

Remember, the mind is that part of us that is solely individual to us, it is our decision maker, our driving force, it is the primary element that actually takes our body where we want it to go.

It is so very important for you to grasp the extent to which the body is merely the servant of the mind that I will now give you 4 examples…

1. Here's Tom again
2. Boulders
3. You are what you think
4. Thought can even control life and death

1. Here's Tom again
Cast your mind back, yet again, to Tom (page 52) and how no conscious thought is required to trigger off arousal. Immediately after Tom had

crashed the cymbals together, you were then likely to have chosen one of three responses…

1. You could have laughed and seen the funny side of Tom's prank. In which case your arousal responses (heartbeat, breathing and so on) would have calmed down quite quickly.

2. You could have sat back down, saying nothing, yet inside feeling very angry with Tom. In which case, your arousal responses would have continued to be stimulated for a while, fading only as your anger faded.

3. You could have been so angry at Tom for frightening you that you screamed and shouted at him, resulting in you both having the most dreadful row. In which case, all your arousal responses would have continued to be high throughout the duration of your anger, calming only when your thoughts and anger had calmed.

Do you see? Immediately after Tom had crashed the cymbals together, if you had chosen to see the funny side of his prank then all your arousal responses would have immediately calmed. If you had chosen to be moderately angry with Tom then all your responses would have partially calmed down. And if you had chosen to be really angry with Tom then all your responses would have continued to be high indefinitely.

So in whichever way you responded to Tom's prank, **you controlled it**. You controlled your own arousal responses. You controlled whether or not your responses calmed, or whether they continued for a short while or whether they continued at a high rate for a long time. And you did it solely by what you were thinking about Tom and his prank.

In short, when your mind told your body to immediately jump, it did so. And when your mind told your body to totally calm, partially calm or stay angry for a while, it did so. **Your body is the servant of your mind**.

2. Boulders

Picture the scene: You are riding a bicycle down a country lane. After a while you notice a large boulder in the distance blocking half the pathway. Your first though is, "My goodness, that's a big boulder" but on quickly assessing the situation, you realise that, even if you stay on your bicycle, you will still have ample space to pass. So you cycle on.

Question: As you cycle closer to the boulder, would you keep your eyes and thoughts fixed firmly onto the boulder and think, "What an unusual sight, I wonder how it got there? I hope I don't crash into it. How very big it looks the closer I get to it." Or whilst frequently glancing over to the boulder to asses your safety, would you keep the main focus of your eyes and thoughts beyond it and through the gap? Of course the latter, for you know that if your eyes and thoughts where focused onto the boulder your mind would draw your body towards it and you would crash into it.

Similarly, if you were driving your car along the road and noticed an enormous articulated lorry in the next lane, you wouldn't focus your eyes and thoughts onto the lorry, for if you did, your mind would then draw your body towards the lorry and you would crash into it. But rather, as soon as you noticed the lorry, whilst frequently glancing over to it and assessing the situation, you would keep the main focus of your eyes and thoughts firmly fixed past the lorry and onto the road in front of you, thereby ensuring your safety. In short, whatever you focus your mind on, your body will be automatically drawn to it.

3. You are what you think
Emotionally

- If you look out of the window, see it raining and think, "Oh no it's raining, I'm going to get wet today." As the thought was negative, your mood would fall and your body would become lethargic.
- On the other hand, if you look out of the window, see it raining and think, "Oh no it's raining, I'm going to get wet today…Never mind, at least tonight I won't have to spend time watering the garden, so I'll be free to enjoy a wonderful leisurely meal." Although your first thought was negative, as you immediately followed it by a positive thought your mood would rise and your body would have more 'oomph.'
- If you were informed that you had only moments to live yet your last thought was similar to, "Oh well, I'm now about to die…but I've done my best and now I'm going to meet my God." Even as you took your last breath, your mood would rise and you would be at peace.
- If both you and your beloved partner had always dreamed of winning the Lottery but sadly your partner had recently died and then you won the Lottery. If your last thoughts were similar to, "Great, I'm a millionaire but this money has no use to me whatsoever now my loved one has died." Even though your lifelong dream had come true, your mood would nevertheless fall and you would become melancholic.

Physically

Try the following proof yourself. You will need someone to assist you…
1. Stand upright with your arms hanging relaxed by your side.
2. With your arms still by your side, tell yourself (for about 30 to 40 seconds) and really mean it, that you are an extremely weak,

pathetic and useless human being: ask your assistant to be your timekeeper.

3. Raise one arm (either arm) and hold it out at shoulder height then, your assistant should gently yet quite firmly press your raised arm downwards and you try to resist – note your power of resistance.

4. Rest for a moment with your arms by your side.

5. With your arms still by your side, tell yourself (for about 30 to 40 seconds) and really mean it, that you are a very strong, powerful, awesome human being: ask your assistant to be your timekeeper.

6. Now, raise the same arm as previously and hold it out at shoulder height then, your assistant should gently yet quite firmly press your raised arm downwards and you try to resist – note your power of resistance.

Need I say more?

4. Thought can even control life and death
Although this example has no relevance to panic attacks whatsoever, it is nevertheless an excellent example of how the mind controls the body...

On being told they have a terminal illness of which an estimated 'time-left' is given, many people feel such a strong desire to reach a particular event, i.e. birthday, wedding, anniversary, the birth of a child or until a certain task is achieved, they actually delay their own death for years. On the other hand, after losing a loved one, some people feel so lost and lose all purpose in life that, within the following two years, they develop a terminal illness and die. The 'will' of the mind is so powerful, it can and often does determine whether the body lives or dies.

Thought: the all powerful
From the above examples, I hope you see that the body itself is not the controlling factor in all this, as it does not, will not and cannot control itself. The body is merely the servant of the mind. So when your thoughts are positive, your body will experience sensations of optimism and be energised. When your thoughts are negative your body will experience sensations of gloom and feel lethargic. When your thoughts are fearful, your body will experience sensations of arousal. When your thoughts are only brief flash thoughts of fear, your body will experience only brief flash seconds of arousal. When your thoughts are fearful and continuous, your body will experience continuous sensations of arousal. When your thoughts are fearful, acute and continuous, your body will experience continuous sensations of full-blown fight or flight. As a result, whether

your thoughts are positive, negative, flash or continuous your body will respond so very fast that your body is, in reality, experiencing what you are thinking, right now!

And to take this subject further. Even if you are 99% surrounded by a positive aspect (like winning the Lottery) but your thoughts are focused onto the 1% negative boulder, your mind will steer your body towards the negative boulder. Likewise, when you are 99% surrounded by a negative boulder (as during a panic attack) but your thoughts are focused onto the 1% positive aspect, your mind will, even then, steer your body towards the positive aspect.

In short, whatever thought you had one second ago, your thoughts are so incredibly fast, you could say, you **are** what you are thinking: right now!

Let-go: using your limited brainpower

The irony of panic attacks is that during a panic attack, when the modern thinking part of the brain has lost virtually all its ability to create rational thought, whether the panic attack continues or whether it calms is actually dependent on thought. Therefore during a panic attack, making **full** use of whatever 'thought ability' you have is absolutely essential...

I have just explained that during a panic attack virtually all rational thought will be lost to you. Please note, the word is **virtually**, which tells you that during a panic attack you do still have **some** degree of ability for thought. And whilst that limited degree of ability is limited in the extreme, it is still enough to free you from any panic attack. Let me explain...

The human brain is designed to experience not only emotions and the extremes of those emotions but also the many levels or degrees within those extremes. Consequently, when the human brain experiences a panic attack, even if it is the worst, severest, most frenzied panic attack ever known. Despite the modern part of the brain then losing virtually all its ability to create, construct, organize and arrange rational thought. **The brain still has enough ability to hold onto six words, if those words do not have to be created, constructed, organized or arranged during the actual panic attack**

To repeat that

When the human brain experiences a panic attack, even if it is the worst, severest, most frenzied panic attack ever known, despite the modern part of the brain then losing virtually all its ability to create, construct, organize and arrange rational thought, **it still has enough ability to hold onto six words, if those words do not have to be created, constructed, organized or arranged during the actual panic attack.**

In short, during a panic attack, whilst your terror is raging and your ability for rational thought is limited in the extreme, instead of trying to force the modern thinking part of your brain to perform a task that it cannot do in the circumstances… you must then make full use of whatever rational thoughts you do have And you do that by focusing it onto six words that you have **already** chosen, thought about and worked out.

Let-go: going to the necessary depth

When a panic attack is throwing its worst at you, you then need to separate yourself from the physical and go to an emotional place inside yourself so deep and meaningful it will carry you above and beyond the panic, the depth of your thoughts can do that. And even if you are experiencing the worst panic attack known, the depth of your thoughts can still do that. Therefore during a panic attack, **the depth of your thought is all-important!**

Reaching the depths…

The human body is centred on balance. Indeed, balance is so integral to the human body that even when forced out of balance by physical, mental, emotional or spiritual distress it will always try to work its way back to balance. In fact the maintenance of balance is so integral to the human body that if a well-balanced person should try to force their own body out of balance and into a state of extreme arousal (ecstatically happy, ragingly angry, passionately in love or frenziedly terrified) they would find it impossible.

Think about it. Before you developed panic attacks (and assuming you were a calm, well-balanced person) how easy would it have been for you to have put yourself into a state of frenzied terror? Of course you might have found it easy to worry, be anxious or even frighten yourself with thoughts of illness and death. But for you to have experienced frenzied terror at will, without external influences, would have been impossible.

Terror is the extreme state of fear and lies at the very core of life itself. We can't simply feel terror at will, it is triggered and sustained only when we believe we are in a life-or-death situation. And because terror is rooted so deep within us, if we wish to influence it, we must firstly go within ourselves to the same depth as it. Once there, we must counterbalance the terror and its importance to us by going exceptionally deep within ourselves then emotionally touching and moving the essence that is seated at our very core. It's little use trying to catch an elephant with a butterfly net, it's little use trying to harness the sea with a bucket and spade and it's little use trying to calm a panic attack by trying to count from one to ten backwards or by trying to imagine oneself on a beach. **Those thoughts are simply not deep enough!**

Do you see? Although terror is the extreme state of arousal and lies deep within the primitive, it can be influenced. And when a panic attack is throwing its worst at you, when the rain is falling, the thunder is crashing, the lightning is flashing and the hurricane of terror is swirling around you. If you then emotionally go to a place inside yourself so meaningful that it touches the deepest part of your being, you will then separate your mind from your symptoms, keep it occupied with your chosen words and by not feeding the terror, it will quickly fade.

Let-go: using the right words for you

You know that during a panic attack virtually all rational thought will be lost to you, nevertheless your mind will still hold six words if those words are **already** thought about, worked out and their content so deep and meaningful they touch the deepest part of your being. So choosing the right words for you personally is all-important. That now being said. Obviously every person has his/her own physical, mental, emotional and spiritual needs. So the meaningful words that touch and move one person may not touch and move another. In which case, there is absolutely no point in me telling you what specific words to use because those words may be totally inappropriate and ineffective for you. But don't despair, many people have never searched inside themselves for deep meaningful words of comfort. Realising that, about 20 years ago, I compiled two lists of the 'type of words' and 'categories' that I thought suitable then I gave both lists to every new sufferer who sought my help. The lists then proved to be so beneficial (as examples) that I still use them today and, once read, most people do tend to grasp the depth and type of thought required.

The three most used and proven categories:
God - A deceased loved one - Fact
1. God
The perception of God to one person is often very different to that of another. Therefore if God, to you, is the God of religion, or an almighty being of goodness, or a universal power of goodness or a vibrating energy

of goodness and if, when thinking of your God, you feel a sense of love, protection, reassurance, strength and comfort then you might consider using this category. And I am not saying to use this category, I am simply suggesting that you might consider using it.

On the other hand, if you say you believe in God, you might even go to church but in your heart you don't feel God, then you might consider using another category. Again, I am not saying to disregard this category. In fact, I recall a number of my clients who, despite doubting their belief in God, but out of sheer desperation, used this category only to find a closeness to God they had never experienced before, they also gained a complete recovery from panic attacks.

The way to use this category is to choose words that give you a deep, soulful, positive feeling then, using your words, ask for help.

2. A deceased loved one

Before you proceed further in this category, I must emphasise that this category does not involve anything connected to the supernatural.

This category is used solely to ask for help (as one would to God) from a 'loved one' who would have helped you if they were still alive today. And although this may sound incredibly weird to some people, I assure you many people do use this category. Indeed some sufferers told me that after their mother, father, grandparent or spouse had died, how they (the sufferer) had felt as if their departed loved one had never really gone away but had stayed close to them for many years, protectively looking out for them, as if waiting to help them.

So if you are fortunate enough to have had a relationship encompassing good, strong, dependable, unselfish love that is felt in the deepest part of your being, and if your 'loved one' is no longer with you in the physical sense yet, whenever you think of them, you feel love, peace, protection, strength, comfort or warmth, then you might consider choosing your 'words of sanctuary' from this category. Again, I am not saying use it, I am simply suggesting that you consider using it.

The way to use this category is to choose words that help you to connect to your loved one then, using your words, ask for help. I do however have two points of caution regarding this category...

- Don't use this category if remembering your 'loved one' causes you any emotional pain. Only ever use it if remembering them gives you a feeling of love, peace, strength, protection and comfort.

- If you have lost a child in death then do not choose words relating to the child, if you do, you will certainly feel a degree of pain.

3. *Fact*

Being a panic attack sufferer, you are being tricked by your own mental and physical sensations, and because, up to now, you have not understood what was happening, why it was happening and how you could stop them, you have become ever more frightened by them. So to use this category, chose words that explain the what's, why's and how's of panic attacks thereby giving your mind an explanation that it will fully accept as being fact; which will give your mind the necessary comfort and reassurance.

The way to use this category is to choose your words containing facts, perhaps relating to just one particular element of panic attacks, or panic attacks as a whole or something relating to you personally. And remember your chosen words must be simple, to the point, absolute fact and give you a deep feeling of reassurance, confidence and understanding.

Words based on those that have worked for others
Below is the list of 'one-liners' based on those used by the clients I spoke of on page 144. But understand, as the following words are those used by other people, they may not be wholly suitable for you. Of course if you would have chosen those very same words for yourself or if, after a few days of thought, you still can't think of alternative words for yourself then use them and have faith in them because **I know** such words have carried people from the absolute terror of panic attacks to complete peace.

When reading the following list, replace a ____ with the name of either a departed loved one or your chosen divinity, i.e. Jesus, Jehovah, God, Mum, Grandma, Kelly, Jim...
____ walk with me
____ hold me
____ I call on you now
Be still, I am ____
I now hand this to you
Know that I am ____
I'm in your hands now
____ be with me now
____ grant me peace
____ give me your strength
I *know* you're with me

_____ I *feel* your peace
_____ stay with me
_____ help me through this
_____ I *feel* you
_____ I *know* you're here
Ponytails (an endearment)
Just *let-go* it's a trick
I'm as free as a bird
These feelings have saved mankind
I now claim back my life
Just 'go with the flow
This is *my* life
Let-go and know
Slowness is the key . . . . (of thought, breathing and movement)
This feeling is only rhubarb . . . . (belittling the panic attack)
I'm safe, let it pass . . . . (*it* being the panic attack)
Just let it pass through . . . . (*it* being the panic attack)
Don't be fooled it's only Tom . . . . (*Tom* crashing his symbols)
You don't frighten me now . . . . (*you* being the panic attack)
You're nothing to me now . . . . (*you're* being the panic attack)
Shirley Valentine . . . . (this lady had been tortured by panic attacks (both indoors and outdoors) for over 30 years. Her words, taken from the film of the same name, gave power and determination to her belief that, once recovered from panic attacks, she also was going to have a brand new life. Once recovered, this lady actually moved to Spain and lived there for about fifteen years; loving every single moment, only recently moving back to the UK for family reasons).

From the above list you will see that the sense of peace, love, protection, reassurance and strength gained from the words need not be in the actual words themselves but rather, in the feelings they evoke. Truly, when a panic attack is throwing its worst at you, it will be your words of sanctuary' that saves you, for they alone will be your shelter. Your 'words of sanctuary' **are** your way out of panic attacks.

Let-go: voicing your words out loud, if possible

There are three main reasons for voicing your words out loud...

1. Whilst the conscious mind can work fast, the subconscious mind can work so fast that the conscious mind is unaware of having had a thought at all. Speech and vocabulary do not have the same ability for

speed. So when voicing your words, your mind will, to a significant degree, slow down your thoughts to synchronize with your speech.

2. Breathing is generally under 'involuntary' control, so during a panic attack, if breathing is left unchecked it can become very rapid indeed. Voicing your words will bring your breathing under voluntary control and thereby actively slow down your thoughts.

3. It has recently been scientifically shown that the human mind absorbs and retains the contents of the words we say in comparison to the words we hear. Therefore it will be much more beneficial, if you actually say your words rather than just thinking them.

Let-go: whispering your words, if need be

There will be situations when a panic attack strikes but it is inappropriate for you to say your 'words of sanctuary' out loud so, if necessary, find a place where you can whisper them: nurses can go to the sluice room - men and women in offices can sit at their computer with their eyes fixed on the screen but concentrating on their words - teachers can go to the staff room - shop assistants can go to the store room - public toilets have proved to be places where many sufferers have whispered their words - shop keepers (once the situation has been explained) will often allow the sufferer to find sanctuary for a few moments - and churches (if you can find one open) have also proved to be exceptionally beneficial places etc.

Let-go: in stillness

To repeat, when a person moves quickly in fear their nervous system will automatically assume danger is present and will therefore stimulate their mind and body even more. So when you feel a panic attack beginning or when you find yourself in a panic attack, although every fibre of your mind and body is then compelling you to run, do not move but try to stand or sit exactly where you are, moving only when the attack has passed. And if you are in a situation where you have to move then move as slowly as you can.

Let-go: at the correct time

Throughout every moment of your day and night, your conscious and subconscious mind will be telling your nervous system, "At any moment, a wild, ferocious panic attack is going to strike me down, hurt me, send me insane or even kill me. So be warned! Don't be found off guard and don't relax," to which your nervous system will respond by keeping your whole bodily system continuously at 'battle ready.' As a result, throughout every moment of the day and night, you will be experiencing various levels of arousal, from anxiety to fear and terror, including all the relating symptoms. So realising how confusing it would be for any panic attack sufferer to have each individual level of their fear analysed, at this point, I simply divide all levels of fear into two...

Fear...as during concern, anxiety, worry and fear

This is the part of your day when you are just going about your daily tasks of life. During this time you will be experiencing various levels of anxiety and symptoms of stress but you will **not** be experiencing a panic attack or knowing that a panic attack is actually on its way.

Terror...as during a panic attack

This is the part of your day when you either know a panic attack is on its way or you are actually experiencing a panic attack.

The trigger that throws you personally from **fear** to **terror** might be a pain, sensation, situation or thought: conscious or subconscious. And the time it takes you to pass from **fear** to **terror** might be a matter of hours, or you might have just enough time to think, "Oh my God, it's here again" or the panic might seem to strike instantaneously. That being so, we will now identify the correct time for you personally to begin to let-go...

1. If you are a sufferer whose panic attacks take hours to build then, once your trigger has occurred and you know a panic attack is beginning to slowly build...**immediately** work on a conscious level, say your 'words of sanctuary' and try to let-go. At this stage, when you are able to let-go correctly, the panic attack will be prevented before it even begins.

2. If you are a sufferer who has just enough time to think, "Oh my God, it's here again," which fortunately gives you a few precious seconds warning that the panic attack is on its way. Then, once your trigger has occurred and you feel your fear speedily rising...**immediately**, work on a conscious level, say your 'words of sanctuary' and try to let-go. ... If you don't manage to let-go within those few precious seconds, therefore you find yourself experiencing a full-blown panic attack. As the 'first flash response' will then have passed, therefore you will then be in the 'sustained response'...**immediately** work on a conscious level, say your 'words of sanctuary' and try to let-go.

3. If you are a sufferer whose panic attacks strike suddenly, without any warning, one moment you are not in panic then the next moment you are in full-blown frenzied terror. Then once your trigger has occurred and you are experiencing a full-blown panic attack. As the 'first flash response' will then have passed, therefore you will then

be in the 'sustained response'...**immediately** work on a conscious level, say your 'words of sanctuary' and try to let-go.

Remember...
First flash response will pass very fast, below the level of consciousness and will be over before you know what's happening. That is why so many panic attack sufferers believe their panic attacks just strike from nowhere.
Sustained response will keep arousal going, can last indefinitely and can be consciously worked on, thus allowing you to determine the duration of the panic attack.

Let-go: and be 'somewhere else'

On seeking help for panic attacks, a significant number of sufferers are told by their therapists, they will never be free of panic attacks until they endure every panic attack and go through the frenzied terror, whilst consciously taking the full blast of the sensations and to do so until every panic attack decides to leave them. By doing so, the therapist is trying to prove to the sufferer how the panic would not hurt them. But after genuinely trying such a therapy and always failing, many sufferers come to fear they will never recover. Wrong! Wrong! Wrong! This is a therapy for phobias not panic attacks.

When a person normally experiences the extreme sensations of frenzied terror, they are usually in a life-or-death situation and mentally occupied trying to free themselves from the danger. Consequently, although they are then experiencing the extreme sensations of frenzied terror they are mentally 'somewhere else.' And that is how you will recover from panic attacks...being mentally and emotionally somewhere else.

Let-go: with a desire to recover

When we feel anger or fear our arousal responses become stimulated and when we feel peaceful and relaxed our arousal responses calm. Therefore, our feelings are the all-important factor in controlling arousal. How do we control our feelings? By thought? What determines thought? 'Will.' What determines 'will?' What is the 'core' determining element that drives us? The answer is, of course, **desire**. And realise, desire is not merely a want or a need but rather, it is a hunger, a prayer of the soul, a yearning of the heart. Desire is absolute. We cannot partially desire something. We either desire something or we do not. Our heart and soul either yearns for something or it does not. Desire is all-powerful, for it alone gives the mind its 'strength of will.'

During any conflict, whilst some warriors fall and stay down, others fall and courageously get back up, and they do so, not because they are physically stronger but because they have a greater desire in their heart and soul. Do you desire recovery? Do you desire recovery so much that every time you fail to let-go you will try again and again and yet again? If so, I absolutely **promise** you, your recovery from panic attacks is there to be claimed.

Seize the moment!

You can read about panic attacks, learn about them and know that other people have recovered from them. People might show you sympathy, care and offer words of reassurance but that still leaves you suffering panic attacks and doubting if you will ever really recover from them. In fact even if every other panic attack sufferer in the world recovered, you would **still** probably question your own ability to free yourself. Which now brings us to where you begin to put your new found knowledge into practise. And you will do that by 'seizing the moment' and letting-go; **once**.

And so...

Firstly, chose your 'words of sanctuary' and don't be surprised if finding the right words for you takes a little while. Once you have your words, the next time you feel your fear rising and you know a panic attack is on its way or when you next find yourself in actual panic attack terror. Then, with both your conscious and subconscious mind knowing how panic attacks are tricking you, how your arousal responses work and how your mind is all-powerful. With fear then throwing its worst at you, with the rain falling, the thunder crashing, the lightning flashing and the hurricane of frenzied terror swirling around you, you will not run, try to fight it or try to rationalise with it but rather...

...with every fibre of your body, with desire in your soul and with every ounce of strength in your spirit, you will then take a giant leap of faith, focus your thoughts onto your words and then let-go...

...and amazingly, as neither your conscious nor subconscious mind are then feeding the terror, the terror will then fade and die away.

And realise...

When you first try to let-go, you might find it difficult, with mixed results and perhaps a little disappointing: – you might lose your words altogether and spiral into another panic attack – you might let-go but only for a few seconds – you might mentally swing back and forward between your words and panic – you might only minimise the sensations slightly – you might only prevent the panic from reaching its peak but not shorten it – or you might only reduce the duration of the panic by a few seconds.

And yes, if you don't completely let-go the first time or even the first few times, you will feel bitterly disappointed, you might feel inclined to give up trying, you might consider yourself a failure or a soft person or you might worry over whether or not you are worse than everyone else. If so, just remember those immortal words of Winston Churchill, "Success is going from failure to failure with enthusiasm."

That being so, if you do find it difficult to let-go or when you do let-go it is with mixed results and leaves you feeling disappointed remember, you are not a soft person, you are not worse than everyone else and you are not a failure. You are, though, an exceptionally courageous person who, like Winston Churchill, when facing great adversity, despite experiencing failure after failure, does not give up but rather, keeps on going with the desire to succeed. And you will succeed because it is within every persons capability to do so; even yours.

It's all simply a knack
To let-go of a panic attack is as easy or as hard as skating, swimming, riding a bike or anything that requires a knack. And whilst it is easy to describe how to put the procedure into practise, it is almost impossible to describe how a knack is actually caught: – some people say it is when a person is no longer merely going through the motions but they are actually experiencing the spirit of the event – some say it is when a person moves from thinking he can't to believing he can – and some say it is when the body puts into practice what the mind is imagining. But whatever the diversity, whether you manage to 'catch the knack' and let-go of your next panic attack or whether it takes you a few attempts. It will not be a matter of can your mind do it because of course it can, there is absolutely no doubt about that. The question is, how soon will you do it?

You might be one of the 30 percent of sufferers who 'catch the knack' and let-go literally within the first few attempts of trying or you might be similar to others who find it more difficult. But in whichever group you find yourself, when you do 'catch the knack' and let-go, you might initially feel a little hesitant to actually believe it. You will, of course, realise that the panic faded away but you might question whether or not it was really you who determined the outcome. It is almost as though you can't allow yourself to believe your luck for fear of tempting fate or risking future disappointment. So if you do initially feel doubtful over whether or not you let-go, don't tie yourself in knots trying to decide because, sooner or later, it will become blatantly clear to you that you are indeed letting-go.

And if you are still unsure about trying to let-go, I will add one final word. Yes you might find excuses why you should not try this programme. You might find someone who will offer you a magic wand. You can turn to drink or drugs and spend the rest of your life in oblivion. You can stay exactly as you are and spend the rest of your life imprisoned by terror; even though you have the option to be free. And you can forfeit all chance of ever being the person you were born to be. It is your life after all.

But realise...

Recovery from panic attacks is not lost in setbacks but in excuses. So if you now choose to settle for any option other than total recovery, "It will not be panic attacks that has defeated you, it will be you who has forfeited your own self to panic attacks!"

Your likely responses: positive and negative

At this point of my programme, I expect you to respond very strongly to what I have just explained about letting-go. And I expect your comments to fall in one of the following 4 categories...

1. You might breakdown in tears saying, "I get it! Now I see how this whole programme works. Oh thank God. I really do see a ray of hope."

2. You might say, "Yes I now see how this programme works and in the future I'll try it **but** at the moment I can't because if I do and fail then I'll feel worse than ever," or "I'll try it **but** if it doesn't work fast then I'll have to leave it," or "I am prepared to give it a try **but** I'm ill you know, so I can only do what I can" or "I'll try it **but**...

3. You might angrily state, "Forget it! No Way! Absolutely no way could I ever experience a panic attack and me just stand there and not fight it."

4. You might scream out at me, "What a load of rubbish! No way will six stupid words hold me! How can you lift my hopes so very high only to say something so foolish? I really thought you understood how ill I'm feeling but obviously not. I've consulted the most eminent specialists, I've had years in therapy and I've spent thousands of pounds to escape panic attacks, surely you don't expect me to now take this seriously? Absolutely no way will this rubbish help me."

So realising your response to my suggestion of letting-go will be similar to one of the above, I remind you that, at the beginning of this chapter, I asked you to promise you would stay with me to the end of this chapter. So if you gave your promise, **please**, keep to it and read on. If you didn't give your promise but you still desire recovery then read on anyway, what have you got to lose?

Category 1. "I get it!"

I will make only 1 point

1. Now you are able to see the full picture, your body will take a breath of relief, your mind will feel a degree of optimism and your spirit will see a ray of light at the end of your very deep and dark tunnel. You are now on your way to recovery.

Category 2. "I'll try it, but..."

I will make 4 points for you to consider...

1. In their desperate need to find freedom from panic attacks, some sufferers have undergone electric shock treatment, some have sold their homes to raise money for clinics and therapy fees and some have left their families to suffer alone for fear of distressing their children too much. Yet all I am asking of you is to try to let-go of one panic attack and you are even reluctant to try that.

2. When a panic attack sufferer is working on recovery, two elements are essential. Firstly, they need the desire to recover. And again, the word is desire, not determination. Desire will involve them being fully prepared to do the best they can and if, at first, they don't succeed, to then try and try until they do. Secondly, they need 100% confidence in **both** their adviser and their programme. If they don't have such confidence then, as soon as they feel the fear rising and know a panic attack is on it way, their confidence will fail, doubts and fears will take over and they will end up in panic. So ask yourself: Do you desire recovery and do you have 100% confidence in me and this programme?

3. Panic attacks are like bullies, when they know you fear them they pick on you all the more but when they know you don't fear them, they will leave you alone.

4. If you are a 'but but' person, I suspect that (with respect) you are not yet ill enough, desperate enough, frightened enough, determined

enough or desire freedom enough because if you were, you would try literally anything. However as you continue to travel your journey of panic attacks, in all probability, sooner or later, you will find yourself at the point of being desperate, frightened and determined enough to give all avenues of recovery your hundred percent best effort. And come that day, I will still be here waiting for you.

Category 3. "I can't do that!"
I will make 5 points for you to consider...

1. Panic attacks now control you to some degree and if you are suffering severely then panic attacks will now have total control over you: – your mood – your quality of life – your personal, domestic and financial stability – your mental, emotional and physical health – and your freedom. They control: – if you will panic – when you will panic – the intensity of each panic – and the duration of each panic. In fact depending on how severely you are affected, panic attacks might now be the one controlling factor in your whole life, you being the servant of them and they being the master of you. And because panic attacks are such a very cruel master, you now live in absolute fear and terror of their wrath. Yet you still have doubts about trying to let go?

2. When you watch a magic trick, even though you know it's a trick, you still think it impossible. But once the trick is explained to you, more so if you perform it yourself, you then think, "How could I have been so easily fooled by something so obvious." Panic attacks are similar to magic tricks. Once they are explained and you are able to let-go, you then think, "How could I have been fooled by something so obvious."

3. Think of the film, 'The Wizard of Oz.' There was Dorothy, knowing that if she was ever to return home she must firstly speak to the Wizard. But when entering Oz she hears a terrifying voice, and assuming it to be the Wizard, she is overcome with fear. Nevertheless, despite her fear, in her 'desire' to go home, she valiantly yet tentatively walks into the room where she knows the Wizard will be. And as she stands there quaking with fear, believing the wrath of the Wizard will surely fall on her at any moment, her little dog Toto begins to tug on a curtain. "No Toto! No!" cries Dorothy; fearing that her little dog will surely make matters worse. But as Toto tugs again, the curtain falls to the floor and the Wizard is unveiled. Wow!

What a con trick! The so-called terrifying Wizard that Dorothy was so afraid of is shown to be a timid, insignificant little man speaking through a megaphone. How easy it is to be frightened of something, believing it is one thing when, in fact, it is something else altogether.

4. Yes I know you have spent years avoiding panic attacks, fighting them, running from them, suppressing them and keeping a tight grip on them. And yes, when you are next on the street, in the supermarket, at work, on the motorway, with other people or on your own and you know a panic attack is on its way or you find yourself in full-blown frenzied terror. Your body will pulsate, your mind will be frenzied, you believe you are about to die and the driving force of primitive arousal will be compelling you to fight or run for your life. To then not fight or run will take every drop of courage you possess. But do you really think that by trying to fight or run from the panic attack you will ever be free of them? Of course not! So why do it?

5. Many panic attack sufferers live in the hope of finding a magic wand and it freeing them from panic attacks forever. And on occasion, some sufferers believe they have actually found one, as magic wands can seem to appear in many guises: alcohol, drugs, a change of lifestyle, medication, hypnotherapy, acupuncture, finding a new partner, freeing oneself of a partner, going away on a holiday, acquiring a pet or changing occupation etc.

    However, after a period of freedom they again experience a period of stress which, after more time, is followed by a sudden wave of panic. Of course immediately they again reach for their magic wand but then it no longer works for them, perhaps: – their previous medication or therapy is no longer available – their symptoms have change from previously, making both their new medication and treatment ineffective – their previous doctor or therapist has moved – or their financial situation has changed to where they can no longer afford the medication, therapy, holiday and so on. So for whatever reason, their magic wand no longer works, which leaves them with no other option but to, yet again, go in search for another magic wand.

Like many panic attack sufferers, you also might now be hoping to find a magic wand and it freeing you from panic attacks forever. But what if you did? What if 4 weeks ago you found a magic wand. You whispered a few magical words and 'hey presto' you suddenly found yourself free from panic attacks. One moment you were a panic attack sufferer and the next you are free. Sounds good doesn't it? But then, after enjoying a wonderful week of freedom, 3 weeks ago, you again experienced an unexpected domestic, financial or personal problem; from which 2 weeks ago, you experienced a few minor symptoms of stress. Of course initially you tried to shrug them off but alas, as the days passed, matters worsened and moments ago you experienced a seemingly motiveless wave of terror. What thoughts now flash through your mind? What scenario do you see? What is your new plan of action? How do you now prevent yourself from being dragged back into the dreaded panic attacks? Did I hear someone mention a magic wand? And assuming you do find yet another magic wand and it works for you today. What about tomorrow?

Do you see? If your freedom from panic attacks is dependent on a magic wand, you will then be forced to carry it around for protection for the rest of your life, never feeling safe without it and always having to live in hope it will continue to work. And yes, of course, you might say, "Well it's only a little stick and if carrying it around for the rest of my life will protect me from panic attacks then so be it." But what if your little stick should break? What if you lose it? What if it only works three times, or on specific days or at specific times of the year? And even if your magic wand worked time and time again or you lost it but found another and another. Is that **really** what you call freedom?

No my friend. If you are suffering panic attacks then magic wands are not the answer! They fail! They fail because they are that someone or something outside of 'you.' They fail because, if the magic wand is controlling the panic attacks then **it** is controlling you; you are still subservient, only then, to that someone or something that is 'the magic wand.' They fail because, too often, what initially appears to be a magic wand turns out to be a stick of dynamite. And they fail because, **if your freedom from panic attacks is dependent on anything outside of your own direct control, then your freedom is still dependent on chance**, and come the day when chance fails you, what then?

Your true freedom from panic attacks will never be gained by magic wands. Your true freedom will only be gained by you fully understanding what's happening to you and then you putting that understanding into practice. Then, not only will you be gaining your freedom in the short term but for the rest of your life.

Category 4 "What a load of absolute rubbish!"

I will make 4 points for you to consider...

1. Yes you might have screamed such dismissive comments at me. Even so, if I can convince you to 'stay with it' and continue to follow this programme through, you **will** become an ex-panic attack sufferer, all mended by this very programme.

2. You cannot, do not and will never change the fundamental principle of life. Which is, if you feed fear with fearful thoughts then both the fear and the sensations of fear will intensify. And if you don't feed fear with fearful thought then the fear and the sensations of fear will die.

3. Of course I realise you have consulted eminent doctors, you have spent countless hours in therapy and you have spent thousands of pounds on programmes, treatments and therapies. But ask yourself, "Am I now totally and permanently free of panic attacks and all fear related to them?" Because, as you are now reading this book I am tempted to assume you are not, and if not, what's your point?

4. Think back over the doctors, psychiatrists, psychologists and therapists that you have turned to for help regarding panic attacks. Surely, by now, you must realise that my words and this programme do not simply come from textbooks or the hypotheses of others but rather, they come from the experience, the suffering and the found freedom of countless panic attack sufferers, all mended by this very programme.

   Do you see? I know more about panic attacks than most. I know exactly how you are feeling, I know exactly how to free you and I know exactly how to prevent you from ever suffering and fearing panic attacks again. So please realise, by following this programme, you have absolutely nothing to lose yet everything to gain.

A few reminders and helpful tips

Reminders...

- If you have now lost control of yourself to panic attacks then you are now at their mercy. But should the balance of power change to where you are in control, to where you feel master of the panic attacks and to where the panic attacks are now at your mercy then your fear towards the panic attacks will quickly die away.
- Even during the severest panic attack known, the human brain **will** hold up to six words.

- Your 'words of sanctuary' are intended to bring you a feeling of calm, so don't choose words that might cause you pain or words that could act as fighting talk.
- Voice your 'words of sanctuary' at every opportunity, as doing so will help to slowdown both your mind and breathing, it will also help your mind to hold onto the content of your words to a greater degree.
- Don't just mouth your 'words of sanctuary' whilst looking around the room but rather, close your eyes or focus them onto a specific object or into the eyes of another person, as that will both eliminate distraction and help your mind to hold its focus.
- During a panic attack don't move or at least move very slowly.
- Remember, there are no prizes for being the first to let-go. The only prize is your full and permanent freedom from panic attacks. And in a few weeks or months, when you are completely free of not only panic attacks but also all fear of them, what will it matter if your recovery took the longest time? The fact will still remain that you did it! And you did it at your own pace and in your own time.
- Know you cannot fail! As long as you desire recovery, you can never fail. In this matter, practise really does make perfect.
- My suggestion of 'letting-go' is not a means of trying to runaway from the panic attack, it is though, the means by which you can allow the panic attack to do its worst whilst you are mentally 'somewhere else,' and by doing so, you control the panic.

Tips...
- When choosing your 'words of sanctuary' you need not stick rigidly to six words, as 1-2-3-4 or 5 words work equally as well. Indeed, more than 6 words can sometimes work but I don't suggest you try that. Just keep to a maximum of six words, as I know, beyond any shadow of doubt, that your mind can hold onto that amount, even during the most frenzied of panic attacks.
- Your 'words of sanctuary' are of the greatest importance. So although you are impatient to begin recovery, take the time to find the right words for you, and don't be surprised if finding your words takes you a little time.
- If there are certain places or situations where you feel overly vulnerable to panic attacks then, if possible, temporarily avoid them until later in the programme. But, if you can't avoid those places or situations then when in them, use your 'words of sanctuary' and try to let-go. After a few moments however, if you can't let-go, then walk away

as slowly as you can. Once you are away from the situation then again, say your 'words of sanctuary' and again try to let-go. But note: Don't say your 'words of sanctuary' whilst running away, as the association you will then make in your mind between your words and you fleeing will not help you in the long term.

Good-days/bad-days

In all probability, your panic attacks and symptoms of stress will continue for a while so, as such, for a while, you are likely to feel as if you are on an emotional roller-coaster ride of good-days and bad-days; one day feeling 'not too bad' then the next day feeling 'worse than ever.' That being so, the following chapter will be of tremendous use to you: – it will explain that, although some boulders attached to panic attacks are obvious, others might not be – it will help you to recognise the issues that make up your boulders – it will draw your attention to how you might now be feeding your bad-days by inadvertently focusing your mind onto your boulders rather than on your recovery – and it will offer suggestions on how you might organise 'a plan of action;' as whilst your good-days will take care of themselves, your OK and bad-days will need planning for.

The Roller-Coaster Ride of 'Good-Days/Bad-Days'

For most panic attack sufferers, particularly those suffering severely, the road to recovery rarely proves to be a nice steady ride, where every day they see the light at the end of the tunnel becoming ever brighter. Indeed for most sufferers, recovery is an emotional roller-coaster ride of good-days/bad-days, where one day they feel they are taking a big stride forward then the next day three strides backwards. So I hope this following section will go a long way towards smoothing your journey to recovery.

Boulders

We previously spoke of 'boulders' and how, when riding a bicycle, driving a car, experiencing illness or indeed during any negative or potentially negative life situation, if you focus your mind onto its negative elements, you are then more likely to experience them.

Being a panic attack sufferer, particularly if you are suffering ongoing, acute stress, severe symptoms of stress, pain, debilitation, worry and fear, then the focus of your mind will now be on those negative elements; your boulders. And as boulders are big, otherwise they would only be pebbles, at this point we will highlight five main areas that are probably making up your boulders; for whilst a few are obvious, others might not be...

Boulder 1: Your general life stresses
Worry is worry, whatever the cause, so any worry is, in itself a boulder. And if worrying is acute, it will make a very big boulder indeed. Therefore, depending on how difficult your life circumstances are, you worrying over them might now be one of the main boulders in your life.

Boulder 2: Panic attacks
If you are only suffering mildly with panic attacks, your life will still be restricted in some way, the resulting frustration will affect your psyche on some level and the resulting strain will contribute to you experiencing bad-days. On the other hand, if you are suffering panic attacks severely

then, in all probability, they will have become the one controlling factor in your whole life...which makes them a very big boulder indeed.

Boulder 3: Symptoms of stress

The sheer relentlessness of your symptoms of stress could be causing you such distress that your energy is sapped, you feel utterly exhausted, your spirit is at its lowest and all hope of recovery feels lost to you...making your symptoms of stress a very big boulder indeed.

Boulder 4: Flashbacks

Imagine yourself in a car approaching a road junction that you have crossed many times before. The traffic lights show green so you drive on. Suddenly, crash! A car has smashed into you. Instantly your body is jolted forward causing shock to reverberate throughout your body, your head smashes onto the windscreen causing blood to gush down your face, the steering wheel is embedded into your chest forcing you to gasp for air, the windows shatter, showering you from head to toe in broken glass and as the front of the car concertinas, numbness slowly takes over where you know your legs to be.

After sitting there for seemingly hours experiencing pain, fear and distress, the emergency services arrive and go through the formalities of rescue. You are then whisked off to hospital where doctors examine you, tests and x-rays are performed on you, your cuts and bruises are attended to and you are monitored, told to rest, relax and not to worry. A few days of pain and anxiety then pass only to be told, "You are suffering with nothing other than slight concussion, a few abrasions and bodily bruising but overall nothing really to worry about. So go home, get plenty of rest and go back to work as soon as you are able."

Question: After such an accident, once mended, how easy would it be for you to forget the accident? How soon would the memory of it fade? And how would you feel the next time you approach that same junction? I don't think it an exaggeration to say that, despite you having previously crossed that junction many times before, never giving it a second thought, you would now view it with apprehension, trepidation, even fear. In fact you might choose to avoid the 'accident spot' altogether.

Of course the reason for your trepidation and fear towards the 'accident spot' is not because you are a soft, silly person but because, to your mind, the junction now equates to danger and a threat to life. As a consequence, if you did go near that same junction again, your mind would recognise it, remember the accident, realise that another accident is a real possibility and will therefore alert you, via mental flashbacks, thoughts of danger and memories of past suffering; all in the attempt to forewarn you, forearm you and thereby keep you safe.

So whenever you are in a situation where you once experienced acute pain, distress or terror then, in the attempt to forewarn and forearm you, your survival responses will give you flashbacks of your past suffering.

You are currently suffering panic attacks and symptoms of stress, which are painful, distressing and terrifying. And you could have experienced them in every area of your life: – in every shop – on your local street – at work – at every set of traffic lights – in your friend's home – in your own home – and in your own bed. Therefore every time you now go into those places, your mind will give you flashbacks, thoughts of danger and memories of that past suffering. However, being a stress sufferer, **your** flashbacks, thoughts of danger and memories of past suffering will not forewarn you and help save your life but they will forearm you, arouse you and possibly throw your already oversensitive nervous system further into arousal… making your flashbacks potentially big boulders also.

Boulder 5: Re-balancing

One of the main functions of the brain is to sustain and when necessary regain bodily balance, which is achieved by the ongoing adjustment of the body's nerve impulses, thought patterns and hormone levels. And whilst the normal bodily balancing process is usually unfelt, when a person has been stressed for a prolonged period of time and then begins to calm, the re-balancing process itself can often be felt and feel strange. All of which could very easily trick an unsuspecting mind back into much unnecessary worry, fear and panic attacks; leaving them feeling as though an even bigger boulder has suddenly fallen on their head.

So, to cover the sensations of re-balancing and enlighten you to what you can expect and thus what to ignore over the next few weeks, I will now give you an idea of what the sensations of re-balancing feels like…

"Relax, never again!"

On your bad days, which, for a little while, might be every day, you will expect panic attacks to strike, or various aches and pains to be present or possibly for new symptoms to develop. But on your good days, when trying to relax, perhaps when listening to soothing music, dozing in front of the fire having a luxurious bath or going out for a walk, whether your relaxation time is for only a few moments or many days, for you to then experience a sudden and unexpected twinge, ache, pain, mood swing or flashback could easily frighten you and throw you back into full-blown panic, leaving you thinking, "Relax; never again!"

You might find this segment easier to relate to if you compare it to nicotine withdrawal. For example, if you are a smoker of about 20 cigarettes a day. On any average day, when smoking your 20 cigarettes, your body will go about its normal life. But if you then decide to reduce or stop smoking, thereby reducing your intake of nicotine, your body will then give you symptoms by way of saying, "Come on mate, give me my fix of nicotine." After all, if you are a person whose usual nicotine withdrawal symptoms are cravings, anxiety, headaches, anger, restlessness and so on, and your usual response to those symptoms is to have a cigarette. Then all your body has to do to trick you back into smoking (and thereby give itself a shot of nicotine) is to give you cravings, restlessness, anxiety, headaches, anger and so on and 'bingo,' you are again smoking.

Do you see? On your bad-days, when your symptoms of stress are severe and thereby you are then feeding yourself buckets of adrenalin, your body will go about its normal day. But on your good-days, when your adrenalin level is lowering, although you might feel a degree of calm, your body will then give you symptoms by way of saying, "Come on mate, give me my fix of adrenalin." After all, if your usual symptoms of stress are pains in your head and your usual response to such pain is to worry about them. Then all your body needs to do to trick you back into worry (and thereby feed itself extra adrenalin) is to give you a few minor aches, pains, twinges or some other head pain and 'bingo,' you are again worrying and feeding your body its fix of adrenalin.

Note: The concept of adrenalin withdrawal is not a normal term used regarding mind issues. It is, though, a term that I have used for many years because it is the means by which most people are able to relate to.

Twinges

These symptoms are acute moments of pain that you might have experienced before. They are strong enough to attract your attention and can be so strong they stop you in your track. Moments later, once they have passed, you are left wondering, "Whoa! What was that?"

Twinges last for only a few moments.

"Oh no, what now?"

These symptoms are so called because that is precisely how you will feel if you experience them. They are the brief appearance of completely new mental, emotional and/or physical symptoms of stress, which are similar in degree to those you are experiencing at the time.

These symptoms can last from hours to a few days.

Old Foes

These symptoms are not of a physical nature but are emotional, being similar in both nature and severity to when you briefly glimpse a person from your past that once caused you pain, fear and distress. One moment you see them and immediately all your old feelings of apprehension, anger, weepiness and fear swell up inside you. Then the next moment they are gone, leaving you thinking, "Where on earth did they come from?"

Old Foes usually last for only a few moments.

Glimpses of today - Shadows of yesterday

These symptoms are physical, they are, in themselves, like those you have experienced many times before. Their differnce being...

Whilst your life is now overshadowed by fear, although your symptoms of stress are not wanted they don't really come as a shock to you. But as you recover to where you are virtually free of stress thus free to appreciate the trees, flowers, conversations and truly feel alive. To then experience a sudden twinge, pain, funny turn, emotional plummet or wave of fear, anger or frustration, could easily shock you and seem much worse than you previously experienced. Which, could leave you feeling devastated and fearing that your recovery will never happen.

Shadows of yesterday usually last for only a few moments.

After-effects

When a pebble is thrown into a pond, for a short time afterwards, ripples are seen on the surface of the water. When a taut peace of elastic is plucked, for a short time afterwards, the elastic reverberates. And when a bell is struck, for a short time afterwards, its sound can still be heard.

Those few examples are similar to many events of nature in that once a particular event has occurred, for a short time afterwards, a continuation of the event will occur in ever lessening degrees until it is no more. And so it is with panic attacks and symptoms of stress. For as they are due to stress, when a person is recovering from them (even when the person has reached the point where they are no longer experiencing panic attacks) for a short time afterwards, they will still experience symptoms of stress in ever lessening degrees until they also are no more.

After-effects in nature are numerous: ripples, lingering sounds and vibrations. After-effects of 'prolonged arousal' are also numerous: aches, pains, twinges, bodily trembling, feeling jittery, butterflies in the stomach, apprehension and, in fact, any one of the many symptoms of stress.

And so, when you are reaching the end of Step Four and into Step Five, if you experience after-effects, just hang-in; for they will be no worse than you have experienced many times before. They can't harm you and they are not a sign that you are falling two steps back. They are, however, the result of a previously overstressed nervous system. And like all other after-effects, they too **will** fade in ever lessening degrees until they are no more.

After-effects can last from minutes to days.

Again realise...
Like all other sensations of arousal, the sensations of re-balancing are not usually experienced one at a time but are accompanied with others, each being felt in varying degrees and lasting different lengths of time. But, if not fed with worry and fear they will only last for the time stated.

Have a 'plan of action'

Make your recovery a smoother ride by following the suggestions below and, with your befriender, structure a 'plan of action'...

Every day, whether it is good, bad or OK

- Try to let-go at every opportunity and begin to build your confidence; at this stage, confidence is a priority.
- Tiredness, illness and disharmony will steal your energy and whatever stamina you have. So ensure you have plenty of rest.
- Try setting yourself a daily target, when you reach it, be proud of yourself for succeeding and if you don't, be proud of yourself for trying. But if having a daily target is too much for you at the moment, then omit it for a little while until your confidence has built-up.
- During the day, when not in panic attack, say your 'words of sanctuary' and familiarise yourself with them as often as you can. Let them become your friend so that when a panic attack strikes, your words will not feel strange to you.
- If you are suffering severely with prolonged mental symptoms of stress, perhaps to the point of nervous exhaustion/breakdown then try the useful 1 to 5 approach: – 1 apprehensive – 2 anxious – 3 frightened – 4 very frightened – and 5 terrified.

    So during the day, when the degree of your fear is on or below level 3, try to focus your mind beyond it and onto the stress buster (see next chapter). And when the degree of your fear has risen onto level 4 or 5 then try to focus your mind onto your 'words of sanctuary' because whilst they are your safe haven during your panic attacks they can also be used anywhere, anytime and as often as you wish.

• Live and recover to no one's yardstick but your own.

On your good days

• If your optimism is high, don't make arrangements where you could let someone down because if you do, as the day of the arrangement draws near, you will put pressure on yourself to honour your commitment, which may result in you disappointing yourself and upsetting others. So, at this stage, just leave all plans open-ended.

• With your befriender, devise a temporary 'plan of action' for your OK and bad days: you could arrange for someone to help you with childcare, or be with you for moral support, or go shopping for you, or accompany you whilst outside or drive you to and from the shop, school or workplace or if necessary (and only until later in this programme) designate a 'place of safety' for you to retreat to when outdoors, i.e. an understanding shopkeeper, a neighbour and so on.

• Carrying many small chains of negativity can be just as heavy and take just as much energy as carrying one big one. So if you have any unresolved pressing issues, evaluate, designate and try to deal with them as soon as possible. However, if you don't feel well enough to deal with such matters at this point then ask your befriender to either deal with them for you or find someone who will. (Unresolved health, personal and life issues are discussed in Step Five).

On your bad days

• Try to live one day at a time and do not put 'time limits' on yourself.

• If you feel inclined to hibernate, please don't but instead, throw yourself into your stress buster (see next chapter) it has something to offer even the severest sufferer.

• Allow your 'plan of action' to take over.

• 'Hope springs eternal.' I have known many sufferers who, due to panic attacks, had lost so very much. Yet during their darkest days, when the panic attacks and symptoms were all consuming, it was hope, alone, that carried them through. Do you have hope in something? Maybe you hope to: - stand-tall again in front of your family and friends - go to college one day - give birth to a healthy baby - simply 'enjoy' your family - or even just see spring again. If you don't have hope in something then you're not looking hard enough. **Find hope**, for it will be your saviour.

Do you love someone or something more than you hate panic attacks? If so, cling to them/it! If not, find **something**! For during panic attacks, when you have love you have hope and when you have hope you have recovery.

Remember...
Whilst you will understandably wish to let-go of every panic attack and symptom of stress, initially there will possibly be times when you cannot. And on those occasions, yes, you might 'lose it,' cry, feel overwhelmed, frightened, frustrated, disheartened and impatient, yes, the sensations will remind you of past suffering, they might come and go, last from moments to days, disappear only to re-appear days later and yes, symptoms will be experienced until your whole nervous system has calmed; which could possibly take weeks. Nevertheless, even if all that happens remember, they are only the normal, natural sensations of high arousal and being such, whilst they might be distressing, they are not a death sentence!

Again, I know I am asking such a very lot from you but, if your desire to recover and your love for someone or something is stronger than your hatred for panic attacks then **I promise you**, slowly but surely, panic attack by panic attack and symptom by symptom you will let-go of it all. Your disappointments will fade. Your frustrations will ease. Your successes will increase. Your confidence will grow. And you will self-witness how you also can rise above adversity to become ever stronger for having had the experience.

Good-days and Golden moments
If panic attacks, your terror, your boulders and your bad-days feel impossible to pass, I give you my word they are not. For the mind is a wondrous thing and in a very short while, just as you collected negative memories of suffering, so you will collect positive memories of success. And yes, each time you let-go of a panic attack or symptom, it will be a 'golden moment' for you. But 'golden moments' can be much more personal.

After weeks, months or years of feeling detached from life, to then 'touch life,' even if only for a moment, and perform an ordinary task that has been out of your reach for so long, will feel almost beyond description. But as 'golden moments' are precious, irreplaceable, integral to recovery yet will differ from person to person, I will now try to describe one of my own 'golden moments' of recovery, in the hope it will help to lift your spirit until you start to have 'golden moments' of your own.

My golden moments

Please realise. These 'golden moments' happened over forty-five years ago, so the exact facts around those few days and the exact words spoken are quite hazy. Nevertheless, based on what I remember, I will paint the picture as best I can. To show you what I mean by 'golden moments'...

I was living with my Mum and Dad and, due to panic attacks, I had been totally housebound for about twelve months. Then one afternoon my Mum said that, as the sun was shining and indoors felt stuffy, she wished to open the back door to allow some fresh air into the house, so how did I feel about it. I said I didn't think the open space would be too distressing, so the door was opened.

After about an hour, on seeing the sunshine stream through the door and fall onto the carpet, I realised that if I sat on the carpet I would be in sunshine. So I did it. What a wonderful sensation to feel the sun's warmth on my face and arms once again.

A few hours later, once the sun had moved and whilst thinking how wonderful the sunshine had felt on my skin, I just said to my Mum, "I hope the sun shines tomorrow." "What did you say?" my Mum asked, surprised at my optimism, "I hope the sun shines tomorrow, if it does, I'm going to sit in it again," I replied. My Mum then smiled and said, "I'll tell you what, if the sun does shine tomorrow, not only can you sit in it, but we'll swing the two armchairs round and sit in the sunshine together. In fact we'll do better than that, we'll have a cup of tea, a piece of cake and have ourselves a picnic whilst looking over the garden." And in that one moment, I had my very first fleeting glimpse and memory of what it felt like to be 'normal' again; a golden moment indeed.

The sun shone the following day and, in fact, the day after that. But throughout those days and nights I had one panic attack after the other and was left feeling too ill to bother with anything, let alone a picnic. What a disappointment that must have been for my Mum! And although I did feel a little better on the third day, the day itself was grey and overcast.

On the fourth day the sun shone brightly and although I had a couple of very bad panic attacks through the previous night, come the day, I felt OK. And so, once the sun had moved into position and was shining through my Mum's back door, we then moved the two armchairs round and sat in the sunshine, enjoying a cup of tea and a piece of cake; an exceptionally golden moment indeed.

After enjoying our picnic for about an hour my Mum returned to the housework, and as I sat there resting in the sunshine and looking out over the garden, I had an urge to move my chair near to the doorway and on impulse I did it then sat down again in my usual position with my bare feet crossed underneath me. A little while passed then, strangely for me, I began to feel pins and needles in my left leg, so I quickly uncrossed my legs then put them down onto the floor. Instantly, I felt heat beneath my my bare feet! And on looking down I saw that my feet were on the garden paving stones. I was outside! Well my feet were outside, I, of course, was still sitting in the armchair inside the doorway. Even so, I was physically feeling the outside beneath my feet. On realising what I was doing (and maybe out of shock) I called out to my Mum, and as she came towards me I jokingly said to her, "Who can't go outside then?" And there it was, in that one brief moment, as I saw my Mum's face filled with pleasure, I knew we were experiencing one of life's rare 'golden moments;' perhaps even my turning point.

Begin to build your own 'golden moments'

As you know, to the mind, good health equates to a long life, symptoms equate to ill health and ill health equates to a potential threat to life. So if you have any mental, emotional or physical symptoms, your mind will be inclined to focus on them as it would a potential threat. In which case, when suffering prolonged symptoms of stress, you need to distract your mind from your symptoms as much as possible.

The following chapter is very powerful, as, working on many levels, it will help to distract your mind from your negative boulders by occupying it with positive thoughts and actions. It will also aid mind-rest, help you to take control of your thoughts, teach you how to relax, allow you to feel what relaxation feels like, slowdown your production of nervous energy, physically release whatever nervous energy has built up in your body and help to steer both your mind and body to where you want them to go, and thereby help you to begin to build your own golden moments.

The Stress-Buster

As the boulders of panic attacks and symptoms of stress are currently in your path then worrying on how best to fight them, how best to avoid their worst scenario and how best to free yourself of them will actually put you on a collision course to crash straight into them. On the other hand, although such boulders are currently in your path, if you focus your mind beyond them onto the more positive aspects of life then your journey through the condition of panic attacks will be far less harrowing and considerably faster.

The stress-buster

If you were in life-or-death danger, although your body would produce a massive burst of energy, you would quickly use up that energy fighting or fleeing for your life. However, being a stress sufferer, although your body is currently producing a significant amount of nervous energy, you are not using that energy but rather, you are actually increasing it then stockpiling it in massive amounts. In which case, you now need to dramatically slow down your production of nervous energy and physically release whatever nervous energy has built up in your body. And you can do just that by distracting your mind from your symptoms and occupying it with positive thoughts and actions.

As you see below, the stress-buster itself consists of 3 categories and 21 elements, all of which will play a major part in both slowing down your production of nervous energy and physically releasing whatever nervous energy has built up in your body. So read all 21 elements, decide which ones you feel will work best for you, then throughout the day (and if need be, the night too) partake in as many as you can, as often as you can.

To slow down your production of nervous energy
1. Try to develop a more philosophical approach
2. Avoid added stimulants
3. Generally slowdown
4. Talk to yourself
5. 'Hold-it'

6. Deep yoga breathing
7. 'Sound' via Mantra
8. Negative thought strategy
9. Moments of affirmation
10. Worldly distraction
11. Visualisation
12. Listen to a verbal relaxation tape
13. Play calming background sounds
14. 'My time' moments of peace
15. Avoid added negativity
16. Little changes
17. Make lists

Physically release your built-up nervous energy
18. Controlled physical exercise
19. Sing, scream, 'ouch' it out

Additional benefits
20. Keep a journal
21. Ensure your body maintenance

To slow down your production of nervous energy

1. Try to develop a philosophical approach

Many people go through life fearing all kinds of things when, in reality, their fears simply don't happen 99.99% of the time, and even on those rare occasions when a fear does come true, those few occasions certainly do not warrant spending a lifetime in fear.

Your symptoms of stress are nothing more than sensations of arousal, therefore your fear towards them is not due to you actually experiencing them, as everyone on the planet experiences them many times over, they are, after all, the lifesavers of mankind. You fearing your symptoms of stress is, however, founded in your mistaken belief that they will do you harm. Of course, to you, your fear towards your symptoms will seem appropriate but, in truth, it is not. Remember, throughout the time 'man' has roamed this earth those very sensations have protected his life not killed him off.

If you had influenza, although you would not like the symptoms of head pain, breathlessness, muscular aches and bodily weakness, you would not try to fight them or run from them but rather, you would experience them without resistance and just wait for recovery.

Anxiety is just another condition with its own symptoms: the higher the anxiety, the more severe the sensations of arousal. That's a fact of life! There is nothing surer, nothing anyone can do to change it and although, on a personal level, you might not want it, need it or like it, you do know it. So you hoping you won't experience sensations of arousal during a period of high arousal is futile and you feeling disappointed, frustrated, angry or frightened by them is a total waste of your time, emotions and energy.

That which cannot be changed must be accepted; otherwise we live a very unhappy life. And as your symptoms of stress will not disappear overnight, your ideal philosophical approach towards them would be to simply accept them and get on with your life. However this being the real world and you being a panic attack sufferer, you simply accepting your symptoms will be much easier said than done but as life really does go on with them, despite them and thanks to them, you might, at least, try the philosophical approach of acceptance.

2. Avoid added stimulants
Stimulants, including tea, coffee, cola, alcohol and cigarettes increase brain function, heartbeat, blood pressure and so on. So reduce as many of those substances as you can, but do it gradually, because if you reduce any substance too quickly that has been in your body for some time, you risk experiencing withdrawal symptoms such as headache, dizziness, nausea, sweating and flue-like symptoms. If you do experience such symptoms they should last for only about four or five days. If you wish to quicken the withdrawal process, a mild laxative such as Epsom salts (magnesium) or 1 gram of Vitamin C taken twice daily for about three days should help considerably.

Note: If you withdraw from a food or drink then later wish to reintroduce it into your system, you then risk experiencing the symptoms of re-introduction; they being indicative of food and/or chemical intolerance. So seek medical advice before doing so.

3. Generally slow down
Being a stress sufferer you probably live at speed: eat, walk, speak, change nappies, drive and work. However, as you know, when an anxious person moves quickly their primitive survival responses assume danger is present, their nervous system becomes more stimulated, their body becomes more energized and their mental and physical sensations of arousal become

ever more heightened. So help your nervous system to slowdown by making a conscious effort to do everything as slowly as you can.

4. Talk to yourself, if necessary, out of earshot

Contrary to common belief, talking to oneself is not a sign of madness. In fact, sometimes it is the sanest thing we can do. When I was a young girl my Grandmother used to talk to herself all the time. And whenever I said, "Grandma you're talking to yourself again," she would say, "I am, and show me someone who knows me better than I know myself and I'll talk to them as well." And even in her eighties, the lady was as bright as a button and the sanest, most well-balanced person I have ever met.

Talking to oneself can be extremely useful on four counts...

- As you saw earlier, whilst the conscious mind has the ability to work extraordinarily fast, the subconscious mind can work so fast that the conscious mind is oblivious to having had the thought. Speech and vocabulary do not have the same ability for speed. So when a person speaks their thoughts out loud, their mind will then, to some degree, slow down the process of thought to synchronize with the speech.
- You may now be so overwhelmed by fear and negative thoughts that you spend virtually all your days in silence, lost in an internal world in which you feel you cannot escape. By talking to yourself out loud, you then become familiar with both speaking and hearing yourself speak.
- By talking to yourself you can become your own best friend: have a good moan, voice your opinions, comfort and pick yourself up.
- Talking out loud to God or to a departed loved one can be a great help.

5. 'Hold-it'

Previously, in 'Arousal Creating Prolonged Physical Symptoms Of Stress,' regarding the Chest, Over breathing (page 91) I spoke of the findings of Dr Buteyko and how, when breathing is deeper and faster than normal, we can exhale too much carbon dioxide, which lessens our body's uptake of oxygen.

All stress sufferers breathe too quickly and too deeply thereby exhaling too much carbon dioxide, which inhibits their body's uptake of oxygen. A simple test, based on the Buteyko Breathing Test, that can indicate whether or not a person is a likely over-breather, is as follows...

1. Calm yourself for a few moments, gently breathing in and out.
2. Gently breathe out. Once your lungs are empty (taking your timing from the second hand of a clock) mentally count the seconds until

just before you feel discomfort – breathe in – breathe normally – then note your count.

From his research, Dr Buteyko found that, after a relaxed expiration, those with a normal carbon dioxide level could count to 40 seconds. On the other hand, those with asthma could count to about 10. Therefore, if your count was below 25 seconds then your breathing possibly needs attention and if your count was around 10 seconds then a significant breathing problem could exist. But whatever your count, hopefully the following exercise will offer you benefit...

1. Throughout this exercise, and only if your health will allow it, keep your mouth closed, breathing only through your nose.
2. Sit or lie down in a comfortable position.
3. Bring your breathing under voluntary control then breathe normally for about 30-60 seconds.
4. Breathe in very gently and slowly – breathe out gently and slowly then, once your lungs are empty of air, 'hold-it' until just before you feel discomfort – breathe in.
5. Breathe normally for about two minutes.

The above exercise is quite powerful, so only practise it three times at any one session and about 5 sessions a day. If at any time you feel dizzy then you are doing it too much, so stop for a little while then repeat the exercise but fewer times at any one session.

If you wish to look further into the Buteyko Breathing techniques then I suggest you read about Dr Konstantin Pavlovich Buteyko and/ or read the book 'Breathing Free' by Teresa Hale, which is based on the Buteyko Breathing technique. And although, in my opinion, Teresa Hale is truly missing the crux of panic attacks, her book 'Breathing Free' does indicate a significant degree of understanding of Buteyko Breathing.

6. Deep yoga breathing

You now know that, during deep breathing we can exhale too much carbon dioxide, which lessens our body's uptake of oxygen. That being so, the following exercise might initially seem quite contradictory to that suggested by Dr Buteyko, however it is not.

We all deep breathe when angry, afraid or involved in high physical activity, at which point, our breathing is then subconsciously controlled, rapid, strained, thin and mainly from the chest. However when a person is deep yoga breathing, their breathing is focused, slower, relaxed, fuller and involves their diaphragm; all of which greatly helps to balance the body's oxygen/carbon dioxide ratio.

Below is a simple deep breathing yoga exercise which will significantly help to slow down your production of nervous energy...

1. Lie on your back on a semi-hard surface.
2. Place one hand on your chest and the other on your stomach.
3. Bring your breathing under voluntary control by consciously focusing your thoughts onto each breath.
4. This next action is practised in one flowing movement and involves **inflating** the chest and stomach, in that order, and then **deflating** the stomach and chest, in that order...

    Place one hand on your chest and your other hand on your stomach. Next, gently **inhale** through your nose whilst inflating your chest to the slow count of one (that will raise the hand on your chest) then whilst continuing to **inhale**, gently expand your stomach to the slow count of two (that will raise the hand on your stomach) next gently **exhale** through your nose whilst deflating your stomach to the slow count of three (that will lower the hand on your stomach) then whilst continuing to **exhale**, gently deflate your chest to the slow count of four, five (that will lower the hand on your chest).
5. Once you have acquired the timing of this exercise and you are able to carry it out without counting, you might like to try the following...

    With your eyes closed, seeing only with your mind's eye, **inhale** whilst gently breathing in the colour white, then either send the white throughout your body or direct it to a area of your body that is causing you most worry. Then **exhale**, gently blowing out the colour black.

Deep breathing yoga is very powerful, so initially complete each cycle of breath (both inhale and exhale) only three times at any one session and about 4 times throughout the day, building it up gradually to about 10 minutes twice daily. If at any time you feel dizzy then you must stop for a little while then repeat the exercise but fewer times at any one session.

7. 'Sound' via Mantra: man (thought) tra (protection)

Mantra: to repeatedly chant certain sounds or words that have a beneficial 'cause and effect' to the well-being of the person involved.

For many thousands of years, the Eastern cultures of the world have recognised the tremendous value of 'sound,' via mantra. Over the last two thousand years, religious groups also have come to recognise the value of 'sound,' via prayer. And whilst some non-believers of Mantra, repeatedly demand scientific proof before belief, the believers, being unable to provide such scientific proof, have steadfastly held onto their convictions.

Science once argued that the world was flat, that the sun, moon and stars revolved around the Earth and that the atom was the smallest particle in the universe. Yet over time, all those theories and countless more have been proved wrong. So it is with 'sound.' For it has now been found that certain sound frequencies can indeed affect 'so called' solid matter.

I say 'so called' solid matter because it has also been found that solid matter itself does not actually exist. Of course to you and me it appears to exist, for I see you as being solid and you see me the same. But in reality, it does not. When any individual particle is taken to its most infinitesimal, the subatomic matter found are not particles but 'strings of vibrating energy.' Furthermore, it is now thought that from the largest planet in the universe to the most microscopic element in the universe, the same principle is at work: namely, 'the universal energy wave of life.' You might say, we are each a 'string' of light, a golden strand that unites us all in the one heart.

Do you see? The reason why mantra is so very effective is that when practised, the vibration it creates within us, reverberates through us, to influence and balance the vibration that is us.

To practice mantra in its true form, and thereby gain most benefit, one requires many precise warm-up exercises and considerations. But as we are not using mantra for any purposes other than to focus the mind and aid general relaxation, we can eliminate all those considerations and just enjoy the mantra for itself, whilst gladly accepting whatever benefit we receive.

I included the following exercise into the stress-buster about ten years ago, which has since proved to be extremely beneficial...

1. **Preparation exercise**: Softly, gently, sing the sol-fa scale, rising and falling, in order of pitch: i.e. doh – re – me – fah – so – la – tee – doh / doh – tee – la – so – fah – me – re – doh. Repeat the whole scale about 3 times, ending on your lower doh. Hold it, then gently change the doh to A (it sound like 'are') whereupon your pitch might then go even lower but whatever pitch your voice rests on, that is your pitch for this mantra.

2. **Exercise**: Gently inhale through your nose until you have a full breath. **Now the full AUM**: Firstly, focus both your mind and breath onto the A sound (it sound like 'are') then hold it until you have used about one-third of your breath. Next, slowly change the A to the U (as in u for umbrella) then hold it until you have used a further third of

your breath. Then, slowly change the U to the M (m for mother) sound then hold it until you have used the remaining third of your breath.

3. Breath normally for two breaths.
4. Repeat the exercise.

When practicing the AUM mantra, make the transition from the A to U to M as smoothly as you can. If you are doing it correctly you will feel a vibration in your neck and throat, changing slightly with each sound, and if you are very lucky you will feel a slight vibration in your chest.
Also when practising this exercise, even in this basic form, the technique of voicing mantra is only secondary to the feelings you experience when practising. So try to both focus your mind onto the sound itself and also feel it.

Again, this is a very powerful exercise, so initially complete each mantra of AUM only three times at any one session and about 4 times throughout the day, building up gradually to about 10 minutes twice daily. When practicing, if at any time you feel dizzy then you are doing it too much, so stop for a little while then repeat your mantra again but fewer times in any one session. Also when practicing, if you feel calm and/or uplifted then certainly continue but if you feel disturbed then stop immediately.

To look more deeply into the practice of mantra, look into the work and teachings of the incredible Muz Murry. If you feel inclined to buy just any random CD/DVD be careful, there are many half trained, so-called yoga teachers out there.

8. Negative thoughts strategy

Negative thoughts can strike anywhere, at anytime, to anyone. One does not have to be suffering nervous exhaustion or breakdown for negative thoughts to strike. So be prepared for them, not by keeping yourself tense and 'on-guard' but rather, by having a 'negative thoughts strategy.' That is, to have a certain thought, words or action already worked out that will help to distract your mind and keep it occupied for a few moments thereby giving your mind a little time to regain its perspective. And as we are talking of those times when you are not in a panic attack, you need not restrict your words to six but rather, you could have a couple of sentences. For example...

You could use your 'words of sanctuary' or use an affirmation, poem, prayer, hymn or just comforting words such as, 'Holy Father, in the midst of this storm, let me know your peace,' or 'Holy Father, in my weakness, let me know your strength,' or (my own personal words of strength and comfort, by Alistair MacLean) 'If I may hold your hand in this darkness, it is enough.' You could use a 'reason for reassurance.' Or you could use a loved one's name (whether they are alive or dead) and talk to them as if they were stood next to you. Then, whenever a negative thought strikes, just take a moment and re-focus your thoughts onto your positive words.

If you have many worries, I don't recommend using different words for each issue, as that can get quite complicated. You might find it easier to have just one or perhaps two sentences that cover all your issues but, of course, if you feel it will serve you better to have different words for each worrying issue then do so.

Also, if it helps you, try looking upon your negative thoughts as you would the behaviour of a naughty child. That is, when a child is acting naughtily, don't give their naughty behaviour attention but rather, give them something positive to do then praise their good behaviour. Likewise, don't try to force your negative thoughts out of your mind; as that will only give them importance but rather, focus your eyes and thoughts onto something or someone positive; as that will gently guide your thoughts away from the negativity and onto the more positive aspects of your life. And even when other negative thoughts come into your mind, as they surely will, just continue to treat them as you would a child's naughty behaviour; by focusing your attention on something positive.

9. Moments of affirmation

Affirmations are positive, encouraging words that one repeatedly says to oneself. Whilst some people have only one or two affirmations other people have many. And whilst some only use them to calm themselves during a particularly stressful situation, others place them around the house or workplace and use them every day wherever and whenever they pop-up; on your fridge door, on mirrors, in drawers, in your purse, on your desktop or in your car.

The actual words you might use for your affirmation could be: – your 'words of sanctuary' or any other profound, meaningful words that make sense to you – humorous words that bring a smile to your heart – words that give you a 'reason for reassurance' and thereby help you to see your problem from a different and more positive perspective – words that encapsulate everything that is happening to you – or words that remind you of happier times or a particular person, place, object, hobby, ambition or anything that is pleasing, comforting, uplifting or inspiring to you.

But whatever words of affirmation you do use, always use the 'now,' i.e. 'I **am** stronger,' 'I **am** better every day,' 'I **do** love life.'

If you wish, try to combine a mantra and affirmation together by using a one-line affirmation as a mantra.

10. Worldly distraction

When a sufferer is at the point of nervous exhaustion or breakdown, their inclination is to do nothing and think about nothing other than matters associated with their worries. And even though 'life' is going on all around them, they merely go through the motions, becoming evermore mentally and emotionally imprisoned until they eventually become detached from life itself. Yet even at this point, distraction is still the best action to take.

The aim of 'worldly distraction' is to give your mind a few seconds rest by re-focusing it onto the more positive elements of life, thereby breaking through the mental barrier of negativity.

So as you go about your day feeling anxious and afraid, wherever you are and whatever you are doing, use the power of your mind, for just a few seconds, to bring yourself back to the reality of the situation by just focusing your thoughts onto something positive. For example...

You could focus your mind on literally anything: – a special item in your pocket or handbag – window-shop or look into other peoples' gardens and think which plants you would like in your garden – embrace 'love' by hugging your children, and really focus onto the hug, or feel your child's skin, stroke their hair, look into their eyes and really see them – look at a special picture and imagine yourself in it – look at a photograph of a happier time and allow your thoughts to remember how you felt when the photograph was taken or look straight into the eyes of a person in the photograph and talk to them – sing a special song, read a special poem or read a special letter and allow your mind to linger over the words – pick a flower from your garden and allow your thoughts to really focus onto both its form and scent – play a special piece of music and allow yourself to feel the emotion the music evokes – or do anything that might distract your mind from the negativity of worrying.

If you can't think of any aspect of your current life that holds enough interest to entice you back to life then think back to a happier time. Who were you then? What did you like to do? Where did you like to go? What things gave you pleasure? What things were important to you? What had the strength to hold your interest and carry you? What things did you always dream of doing? And where did you always want to go?

11. Visualisation: Grounded and Spiritual

Grounded Visualisation:

Being a panic attack sufferer, whenever you think of yourself in certain situations, you see yourself (in your minds eye) frightened, enduring symptoms of stress and experiencing a panic attack. So instead of allowing such negative imagery to steer your mind, re-train it by seeing yourself in a situations without being frightened. For example, think of any place or situation that frightens you then...

- Whilst using your mind's eye, but staying emotionally detached, see yourself setting off, going to and being in a fearful situation. Really look at yourself experiencing high fear. Then, slowly change the picture from you experiencing sensations of fear to those of calm. Once you see yourself calm, hold the focus for as long as you can; allowing your mind to see you in that feared situation without you feeling fearful but calm.

- Whilst using your mind's eye but feeling the emotions, put yourself into a fearful situation. Feel as if you are there actually experiencing all the sensations of fear and terror then, after a few seconds, try to change your sensations of fear to those of calm. If you are able to do so, hold the feelings for as long as you can and allow your mind to see you, via your mind's eye, in that feared place or situation yet feeling calm.

Spiritual Visualisation:

Whilst using your mind's eye and feeling the emotions, visit a spiritual place where you would love to be. For example...

Visit the heavens and stroll round the 'garden of music' where every shimmering leaf, flower and blade of grass vibrates with its own healing lullaby. – Kneel before the Almighty. – Dance or sing with the magnificent angels of glory. – Have a wondrous conversation with your guardian angel or a deceased loved one. – Go to the golden temple of peace and serenity and sit before the wise men of eons in their saffron, golden and white robes, speak to them of your most pressing concerns then listen to their words of wisdom. – Ride a white cloud edged with shimmering, golden sunshine. – Or float over blue oceans, snow-capped mountains, lush, green valleys and rivers with sparkling clear waters and look down at this wonderful, life-giving, selfless, blue and white planet Earth.

When visualising, make everything to your pleasing, make it as real as you can and also see every element in its finest detail. See the brightness, sharpness, clarity and colour of everything in your environment. Are you in a spiritual realm, or in a town, in the country or by the sea? Is it cool or hot? Are you with someone or on your own? What clothes are people wearing? What are they talking about? Remember, you are only visualising so you are perfectly safe. Change your picture as often as you wish.

12. Listen to a relaxation CD/DVD

If you have a verbal relaxation CD/DVD, listen to it.
(For purchasing details, please see my website: www.lmbookshop.com)

13. Play calming background sounds

Normally, when we go about our daily life we are quite oblivious to the multitude of background sounds around us. But whether or not we are conscious of them, they have a profound effect on both our mental and physical state, often to where the pace and quality of our life is determined by them, i.e. if you were sitting in your garden listening to birds singing, trees rustling or a water fountain trickling, those sounds would have a calming influence on you. Alternatively, if you were sitting in your garden, then suddenly, just beyond your garden wall, workmen descended and began to dig up the road with pneumatic drills, those sounds would have an annoying, stimulating effect on you.

So as you go about your daily life, the sounds around you of children fighting, your husband or wife moaning, people voicing their frustration, machines pounding at speeds much faster than your own heartbeat, music jarring, video games bleeping, house alarms piercing your ears and tense television dialogue of murders, wars, domestic strife and financial ruin, all bring tremendous stress, strain and stimulation to your mind and body. And that is where calming background sounds come into play, as when such sounds are played during the day and, if need be, the night also, they can bring a wondrous degree of tranquillity to the mind, body and environment.

I often play calming sounds: – a Buddhist monastery with its horns, chimes, gongs and chants – a Christian monastery with its bells, chants and singing – a rainforest with its birdsongs, rain and thunder – a cottage garden with its variety of birdsongs – and a family of whales with their squeaks, clicks and great splashes.
(For purchasing details, please see my website: www.lmbookshop.com)

14. 'My time' moments of peace

Have a special time each day to disconnect from 'heart pain' and connect to 'heart pleasure.' You could perhaps practise yoga, Tai Chi, meditation, say prayers, paint, have a relaxing candlelit bath, watch an uplifting or funny film, read a good book or do anything that will offer you 'heart pleasure.'

If you like to express yourself artistically but don't consider yourself talented, remember, 'an artist is not a unique person but every person is a unique artist.' So in whatever way you choose to express yourself, you can't fail, you are simply doing it your own special way.

15. Avoid added negativity
Doom and gloom can be found anywhere, most of which we simply learn to live with. However, being a stress sufferer, particularly if your suffering is severe, you will already have enough negativity to cope with without having to listen to it from others. So avoid all potential gloom from your life: – Cancel your newspapers – don't watch or listen to the news or any negative programmes and avoid those friends and family members who upset you or load their negativity onto you. And instead, encourage into your life everything positive: – watch or listen to uplifting programmes or DVDs – try reading a humorous book, or one with a positive storyline and happy ending or read a children's comic – also, ask your befriender to to tell everyone who upsets you to either stay away for a while or to call but only speak of happy things.

16. Little changes
As you know, whenever a person is in surroundings where they previously had a traumatic time they are likely to experience 'flashbacks.' Being a panic attack sufferer, you have probably experienced more traumatic times than most, so consider changing your surroundings: – redecorate or rearrange all the furniture in a particular room or throughout your home or office – shop in a different store – go to work via a different route – change the colours on your desktop – change your clothes style, hair colour, makeup, toothbrush, handbag – or go on holiday or visit a friend.

If you do make such changes in your life then when you walk into a room, or go to work, or clean your teeth, or look into a mirror or look out the window and it is all different and pleasing to your eye, the emotional uplift could literally carry you for minutes, even hours.

17. Make lists
Whilst I hate to sound patronising, the following will sound exceptionally patronising to those who have a loving, supportive relationship and are not in breakdown. However if you are suffering severely, living alone and in breakdown then I hope the following will be useful to you...

Preparation:

1. Please acquire three writing pads: On the front of one pad write **Pocketbook**, on the second write, **Doing Book** and on the third write, **Befriender**.

2. Keep the **Pocketbook** very near to hand. Keep the **Doing-book** at home handy. And give your befriender the remaining pad.

3. In the **Pocketbook**, list every issue that currently needs attending to until every aspect of your life is out of your head and set out clearly in front of you: – your budget breakdown – your daily and weekly menu – your household and personal shopping – your negative thoughts and worries – points to raise – questions to ask – problems to be dealt with – tasks that need doing or amending – things you would like to do in the future – which people irritate you and which lift your spirit.

4. From your list in the **Pocketbook** transfer into the **Doing Book** every task that you feel you can do yourself, without help.

5. Next, contact your befriender and transfer into their **Befriender** book all remaining tasks; from where your befriender will either attend to them personally or find someone who is able to attend to them for you.

6. Next to each task in the **Doing Book** put a number in order of urgency, one being very urgent and so on down to the least urgent.

Throughout each day:

- **Pocketbook**: When a issue arises that needs attending to, write it down.
- **Doing Book**: Beginning with the task numbered one, do whatever you can to sort it out. Once sorted out then cross it off and move onto the task numbered two and so on.

Every evening or whenever is best for you, amend each list:

- In both your **Pocket Book** and **Doing Book** cross off each task that you have completed that day, leaving the tasks that are not done but which you still feel you can work on yourself.
- Transfer from your **Pocket Book** to your **Doing Book** any new task that has arisen that day which you feel you can work on yourself, without help, renumbering them in order of urgency.
- Contact your befriender and then transfer from your **Pocket Book** to your befriender's list any new task that has arisen that day which you feel you cannot attend to yourself.

- Transfer from your **Doing Book** to your befriender's list any task that you feel you can no longer accomplish yourself.
- Transfer from your befriender's list into your **Doing Book** any task that you now feel you can work on yourself.
- In your **Pocket Book,** cross off any task that your befriender has completed or that someone else has completed for you.

To physically release your built-up nervous tension

18. Controlled physical exercise

Exercise can be extremely beneficial to the stress sufferer because, along with many other benefits, it encourages the production of Serotonin (the feel good hormone) it aids sleep and lowers adrenalin. Circuit training, walking, jogging, cycling, lovemaking, swimming and gymnastics are all perfect. And even though tennis, football, rugby and boxing are highly competitive sports, when they are practiced in the spirit of friendship rather than with the need to win, they too can be of great benefit.

Another exceptionally useful exercise is to hold a cushion or pillow then really bang it on a wall or piece of furniture for 3-5 minutes, as often as you can throughout the day.

19. Sing, Scream, "Ouch" it out

When a person is suffering a long and traumatic experience, it is all too easy for them to become lost in it to where their own self loses both its ability to know its own feeling and its inclination to voice whatever feelings it does have.

To suffer panic attacks is to suffer quietly, to scream in silence, to bury one's fear and to swallow one's terror. But what goes in will come out, in one way or another. So if all your suppressed emotions are not released in a controlled way then, like a volcano, they will, sooner or later, erupt.

The following exercise will enable you to coax out your frustrations, anger and fear, allow you to control the volume to which you do it and allow you to determine the depth of emotion you reach and release...

1. Have a thick cushion or pillow to hand.
2. Turn on your radio or music and set the volume very high.
3. Put your mouth to the pillow then release your emotions by doing any one of the following...
   - Sing out: Chose one of your favourite, uplifting and inspiring songs then, using the words, the passion and the energy of the song, sing as loudly as you possibly can, really blast it out!

- Scream: As loudly as you possibly can.
- Ouch! When an adult is in severe pain, fear and distress, although they are an adult, they will often feel lost, alone, frightened, vulnerable and child-like. In which case, like any child in pain, their cry of 'ouch' will help them to connect to their pain and ultimately release it.

Once you attempt to sing, scream or cry ouch, you may initially have difficulty releasing any sound at all. If so, don't be put off, for this exercise was purposefully devised for you. Just begin slowly, in the softest whisper, gently increasing the volume until you are as loud as you can.

Once you try to sing, scream or cry ouch, don't feel concerned if you have difficulty releasing any emotion. It is only due to you having held-in your emotions for so long that now, to your mind, if you allow even one drop of emotion to be released, the floodgate will open, your emotional tidal wave will be released, of which there might be no stopping and you will be physically, mentally and emotionally thrown 'over the edge.' But that is **exactly** what we are preventing! Yes, your singing, screaming or crying ouch will release a degree of your held-in emotions and built-up physical energy but you are doing so at a time, in a place, to a degree and in the company of your choice, and all in a controlled way!

Finally, once you are able to sing, scream or cry ouch, you might find yourself absolutely sobbing. If so, don't hold back or swallow your tears but rather, allow all that bottled up emotion to come out. And once this exercise is over, expect to feel absolutely elated or totally exhausted. If you do participate in this exercise, take care not to strain your throat.

Additional benefits

20. Keep a journal
There are four main reasons for keeping a journal...
1. From time to time, we all need a good 'heart to heart' talk with a true and trusted friend. But friends are not always on hand when we need them, friends don't always fully understand us and friends sometimes let us down. So, in truth, we all need to become our own best friend. You need to become your own best friend. You need to give yourself as much time as you would give to a best friend. You need to reach the point where nobody knows you better than you know yourself. And you need to be the one with whom you have your 'heart to hearts.' That being so, an extremely useful tool to help you to get to know yourself is to keep a journal.

2. When we experience pain, fear and distress we tend to feel isolated, become morbid, think of all the worst scenarios and feel our life is just a trial to be endured. But when we are low in spirit, we tend to distort the events of our life and shroud them all in darkness and thereby prevent any light from coming through. That is where keeping a journal can be so useful, for it will document any light that enters into your day.

3. When we experience adversity, the way in which we then assess our life is dependent on the degree of morbidity we feel at that time. But when we have kept a journal, we are then able to look back over our happy and sad times, see that our previous endurance's passed when we thought they never would, know that we are stronger today for all our endurance's yesterday, trust that tomorrow we will be stronger for our endurance's today and believe 'this also will pass' and good times will come again. And because it is our diary with our own writing, we will be all the more respondent to it.

4. The Moon influences the ebb and flow of the sea. The sea is, of course, water. The human body is about 60% water and, like the sea, is influenced by the Moon. The issue here, however, is that the Moon has a twenty-eight day cycle and therefore circles the earth thirteen times a year but we do not live with the twenty-eight day, thirteen month lunar cycle, we live against it in a 28 to 31 day, twelve months cycle. Silly isn't it? This, though, can easily be remedied, on a personal level.

    If you keep a journal and note your emotions, i.e. when you feel productive, lazy, short-tempered, accident-prone, antagonistic and so on. After a few months you will be able to look back and identify certain parts of your own twenty-eight day cycle. And although referring to your journal will not give you an exact record (as other elements also come into play such as lifestyle, environment, when and where you were born) you will still be given an indication of your own cycle, your likely mood and your potential aptitude for any given day.

So every evening or whatever time suits you best...

- Have a 'heart to heart' with yourself by talking to your journal from your heart as if it were your most trusted friend. Explain how you felt that day, why you felt the way you did, what hurt you, who hurt you, who made you smile and what you wished for yourself tomorrow.
- List at least three uplifting events that occur each day. They need not be extra special, just nice little moments: – receiving an unexpected

friendly smile, cup of tea or greeting card – witnessing the selflessness of one person caring for another – seeing the miracle of a flower – watching the birds feeding in your garden – listening to the beauty of a poem, lyrics of a song or piece of music – having a good day – doing a small task that you haven't done for a while – or feeling the tenderness of a heartfelt "Thank you" or "I love you."

- If you are suffering severely and often fear that you are going two steps forward and three backwards, then keeping a journal will be very useful for you. As when you have a balanced overview on your reality, (by reading over all your 'good and bad times') you will then be able to to put a more balance perspective on the whole of your life.

21. Ensure your body maintenance

Stress will put demands on the body, often taking from the body that which it cannot afford. So if you have been suffering stress for a while then, sooner or later, your bodily resources will become depleted, which, in turn, will make your body vulnerable to conditions not of stress itself but those secondary to stress, such as allergies, ulcers, asthma, diabetes, high/low blood pressure, lingering colds, sore throats, body infections, irritable bowel, constipation, hormone imbalance and so on. So to help your body cope with its current level of stress…

- Rest as much as you can.
- During each day, find as much time for yourself as you can.
- If possible, eat regularly: morning, mid-day, early evening and perhaps something light during the evening.
- Whenever possible, eat organic, wholesome, fresh, nourishing foods such as whole grain, pulses, vegetables, fruit, fish and chicken.
- Cut out or cut down all refined, processed and packaged food.
- Breathe clean air.
- Partake in regular, appropriate exercise.
- Show kindness to others, be kind to yourself and try your best to think kind thoughts, as often as you possibly can.

To those suffering nervous exhaustion/breakdown…

If you are suffering nervous exhaustion/breakdown you are probably now thinking that to participate in any of the above elements will be impossible for you. In fact I can almost hear you thinking, "Lorraine, what on earth are you expecting from me? I can't hold a positive thought for even one second, so no way will I be able to sustain enough positive thought to be of any significance?" My reply to that is, your mind is merely exhausted, not dead! And the following chapter was purposely designed for you, so I am sure you will find significant benefit.

A few considerations, reminders and tips

Considerations

Each of the stress-buster elements is very powerful in its own right. As a result, before you put any of them into practice, check with your medical doctor that you are perfectly safe to do so.

Whichever elements of the stress-buster you choose, the benefits might not be immediately apparent to you, which might confuse you. Therefore, the guideline that I usually recommend is, once chosen, stay on your element for at least two weeks. By then, you will have a) become familiar with the element itself, b) you will have overcome any strangeness and c) you will then have a good indication as to how it is serving you. After two weeks, if you feel an element is not suitable or not working for you then choose another element and stay on that one for two weeks also and so on.

Reminders

- This programme is about re-educating your mind not to overreact to your arousal responses but rather, for it to respond to them suitably to your reality. And as your arousal responses are only natural bodily functions that your brain has lived with for so many years previously without overreacting. You currently experiencing arousal responses without overreacting is not something that your brain has to learn from new. Your brain only has to remember how it responded to them previously.
- Whilst participating in your stress-buster, if you experience adrenaline withdrawal sensations (see Relax Never Again, page 163) and suddenly feel a wave of fear swell over you, or a compulsion to 'do something' or a panic attack strikes remember, such sensations are an indication that you are on the road to recovery therefore just re-focus your thoughts onto your 'words of sanctuary' or on whatever you were doing and let-go.
- Once you begin to relax, you might find other things happening: – as one fear goes, another one might take its place – as one symptom eases, another one might appear – or one moment you will feel on top of the world then the next moment your emotions plummet. If so, just continue to work the best you can and you will see just how simply and quickly your mind and body will gain rest and become stronger.

- Always ensure your safety: Therefore only ever partake in the stress-buster elements if your medical doctor has sanctioned it and you know you are within your ability.

Tips
- Daily partake in as many of the stress-buster elements as you can, as often as you can and for as long as you feel comfortable.
- It is of greater benefit to set yourself a realistic routine and stick to it than it is to set an unrealistic routine only to give up after a few days.
- The more you are suffering; all the greater is your need to partake in the stress-buster.
- Most panic attack sufferers find it extremely helpful to partake in their own stress-buster frequently throughout the day rather than in one long session. However, whether your time partaking is in one long session or it is divided into many shorter sessions, mind rest is still mind rest.
- Symptoms of stress are not likely to disappear overnight, they will fade away gradually over days and weeks. In which case, you don't need to continuously baby-sit them or supervise their intensity. Indeed, because you know they will still be there five minutes from now, why not give yourself five minutes off from worrying about them. You can always go back to worrying in five minutes time.

Moving ever forwards

If you are not experiencing any mental symptoms of stress other than during your actual panic attacks then, if you wish, omit the following chapter and now go to, 'Re-cap: To Take Your Third Step To Freedom,' which begins on page 202. You can read the following chapter later in the programme.

If you are suffering mental symptoms of stress outside the times of your panic attacks, therefore your mental symptoms of stress are prolonged, then continue to read the following chapter. For although the mind is a complex issue, the mending of prolonged mental symptoms of stress need not be a complicated procedure.

To Ease Prolonged Mental Symptoms of Stress

To remind you

When the boulders of negative thoughts are in your path then you stressing and straining on – how best to rid yourself of them – how best to fight your way through them – and how best to free yourself of them, will create even more problems...

Therefore trying to force your mind away from negative thought is not your best solution.

When the boulders of negative thoughts are in your path, the more you try not to think them, you will, all the more, think them...

Therefore trying not to think negative thoughts is not your best solution

When a person is suffering mental symptoms of stress to the point of nervous exhaustion/breakdown, if they are taken into hospital for mind-rest, rarely will they be tranquillised to the point of a comatose like state...

Therefore being put into any level of a comatose like state is not your best solution.

Mind-rest

After everything we have discussed about mind-rest you might think that, for an exhausted mind to rest, the whole mind or, at least, all the thinking part of the mind, would need to come to a complete stop. That is not so. An exhausted mind, even when in breakdown, does not need to fully stop nor does it need to play dead. It simply needs to rest.

If you are suffering mental symptoms of stress to the point of nervous exhaustion or breakdown then you attaining mind-rest must take priority over everything. And if you feel you have to keep pushing yourself, caring and providing for your family then realise, nothing is more important to the well-being of yourself and your family than you attaining mind-rest.

The following information, when taken with that given previously, will show how to attain mind-rest. For although the mind itself is a complex issue, the attaining of mind-rest need not be a complicated procedure, in fact it can be quite straightforward. So be reassured, for whilst you will understandably need to adapt the following information to suit your own ability and requirements, it will nevertheless go a long way towards helping you.

Positive occupation of the mind
To explain this whole matter as simply as I can...

The thinking part of the mind can be divided into two parts: the negative thinking part and the positive thinking part.

The **negative** thinking part of the mind demands tremendous mind-energy, as a result, overusing it will **deplete** the mind. So, when a person continuously thinks negative thoughts, sooner or later, such thoughts will lead to mental/nervous tiredness, exhaustion and often breakdown. The **positive** thinking part of the mind creates mind-energy, as a result, using it will truly **energise** the mind. When our thoughts are positive they are not negative, indeed positive thinking will not only allow the negative thinking part of our mind to rest but it will actually energise the mind.

For most people, positive thinking does not come easily, indeed for many people, it is very difficult. The reason being that, when left to its own control, the thinking part of the mind is inclined towards negative thoughts and negative thoughts are inclined towards more; which itself is a survival response. That is why negative thinking can easily become a habit and, for some, become out of control.

And so, every person suffering mental symptoms of stress, especially those suffering to the point of mental exhaustion or breakdown, will need to consciously take control of their thoughts then, very deliberately, think positive thoughts. I call this process, **a positive occupation of the mind** but as the overall objective is mind-rest, we will just call it, mind-rest.

And realise
When experiencing a panic attack, your mind will lean on your 'words of sanctuary' for only a matter of moments until the attack has passed. But when suffering mental exhaustion/breakdown, as those conditions do not last for only moments but rather, they last much longer, you will need to gain mind-rest as often as you can, even if you are only able to do so for one moment at a time. And if perhaps you now think, "One moment, why even bother?" I'll tell you why...

Assuming you are awake for 12 hours a day...
30 seconds x twice an hour = 1 minute an hour
1 minute an hour x 12 times per day = 12 minutes per day
12 minutes is a reasonable duration for any meditation session

1 minute x twice an hour = 2 minutes an hour
2 minutes an hour x 12 times per day = 24 minutes a day
24 minutes is the average duration of most relaxation tapes

2 minutes x twice an hour = 4 minutes an hour
4 minutes an hour x 12 times per day = 48 minutes a day
48 minutes is the average duration time of most counselling or
therapy sessions

5 minutes an hour x 12 times per day = 1 hour a day
That is one whole hour a day of you allowing positive thoughts to energise
your mind thus preventing negative thoughts from exhausting it.

Attaining mind-rest
Mind-rest is achieved in two ways, the first being 'general mind-rest,'
which is practised throughout the day as often as possible. The second is
'specific mind-rest,' which is practised during acute moments.

1. General mind-rest
The stress-buster (which begins on page 171) encourages the positive
thinking part of a mind to work harder and thus become more energised
and stronger. So partake in the stress-buster as much as possible, as often
as you can throughout the day and, if need be, the night also. Please, don't
underestimate the power of the stress-buster.

2. Specific mind-rest
If you are suffering with mental exhaustion/breakdown you will need to
adapt the following information to suit your own situation. Even so, you
understanding how 'specific mind-rest' can give your mind a significant
degree of rest will certainly go a long way towards helping you.

And remember, to suffer mental symptoms of stress is not merely to
endure any one of the thought processes mentioned below. It is, however,
to experience any number of thought patterns in varying degrees.

The veil of mental exhaustion

Symptoms relating to this element do not have to be specifically worked on because once the mind is able to rest they simply fade away on their own. But be forewarned. These symptoms have a tendency to linger until the whole mind is rested therefore they are usually amongst the last to go.

Content based fearful thought

Ellen: as covered previously (see page 110)
As Ellen, her mother (being her befriender) and I talked, it very soon became apparent that Ellen needed to know a few medical facts of conception. So our first task was to separate fact from wild imagination.

As we talked and matters were explained such as, the life-span of the human egg and its release from the ovary, Ellen began to realise that, based on facts, she could not be pregnant with the other woman's egg because the two sexual acts were too far apart for the other woman's egg to have still been viable.

Of course, this awareness brought tremendous relief to Ellen but, as expected, after a few minutes, she began to question the validation of the facts. But as I had forewarned both ladies that such a boulder was likely to happen, the disappointment was cushioned a little. Leaving Ellen and her mother to find words that would encapsulate the facts of the situation.

A few hours later, two sentences were found that Ellen knew to be fact and strong enough to counterbalance her fears. And over the following days, Ellen said her words, distracted her mind from fear and reinforced into her mind how the baby she was carrying was indeed her own.

When there seems no solution.

David: as covered previously (see page 113)
During my first two weeks of visiting David, I saw him deteriorating daily. So knowing the urgency of the situation and that David's problem was religiously based, I met with his priest to ensure that he (the priest) had a nature that David needed. He did and a meeting was planned.

The meeting itself, which consisted of David, the parish priest and myself, was held in an atmosphere of warmth and compassion. However for most of the time David gained no benefit at all and, as time passed, with David crying, the priest doing his best and me becoming ever more concerned, things were looking dire. But then, after about 45 minutes, just as we were leaving the church, with David still not having found a solution to his problem, when saying our goodbyes, the kind priest simply patted David on the arm and casually said to him, "You know David, the desire for God's presence is proof that he's already there." Instantly David said, "What was that you said? What did you just say? Say it again. Say it again." The priest repeated, "The desire for God's presence is proof that he is already there." "Is that true? Is that really true?" David appealed to the priest, "Of course it is," the priest said, then continued, "The desire for God's presence is everything." "But are you sure? Are you really sure?" David pleaded. The priest confirmed, "Didn't Jesus himself say that even if we are in the bowels of hell yet cry out to God, God will come into hell itself to save us." "After all," the priest continued, "Desire itself has to come from somewhere, and for you to desire God, then the Holy Spirit of God must be in you now to provide your desires for God." "Like, will always seek out like." "Yes! That's it! That's it!" David cried, knowing he had found the words that made sense to him and he could totally accept.

As the days passed and David repeatedly said his words, "The desire for God's presence is proof that he is already there," his confidence returned, very quickly to where he was reassured that, despite his wrongdoing, God was still inside him, which eased his mind and helped him gain mind-rest.

Deprivation/Hibernation

After winter comes spring, after drought comes rain, after scarcity comes new growth of both plant and livestock and after a time of famine comes the time of feast. So it was for primitive man. As each winter turned into spring, as each drought eased and as each time of deprivation turned into a time of plenty, primitive man experienced moments of 'emotional treat time:' – feeling the sun's warmth on his body – a hearty meal – and a sense of satisfaction. And as primitive man began to enjoy those moments of 'emotional treat time' his mental, physical and emotional inclinations gradually awoke from 'wintertime hibernation' to 'summertime life'.

If you are suffering panic attacks, symptoms of stress and life problems, you will now be living, to some degree, in a state of emotional wintertime. If so, you now need moments of emotional treat time to slowly bring yourself out of hibernation and back to life. And you can begin that by participating in the stress-buster routine explained previously.

Note: When suffering deprivation/hibernation, once a person begins to enjoy little moments of pleasure and little things important to their quality of life, they will automatically 'wake up' on their own. Not so with clinical depression. So after about 3 weeks, if your feelings of depression have not lifted significantly then go back to your medical doctor to seek more help.

Morning strikes

As a stress sufferer, particularly if suffering severely, when you first wake up or soon after waking, your mind will instinctively be drawn towards your aches, pains and worrying thoughts similar to, "Is the pain still there? Has it moved? Has it changed? Surely, as it has not gone yet it must be cancer. I know it's **something** and the doctors are missing it. Perhaps this is the beginning of the end for me?" Therefore...

- Immediately on waking, focus your mind on your 'words of sanctuary.'
- Set up a CD that you know will offer you relaxation and emotional uplift then on waking immediately play it.
- Rearrange and/or redecorate your bedroom then on waking, along with distracting your mind, you will have a nice little surprise, which, in turn, will lift your spirit.
- Set your alarm to the time that you want to wake up, then when your alarm rings, immediately get up; physical health permitting.

Obsessive/Compulsive behaviour

The root cause of any obsession or compulsion is usually extremely complex. Indeed most people who suffer such conditions might have many obsessions/compulsions and on eradicating one, another will take its place. So it must be said that compulsions, like obsessions, are always best dealt with by specifically trained therapists. However, if (for whatever reason) you are not in the position to receive therapy for your obsessions or compulsions then please consider the following, for whilst it is only a few general suggestions, it might help you to some degree...

Whilst it now seems commonplace for people to use the terms obsessive thoughts and compulsive behaviour, in truth, compulsive behaviour itself stems from thought. The body is the servant of the mind. As such, to ease your compulsions you will still need to work on your thoughts.

Philosophically speaking, in life, good things happen and bad things happen; that's a fact of life. To have life is to have problems, illness and death. Nothing can guarantee that your day will be safe, problem free or that you will be alive at the end of it. Knowing that, how can one mentally break free from all the fears of life? One way is to let-go by using either your your 'words of sanctuary' or your 'words of reassurance' For example...

Let's assume you have lost all confidence in your own judgement and, to your thinking, to not follow your ritual would surely put you at risk. In which case, on going to bed in the evening, if your compulsion is to turn the bathroom light off and on ten times, then turn the landing light off and on ten times and then turn your bedroom light off and on ten times, otherwise harm will befall you.

In that situation, you could turn the bathroom light off once, then turn the landing light off once and then turn your main bedroom light off once; all the while focusing your thoughts onto either your 'words of sanctuary' or 'words of reassurance.' And yes, with your ritual then broken, you will feel as if you are taking a tremendous risk, tempting fate and actually inviting doom upon yourself. So you will need to really focus your mind onto your words until the focus of your mind has completely shifted from impending doom. And you will most probably need to go through the same procedure of letting-go for quite a while, maybe weeks. But you see what I mean.

If you are suffering obsessions or compulsions then try to work on the fact that no one can ever bargain with fate. If it is your day for disaster then disaster will come whatever you do. Even if you stay in bed all day, if it is your day for disaster, then it will come.

Having said that, remember, many people go through life fearing all kinds of things when, in reality, their fears simply don't happen 99.99% of the time. And even on those rare occasions when a fear does come true, surely those few occasions don't warrant spending a lifetime in fear. So sometimes in life we just have to take the chance, a leap of faith, otherwise, we really will live a very unhappy life.

Remember, regarding obsessions and compulsions, I am not an expert in this particular field therefore I only speak generally. Nevertheless, based on my experience working with such sufferers, I know that obsessions and compulsions can certainly be de-sensitised by letting-go.

The dreaded darkness

- Brightness indoors emphasizes darkness outdoors therefore, as soon as you notice it becoming dusk, don't keep your curtains open until darkness has fallen but rather, as the light fades, close your curtains and turn on all indoor lighting. By doing so, the darkness will not be quite so apparent.
- Place a few table lights or candles around your home (taking care to site them out of dangers' way) then as soon as you notice it becoming dark outside, light your candles and turn off all the bright electric lights. This will add a warm glow to your evening and help your mind to feel comfortable with the semi-darkness.

- Once darkness has fallen, whilst still in candlelight, please try to enjoy a blissful moment: – listen to your favourite music – sit quietly with someone who is loving to you – focus your mind onto your 'words of sanctuary' – or do whatever you can to find a degree of peace.

- Once darkness has fallen, with only one or two candles flickering, try to feel the majesty of the night: – open the curtains, or a window or a door then look outside – try to step outside or go for a car ride – lift your arms to the heavens, look up at the moon and stars all those millions of miles away and feel the spiritual connection between you and the universe – and just feel the stillness of the night and be uplifted at the majesty and awesomeness of it all.

- When experiencing 'the dreaded darkness' realise that, in this exercise, when outside, your prime objective is not to let-go of a panic attack but rather, it is to familiarize yourself with the night. Therefore, if you wish, use your 'words of sanctuary' for comfort before opening the curtains, before looking outside or before going outside.

Of course if being outside proves to be too stressful then don't force yourself to stay there and, assuming you are not in an actual panic attack, just say your 'words of sanctuary' and slowly walk back indoors.

When you are able to go outdoors, if a panic attack strikes, you will then be dealing with both the fear of the panic attack and the fear of the night. Nevertheless, don't run back indoors but stand or sit exactly where you are and try to let-go. If you do let-go and the panic fades then stay outdoors feeling the night for as long as you wish. But if a panic attack strikes and you feel yourself 'losing it' and need to return indoors, then walk back slowly but don't say your 'words of sanctuary' until you are once again indoors and stationary. Repeat the exercise as often as you can.

Once you are able to feel the stillness of the night, not only will you lose fear of it but you will actually come to love the peace, privacy and sense of oneness it offers. If only everyone would make the effort, take time out from their hectic lives, escape the streetlight pollution, go out into the country or by the sea and feel the energy of the night. It would bring them such an awesome sense of peace and wonderment.

Insomnia

Sleep is the greatest of healers and the best aid to mind-rest. It is also, however, the one thing that is often in short supply for the stress sufferer which, in turn, causes their mind to become even more exhausted; a most vicious circle. Hence, if you do have difficulty sleeping (whether you are unable to fall asleep, or you fall asleep but wake many times throughout the night) you attaining good sleep must be a priority for you. And so…

- Be as physically active as possible throughout the day.
- Have a long, warm, relaxing bath before going to bed.
- Don't try to carry 'things to do' in your head until the following day but during the early evening, list every task that needs attending to. And through the evening or during the night, if any other task comes into your mind then, again, note it down. But whatever you do, don't try to carry things in your head.
- Cut out or cut down added stimulants such as cigarettes, fizzy drinks, coffee, tea etc, especially in the evening.
- Avoid heavy meals, particularly after 6pm.
- Don't go to bed hungry. Instead, have a light supper of sleep inducing food such as a lettuce sandwich or a nice warm milky drink.
- The mind needs about 20 minutes preparation time for sleep, so about 20 minutes before going to bed, programme your mind and encourage the onset of sleep by having a set 20 minute bedtime routine.
- Regulate your bedtime routine by going to bed and getting up at the same time every day.
- The thinking part of the brain will inhibit sleep, so when a mind is worrying, even if about not being able to sleep, sleep will be inhibited. One way to distract the mind from thinking is to use the senses; perhaps listen to the radio, or an audio book, or a relaxation CD/DVD or the sounds outside of the wind, rain or sea. Perhaps read a book or have someone read a story to you so that, in your mind's eye, you can see the events unfolding. Or if you have a vivid imagination, see yourself, via your mind's eye, sitting by a waterfall, or in the kingdom of the angels, or swimming in the golden pool of life energy or floating over mountains, valleys and the sea.
- If you wake in the early hours, don't lie there worrying, trying to force yourself back to sleep but have a plan, perhaps: – get up and have a snack of sleep inducing food then go back to bed and try again – get up and go through your 20 minute 'going to bed routine'– stay in bed but have a 'treat time' of maybe a few biscuits, bar of chocolate or sandwich made of sleep inducing food –read a book –make love.
- If you are awake all night, despite you then being tired, don't cat-nap during the following day but rather, stay awake all day then, in the evening, go through your night time routine.
- If your health allows, sleep in a cool, well ventilated room.

- When in bed, don't block the earths magnetic energy but rather, align your body with it by sleeping north to south or south to north.
- Allow the life-energy that enters your bedroom door to freely flow around the room and not be either reflected straight back out by a mirror placed opposite the door or blocked by furniture, or a bed or even you in the bed opposite the door; thereby stimulating you in your pit of stagnant energy.
- Make your bedroom a place of tranquillity and serenity: – use your bedroom as a sanctuary and a retreat, not as a second living room with a computer, television and full of clutter – a few times every week, have calm and relaxing music playing in your bedroom throughout the day, even though you are not in it – ensure the colours in your bedroom offer calm, not stimulation; absolutely no reds.
- Finally, with your own medical doctors agreement, consider trying a complementary remedy such as Nelsons homeopathic Noctura. Or try a natural remedy such as Chamomile or Fennel tea. Or, if possible, have a massage with aromatic oils such as Lavender, Rose, Chamomile, Sandalwood, Jasmine, Lemon Balm or Marjoram (ensuring you are not allergic to it and you dilute it as recommended on the label). Or try a complementary therapy: such as acupuncture, reflexology, yoga. Or try conventional medicine: speak to your pharmacist and discuss you trying an over-the-counter medicine. Or go to your doctor and discuss you trying a course of mild sleep inducing medication. Some sufferers find great benefit from taking a small dose of Amitriptyline 10/25 mg taken only at night, particularly as it has been in use for over 30 years and has shown to be none addictive, so it might be worth discussing that with your medical doctor. If you do try Amitriptyline, although it really can offer great benefit, it can also take up to two weeks before it reaches its full benefit and sleep comes easier.

Nervous breakdown/Suicidal thoughts

At this point, I need to mention the following...

Many people watch medical dramas on television, as a result, they see the inside of psychiatric hospitals filled with patients shuffling around and looking like zombies with glazed expressions on their faces. And to a family member or friend, seeing their loved one in such plight, can be very distressing. However, when a person is admitted into hospital for mind-rest they might be given extremely strong medication. And whilst such drugs tranquillize the mind they do not always impair consciousness. So when a person is hospitalised for mind-rest and is seen walking around the ward with a glazed expression on their face, they are then probably experiencing more mind-rest than they have had in months.

If you are suffering severely with mental distress but not responding to any form of medication, treatment or therapy and, as a consequence, you are offered hospitalisation then, at least, consider it: – how do you feel about the whole thing – to what degree are you affected – does the staff professionalism and the nature of the hospital itself stand-up to scrutiny regarding panic attacks and other mind issues – and does the overall success rate of the hospital itself compare to the success rate of the best hospitals?

A few reminders

Once you begin to work through your worries, fears and negative thoughts then, due to the nature of mental symptoms of stress, you might find that as one issue goes, another will take its place or that, from time-to-time, you might need to change your words. If so, just continue to work the best you can and you will be amazed at how quickly your mind will gain its much needed rest until eventually it will be strong enough to work out any issue you present it with.

Also, if you have many worries, rather than having different words for each individual issue, try having just one or two sentences that cover all your issues. But, of course, if you feel it will serve you better to have different words for each issue then do so.

Finally, the mind is not a place where we should choose to live all of the time. Yes, of course, 'life' happens, problems arise and for many of us, our career involves 'mind work.' But if we are wise we will do such deep 'mind work' in time-slots, taking a break occasionally and thereby avoiding stress-related mind problems altogether.

Re-cap:
To Take Your Third Step
To Freedom

1. Chose your 'words of sanctuary' and don't be surprised if it takes you a few days to find the right words for you.

2. Have a plan of action for your OK and bad days then lean on it.

3. Devise a stress-buster routine for yourself then find sanctuary in it as often as possible throughout the day and, if necessary, the night also.

4. If you are suffering mental symptoms of stress then, as soon as you can, choose your comforting/reassuring words and gain mind-rest.

5. When the next panic attack strikes or tries to strike, despite all the shakes, sweats, palpitations, dizziness and so on, with every fibre of your being, with every ounce of courage left in your heart and with the limited degree of ability left in your mind: – don't move or at least move very slowly – focus your thoughts onto your 'words of sanctuary' – cocoon yourself in their emotional shelter – take a giant leap of faith – and let-go. If you let-go, good! If you don't that is still OK, just keep on trying until you succeed.

6. A major part of this step is you letting-go of one panic attack. So if you rarely experience a panic attack you will need to put yourself into a place or situation where you feel overly vulnerable to them then take it from there. However always ensure that you are able to remove yourself from the place or situation should you need to.

7. Try to work on the attitude of, "OK, I know what's happening to me. So I will shake out my arms and legs, relax my jaw and focus my mind on life. And if a panic attack strikes or during any acute moments, I will use the refuge of my 'words of sanctuary' then get back to life."

8. Throughout this step, whether it takes you hours, days or weeks, the 'boulders' of panic attacks, symptoms of stress, flashbacks and worry will possibly be your constant companion. So when you feel as if you are being dragged along on an emotional roller-coaster remember, your systems of stress are merely sensations of arousal, so try to let-go of them by focusing on to other things.

9. Remember, after one of your best days, you might have one of your worst and after one of your worst days, you might have your best.

10. If someone is bullying you to fight your fear or dragging you outside insisting, "If I don't drag you out, you'll never go out" then, a) ask them to read this book, b) quietly explain to them that whilst their support and encouragement is invaluable to you, you must now be given the mental, physical and emotional freedom to venture forward in your own time and at your own pace.

11. Whether you have read this step yourself or someone has read it with you or to you, do not have anyone read it instead of you then they give their interpretation of it to you.

12. If you had any difficulty understanding any part of it then read the relevant section or sections again and perhaps a further time. But after your third attempt, if you still have difficulty understanding any part of it or if you don't identify with it, then I urge you to discuss the matter further with both your befriender and doctor.

13. If you have not read, understood and thought about the information in this step (irrespective of whether or not you think it relevant to you) then you have not yet taken this step.

14. Once you have read, understood and thought about the information in this step then move onto Step Four.

    Step Four will empower you: It will show you that – whilst you have already let-go of one panic attack, you now need to let-go again – you don't need to carry one drop of guilt or shame for suffering panic attacks because you have already shown yourself to possess sensitivity and a tremendously strong strength of spirit – and if blame is to be apportioned for your ongoing suffering of panic attacks, the fault was never yours.

Step Four

Empower yourself... by putting your
newly found knowledge into practise

Panic attacks: Do it again

Your likely guilt and shame for suffering panic attacks

The failure was never you

Re-cap: To take your fourth step to freedom...

Panic Attacks: Do It Again

From the very first moment of your very first panic attack, the only thing you thought you could do to protect and defend yourself was to fight, run, hide, live in fear, keep yourself 'on guard' and be as subservient to panic attacks as you could, in whatever way you could, in every aspect of your life. But now things have changed! Even at this early stage, things have changed because now, you have provided the proof positive evidence to yourself that panic attacks are controllable and that you have the ability to control one. And you acquired that evidence not by fighting, freezing or fleeing in terror but by using your desire to recover, then digging deep within yourself, finding whatever strength of spirit you had, taking a giant leap of faith, valiantly standing face to face with terror, looking it straight in the eye, recognising it for what it was then dismissing it by letting-go of it. Well done! By the way, irrespective of whether or not you actually believe it, you are now no longer helpless to panic attacks. You doubt me?

The Oxford Dictionary defines helpless as, "Not able to take care of oneself, weak, dependent." Accordingly, when the panic attack struck or tried to strike, did you fail to take care of yourself? No! Did you display weakness? No! Did you depend on anyone or anything other than yourself? No! Are you still helpless to panic attacks? No!

So now, do it again

You have now let-go of one panic attack, and not wishing to dampen your enthusiasm but trying to keep your objectives realistic, I must explain that letting-go of that first panic attack might not necessarily free you from panic attacks forever, although it might. In which case, you will probably need to repeat letting-go a few more times yet. And I will immediately follow that by saying, if I could have one wish for you now it would be for a few more panic attacks to strike or at least try to strike. And I know that sounds cruel, in fact virtually every time I say that to a client, they half sarcastically say, "Thanks a lot Lorraine." So before going any further I will now explain two key points...

1. Your mind needs to be re-educated

When a person repeatedly performs a task or body function over a relatively short period of time, their brain, then concluding there must be a need for it, takes over the task to lighten the load, i.e. On first learning to drive a gear stick car, you need to consciously and deliberately put each individual manoeuvre into operation, which initially proves to be very difficult. But once you have practised the manoeuvres a few times, it all becomes easier until, eventually, you only have to think of turning right, turning left or stopping for your mind to then direct your body and make it happen. So it is with panic attacks.

Recently, you have been responding to panic attacks by fighting, freezing or fleeing in fear but once you can consciously let-go a few times, your brain (then concluding there must be a need for it) will take over the task to lighten the load. Upon which you will then find the task of letting-go considerably easier until the panic attacks go altogether.

And remember, your symptoms of terror during panic attacks are only sensations of arousal, so they are natural bodily functions that your brain has lived with for many years previously without overreacting. So you experiencing them without overreacting is not something that your brain has to learn from new, it only has to remember how it was previously, unlike when initially learning how to drive a car.

2. Your self-confidence needs to build

As long as you hold fear towards panic attacks you are not free of them. Personally speaking, I only consider a person to be free of panic attacks when they have reached the point where they can go off into the world, take everything the world throws at them, yet still feel 100% secure in the knowledge that they will never experience a panic attack again. Anything less is surely only a token recovery.

So, although you are now hoping that you will never experience another panic attack, that is not good enough! You need to **know** that you won't. And the only way you will ever know that is, if you also know that, when the force of panic attacks was previously threatening you, you didn't hand the control over to them and allow them to become master of you but rather, you took control of them, you became master of them and then you simply dismissed them by letting-go. So although you have let-go once, be honest. Do you now **know** that if a panic attack should suddenly strike, you will, without doubt, let-go of it? Do you now feel totally free of not only panic attacks but all fear of them? And do you know that your ability to let-go of panic attacks will now carry you to any part of the world you want to go or, in truth, are you still unsure, "Did I really let-go? Was it a fluke? If another panic attack strikes will I really be able to let-go of it? Am I really sure that I will never experience another panic attack again? Do I truly feel free?"

Do you see? To be totally free of panic attacks is to feel free of not only panic attacks but all fear of them. To reach that point, you need to prove to yourself that you are no longer vulnerable to them. To acquire that proof, you need to let-go. And although you have now let-go once, the more you can let-go at this stage, all the more your ability to let-go will become entrenched into your conscious and subconscious mind. And to do that you need the 'golden opportunity' of panic attacks.

Also note, during this step, I am not asking you to purposefully go out looking for panic attacks thereby putting yourself into a place or situation where you know you are overly vulnerable and susceptible to them: such as lifts, crowded places, open spaces and so on. I am simply asking you to try to let-go of the panic attacks that strike during your normal everyday life. Having said that, however, if you happen to live in a high rise flat and going into a lift is essential or if your home is situated in a busy area and when just stepping outside your front door you find yourself in the middle of a mass of people. Then, if possible, give yourself a little breathing-space somehow. But, of course, if the demands on you are such that you are daily forced to face those overly stressful situations without any breathing-space then whilst your journey to recovery will be more difficult, your total recovery is still very much within your reach.

For some people, the whole process of letting-go will take only a few days, for others it will take a few weeks and for others it will take a few months; making it a very long slog indeed. But however quickly or slowly your journey through this step proves to be, whilst you will, of course, wish to let-go of every panic attack and symptom of stress, there will probably be times when you don't. And on those occasions, yes you will feel frightened, frustrated, disappointed, disillusioned and disheartened but realise, those boulders are only setbacks and recovery is never lost in setbacks but in excuses.

Therefore do you still desire recovery more than you hate panic attacks? Are you a person who, when fallen, stays down or will you get up and keep getting up time and time again? If the latter then I absolutely assure you, the occasions when you don't manage to let-go will become wider apart. The disappointments will fade. The frustrations will ease. The successes will become more frequent. Your confidence will grow. And you will self-witness how, with perseverance, the human spirit can indeed rise above any adversity to become ever stronger for the experience.

A few reminders on how to let-go

- Ensure you have your 'words of sanctuary' ready, on hand, for when the next wave of panic strikes.
- Know that even during the severest panic attack, the human brain will hold up to six words.
- Your 'words of sanctuary' are intended to bring you a feeling of calm, so don't say them in an angry way similar to fighting talk because that will certainly psyche you up even further.
- Voice your 'words of sanctuary' at every opportunity, as doing so will help to slow down both your mind and breathing, it will also help your mind to hold onto the contents of your words.
- Don't just voice your 'words of sanctuary' whilst looking around the room but close your eyes, or focus your eyes onto a specific object or into the eyes of another person. This will eliminate distraction and thereby help your mind to hold its focus.
- During every panic attack, don't move or, at least, move very slowly.
- If there are certain situations were you feel overly vulnerable to panic attacks, therefore you feel you need a place of safety, then have one but only if you really do have no other choice. And realise, using a place of safety is only a temporary course of action. It is certainly not a permanent sanctuary. In fact, as you will see, you will not be able to move from this step onto step four until you have stopped depending on a place of safety.

  So when a panic attack begins, use your 'words of sanctuary' and try to let-go but, after a few moments, if you feel you have no other choice but to escape from the situation then walk to your place of safety as slowly as you can. Once you have walked from your overly vulnerable situation, then again, say your 'words' and try to let go. However, never say your 'words of sanctuary' whilst walking away because the association your mind will then make between your words and you fleeing will not help you in the long run.
- Remember, there are no prizes for being the first to let-go. The only prize is for you to claim your freedom from panic attacks. And in a few weeks or months time, when you are totally free of not only panic attacks but also free of all fear associated to them, what will it matter if your recovery took longer than other people. The fact will still be that you are free and you did it at your own pace and in your own time.

- Know, as long as you desire recovery you will never fail. So, each time a panic attack strikes, use the experience as a golden opportunity to put letting-go into practise. In this case, practise really does make perfect.

Are you carrying baggage that doesn't belong to you?

Every panic attack sufferer will experience feelings of guilt and shame, to some degree, for suffering panic attacks but many spend so much mental, emotional and physical energy trying to cope with their guilt and shame their recovery is actually hampered. Therefore, as you journey through this step, give thought to the following chapter, for whilst your experience with panic attacks has caused you much fear, suffering and despair and none of it being your fault, why are you now feeling so guilty and ashamed? I truly believe that after reading the following chapter you will no longer feel such destructive emotions any more.

Your Likely Feelings Of Guilt and Shame

Guilt is felt when we have done something which we **feel** is wrong. Shame is felt when we have done something which we **feel** is wrong but which is then made public knowledge.

That being so, every person who suffers panic attacks will, to some degree, feel both guilt and/or shame. Indeed such feelings may now be built into every fabric of your life. If so, whatever feelings of guilt and/or shame you do have, relating to panic attacks, needs to be looked at, dealt with and very quickly eliminated. Otherwise you leave yourself open to both use them against yourself and allow others to use them against you.

There are four main reasons why you might now be feeling guilt and/or shame…

1. Suspecting you are pre-disposed towards stress related illness and, as such, you are likely to pass such illness onto your offspring.
2. Feeling you must be a very weak person and therefore a burden on society and life.
3. You having panic attacks in the first place.
4. You putting additional strain on your family.

1. Suspecting you are pre-disposed towards stress related illness, as such, you are likely to pass panic attacks onto your offspring

Imagine that one of your ancestors was an artist and their talent lay in painting landscapes. As your artistic ancestor obviously had children, grandchildren, great-grandchildren and so on, it is likely that a number of those offspring were also artistic. That being so, those artistic offspring would not necessarily paint landscapes, in fact their individual talent might not lie in painting at all. It might lie in drawing, lettering, carving or sculpting. In other words, those offspring who inherited an artistic talent would not automatically have inherited the actual painting style or technique but rather, they would have inherited the basic artistic talent, the artistic streak, the artistic aptitude.

Likewise, the fact that you are now suffering panic attacks does not mean that you have inherited them or indeed inherited any other stress related condition. Nor does your inherent predisposition lean toward you being over susceptible to stress related illness, even though you might know, or know of, other family members who have also suffered stress and even panic attacks. But it does suggest that, just as in my case, you might have inherited the precious quality of sensitivity.

And let me immediately clarify that statement by saying, "That is not an insult but a compliment!" You being sensitive does not mean that you are a soft, neurotic, demented, deranged, certifiable, head-banging nutcase. Absolutely not, in fact very much the opposite! You being sensitive simply means that your inherent tendency may lean more towards you having a caring, loving, 'giving of yourself' nature. So whereas the seemingly harder people of this world find it more in their nature to be aggressive and unmoved to pain, suffering and distress, your inherent disposition may lean towards you being attentive, empathic and responsive to suffering and distress. And whether the suffering and distress is experienced by other people, animals, the planet or you, it is irrelevant. Any suffering, any distress and any disharmony will touch and affect you far more than it will affect others who are themselves not of a sensitive disposition.

Having said that, never make the mistake of thinking that to be sensitive is to be soft and someone to be taken advantage of. Absolutely not! For when many sensitive people are forced, through life events, to block-off their sensitivity, they are outstandingly capable of taking on the role of the hard man, they are exceptionally capable of driving themselves and others forward towards what they believe is success and they are notorious for being totally ruthless with both themselves and others.

Yet despite their ability to be hard, whenever a sensitive person tries to deny their own sensitivity (by continuously driving themselves forward into the more inharmonious, antagonistic and confrontational way of life) as their true self then feels in conflict with that type of lifestyle, all the more their true self feels suppressed and eventually screams out to be heard, as perhaps you now know to your cost.

So be reassured. Panic attacks are not inherited. They are not something 'in the blood.' You have not inherited a stress related illness. You have not inherited a mental disorder manifesting in panic attacks. No one passed panic attacks to you. You do not, cannot and will not pass panic attacks onto your future offspring. And you are not pre-disposed to pass any so-called 'family weakness' onto others. Indeed when you eventually come to know sensitivity to be the precious quality it is, rather than blaming others for passing it onto you, you will be thankful. And rather than feeling guilt or shame for passing sensitivity onto your future offspring, you will feel honoured to do so.

2. Feeling that you must be a very weak person and therefore a burden on society and life

If you are of a sensitive nature and, due to panic attacks, now feel you must be a very weak person and a burden on others, society and this world. I beg you to realise, you are not a burden on anything or anyone but rather, you are a blessing and very precious indeed. In fact the two elements this world and its people need right now are to be found in you. You doubt me? Then let me prove it to you...

Think back over history up to today. Which people are remembered as being of quality and integrity, an inspiration, a role model, a positive influence, courageous in the face of adversity, an asset to the planet, a benefit to 'man' and the epitome of mankind at its very best: Hitler, The Borgias, Ivan the Terrible, Rasputin, Attila the Hun, Mussolini, Stalin, Genghis Khan? I think not! Yet think of the most sensitive people: Jesus Christ, Buddha, The Dalai Lama, The Mahatma Gandhi and Martin Luther King. Surely each of those people are known, loved, respected, remembered and recognised world wide, not for being rich, not for being powerful and certainly not for being so-called 'tough men' but rather, because each one, in their own way, displayed both sensitivity and a tremendously strong strength of spirit.

And realise, 'strength of spirit' takes many forms...
To experience panic attacks feels similar to being in a war situation, fighting 'something' that is wholly capable of inflicting horrendous pain, suffering and terror. But when a person is normally in a war situation, fighting an enemy who they believe is capable of inflicting horrendous suffering, they usually have the choice to fight, runaway or surrender. Of course, initially, if they have any courage, they will choose to fight with a brave heart. However, as time passes, as the war relentlessly continues, as fatigue sets in, as the prospects of winning feels ever more remote and as the point is reached of having no fight left, the battle weary warrior will come face to face with his biggest test of courage yet. Does he try to run away and flee the conflict? Does he surrender to whatever his enemy chooses to inflict on him? Or does he, even then, courageously choose to fight until he drops?

At present, minute by minute, particularly if your suffering is severe, you are experiencing the continuous and unyielding pain, worry, fear and terror of panic attacks. You are being forced to fight a war that is not of your making, not of your choice and not of your heart. Of course, initially, you choose to fight with a brave heart but as time passed, as the panic attacks relentlessly continued, as exhaustion set in and as the prospect of recovery seemed ever more remote, you also might have reached the point of feeling that no more fight was left in you, if so you too would have faced your biggest test of courage yet.

How does one escape from or surrender to panic attacks? How does one escape from or surrender to something that is so illusive it cannot be seen or heard? And how does one escape from or surrender to something that is inside oneself? This is such a ruthless condition.

Some sufferers try to escape panic attacks by throwing themselves into drink, drugs, staying in bed, heavy medication or sex etc. Some suffers try to surrender themselves to panic attacks by attempting to take their own life. And some sufferers just cling onto life enduring whatever the panic attacks throw at them.

So in whatever way you personally are trying to get through panic attacks, weakness doesn't come into it in any way, shape or form! How can it when, even now, you are still courageously choosing to fight? You are still courageously choosing to get up every morning and fight your way through each day, the very best you can, in whatever way you can and you are still courageously choosing to fight your way through one of life's most torturous battles with every ounce of courage you possess, simply because you don't know how else to survive. Weakness? No my friend, you are certainly not a weak person. Indeed, you are now displaying a degree of grit, courage and heart that belongs only to those who have the strongest spirit of all.

Therefore, if you are now feeling weak, a burden, a nervous wreck and at the end of your tether then realise. As you are still bravely choosing not to give in to panic attacks but to fight them in the only way you know how, you are now displaying yourself to be a person blessed with both sensitivity and a very strong strength of spirit, making you a tremendous human being and an example of mankind at its very best.

Please realise, the fast-track, materialistic, callous and spiritually void people of this world are not of more value to 'life' than you. In fact, it is now realised by literally millions of people worldwide that the saving of mankind and this planet can only be by the hearts, minds and actions of those who, like yourself, are blessed with both sensitivity and an extremely strong strength of spirit.

3. You having panic attacks in the first place

By now you will know that I suffered panic attacks quite severely, in which case, I hope you take the following comments in the spirit in which I give them and not take offence by them. I mention them only in the attempt to bring a little lightness to the issue, yet still convey a particularly valid point regarding sensitiveness.

As a panic attack sufferer, particularly if you are affected severely, you might have had derogatory comments aimed at you such as you being: – a nervous wreck – a bag of nerves – a nutcase – having a screw loose – and neurotic. However, do you remember the old, crude, yet apt saying, "As the madhouse is filled with those who think they are sane, then one must be sane to think oneself mad." Well my observations on the matter are…

Whilst the general populous have not yet awakened from the malaise of life and are therefore unable to see just how crazy their lives and 'life' has become. Many of us have wakened and are able to see the craziness of modern-day life; which often feels like the lunatics have taken over the asylum. So in the attempt to escape the madness of 'life' but not knowing what else to do, many sensitive and very sane people are now locking themselves away in their attempt to escape. And whether their escape is by drink, drugs, sex, work, uppers, downers or whatever, it is irrelevant.

Countless times throughout history right up to date, we have seen that when we sensitive ones are empowered by strong mental balance and ethics, it is we, above all others, who are prepared to stand up, speak out and fight for what we believe in. So when, out of sheer ignorance, the harder people of this world mistake your sensitivity as being an indication of weakness, let them! When they tell you that being sensitive is out of step with modern-day life, ignore them! And when they find it more in their nature to be aggressive, deaf, dumb, blind and unmoved to pain, suffering and distress, pity them! For it is they who are weak, it is they who are out of step, it is they who are to be pitied, it is they who are the burden and it is they who ought to carry guilt and shame, **not you!**

4. You putting additional strain onto your family

In the aftermath of a deliberate wrongdoing or foolhardy act, **guilt** is not meant to be a negative, stagnant place: – it is supposed to be the driving force that persuades the wrongdoer to atone for their wrongdoing – it is supposed to be the emotion that turns negative into positive – and it is supposed to be the middle ground before action takes place. But when no deliberate wrongdoing has occurred yet feelings of guilt are experienced (as during illness) then such feelings can become the ever-consuming pit of negativity from which it feels there is no escape.

When a person is unwell and sees their loved one suffering the resulting strain, whilst a harder person might say, "Well he/she is my partner and it's their job to look after me," or "I know the children miss out on things but hey, life's tough, they'll just have to get over it." The sensitive person, who does not understand their own sensitivity, will often misread their feelings of compassion for those of guilt and responsibility.

As a result, if you are a sensitive person suffering an illness (any illness) to where you need the help of another person. Whilst your private, inner feelings towards your helper might be, "I'm so sorry for involving you in my troubles but know that none of this is my fault. I didn't want it, need it, ask for it or deserve it, but from the bottom of my heart and the essence of my being, I am truly grateful to you for going through this with me." Your outer expression of gratitude is likely to be the no-nonsense verbal apology of, "I'm sorry." The effect of saying, I'm sorry, however, even when due to illness, is to feel a degree of guilt.

Therefore if, due to illness, you tend to constantly apologise to your helper, try changing your vocabulary from, "I'm sorry," to "Thank you," as by doing so, you will begin to change the energy around you both from negative to positive.

Despite your reluctance to involve another person in your suffering, the fact remains that another person is probably involved. So read this book, follow its programme, recover from panic attacks and learn how to utilize both your strength of spirit and sensitivity to not only survive life but to be the shields that enable you to live life to the full. By doing so, you will show your loved one or friend that the person you were yesterday is not half the person you are today and the person you are today is not half the person you can be tomorrow. From which your loved one or friend will become empowered by the knowledge that, when faced with adversity, they too did so with great integrity.

If my comments have outraged you

Of course, not all sensitive people develop panic attacks and not all panic attack sufferers are gifted with sensitivity. Indeed, you might consider yourself to be anything but sensitive. To you, your panic attacks are the result of a one-off period of weakness and, once free of them, you don't expect to experience a moment of 'weakness' again. That being so, if this last section has offended you in any way then please accept my apology, for it was never my intention to insult anyone. Having said that, however, and certainly not wishing to offend you further, I will simply say to you, "To recognise one's vulnerabilities is not an indication of weakness but rather, it is an indication of strength and an opportunity to grow."

The fault was never you

Whilst blame for you suffering panic attacks cannot be apportioned to you or indeed to any one person, we must nevertheless acknowledge that needless suffering has, and is still being endured by you and countless thousands of people. In which case, the responsibility for that suffering must be identified, otherwise it will continue and many more thousands will follow the same or similar needless path.

Therefore, the following chapter will explain exactly who, why and what failed you regarding panic attacks; for whilst the fault was never yours, you are now left to deal with the repercussions. So whilst no blame can ever be apportioned to any one person, you do, at the very least, have the right to know why your panic attacks were not dealt with sooner.

The Failure Was Never You

During the course of my work with panic attacks and panic attack sufferers, I have either heard of, or actually seen, so many people enduring the most horrendous plight...

Some sufferers had literally begged for help only to be abandoned by family and friends, leaving them having to battle and claw their way alone through each and every torturous day. Some were in such physical pain that, every moment, they believed death was only seconds away. Some so lost and spirit broken, they were forced to live in what can only be described as a living hell. Some believed their sanity and life itself would last only until the next panic attack. Some suffered for years, genuinely believing that, as their doctor could not understand how ill and terror struck they were, then no one would, leaving them feeling doomed to spend the rest of their days without hope. Some had endured such extreme worry, fear, terror and despair that, to them, dying seemed their only chance for peace. Some so frightened by their symptoms and exhausted by panic attacks they felt forced to stay in bed for months. Some women gaunt and aged whilst still in their twenties and some men, who once stood proud, wept with shame at feeling reduced to nervous wrecks. Some looking so pale (even in the height of summer) because they had never dared walk through their own doorway and into the sunshine for over 30 years. Some whose children cowered in corners, traumatised at seeing their parent in panic attacks. Some with careers ruined, business lost and genuinely believing their life and hopes were wrecked. Some believing their sanity rested solely on their medication and some so lost in medication they didn't even know what day, month or year it was.

So with each one of those people in my mind, I now feel duty bound to explain the following...

Like those sufferers mentioned above, you also might have had the greatest difficulty in finding the right kind of help to free you from panic attacks. If so, then the next element is certainly for you. So I will now try to fill-in as many erroneous areas as I can...

1. Your doctor
2. Your medication
3. Your treatment/therapy

1. Your doctor

Somewhere along your path into panic attacks, whether sooner or later, and despite your possible embarrassment and need for privacy, you are likely to have sought help from your medical doctor. However the help you then received is quite unpredictable because...

At worst, if your doctor was 'of the old school' and considered panic attacks to be the ravings of the neurotic then, once you had described your symptoms and explained how confused and frightened you were, he/she was likely to have shown no understanding but with an attitude similar to, "I know you would feel greatly reassured if all your questions were answered in full but I have neither the time nor inclination to sit here and explain to you and to every other neurotic worrier, the exact details of what is happening to you. So, although I seem to have no care towards you, no understanding of your suffering, no knowledge of your condition and no empathy towards you for enduring such severe pain, fear and distress, I nevertheless expect you to unquestioningly trust my judgment and accept the diagnosis I give you, which is:- You are not about to die or go insane, indeed you are not ill at all. You are, however, suffering from nerves. You are bringing the panic attacks and symptoms onto yourself by worrying about them. So stop worrying! Pull yourself together! Forget about your aches, pains or whatever! Go home! Stop wasting my time! And allow me to help those people who are really ill! In addition, I am your doctor, therefore if you doubt the diagnosis or question my manner, I will take that criticism as a deeply personal insult from which I am likely to display annoyance and great displeasure."

Needless to say, if you had that type of doctor (of whom many are still practising) then your recovery would have been in question and your wellbeing would have been put at great risk.

At best, if your doctor was not 'of the old school' but rather, he/she was caring of your pain, empathic to your distress and knowledgeable of panic attacks then, once you had described your symptoms, he/she would have been extremely patient. In fact, over a number of consultations, he/she would have treated you with absolute proficiency: – explained what stress is and its effect on you – given you leaflets on stress – referred you to a stress counsellor – arranged for you to undergo a barrage of tests and medical examinations – and finally, prescribed temporary medication.

Days/weeks later, once your test results were back and showed there were no irregularities then, in the attempt to reassure you further, your doctor might have shown you the actual test results. Yet despite such proof of what you were **not** suffering from, did it convince you of what you where (and still are) suffering from and also how to recover from it? I doubt it!

You being a panic attack sufferer made you no different from any other sufferer in as much as, it wasn't enough that your doctor treated you you with patience and understanding. It wasn't enough for you to be told compassionately and reassuringly, "Don't worry it's only stress!" And it wasn't enough to be told of all the illnesses and conditions that you were not suffering from, as if that would somehow convince you of what you were suffering from because then, you needed your very own accurate, conclusive, convincing, unquestionable diagnosis...

You needed a diagnosis with symptoms that matched every one of your symptoms. You needed convincing that your symptoms were not imagined, nor signs of madness, imminent collapse or death but rather, they were the very real, normal, natural and expected symptoms of high stress. You needed all your questions and fears answered with relevant pamphlets, books or audio information covering every aspect of stress; what it is, why we humans experience it and the numerous symptoms that it can and does induce. You needed a full explanation on how to minimize your own stress level and how you personally could eradicate panic attacks from your life forever. You needed full access to all relevant information, thus allowing you to look, listen, understand and digest it all in your own home and at your own pace. You needed preparing for the probability of your symptoms continuing for a while. And you needed lots and lots of encouragement and reassurance, because once your consultation with the doctor was over, sooner or later, all your worries and fears would suddenly jump out from their hiding place and hit you straight in the chest, head, stomach or wherever else you carry your stress.

The crux of the matter...
You **know** that your doctor is human and can make mistakes; **that's** the crux of the matter!

When you initially experienced your symptoms of stress, you probably felt confused and concerned, so if your doctor was 'of the old school' and immediately dismissed you then his/her fallibility would have soon become obvious. However if your doctor was patient, understanding and offered you practical, relevant help and support then, although initially, you probably disregarded his/her fallibility and left the consultations feeling secure in the diagnosis. As the weeks passed and you had one consultation after another but felt no better then, knowing your doctor was fallible and could make mistakes, you began to have doubts about the accuracy of his/her diagnosis. Even to where your doctor's words of reassurance, that once gave you comfort, might then have sounded very hollow indeed. All creating the perfect breeding ground in both your conscious and subconscious mind for the notorious "What ifs?"...

"What if my doctor has made a mistake? What if he/she does not fully understand my condition? What if he/she has overlooked a significant symptom which would show my true condition? What if my condition is rare and my doctor has never come across it before, therefore he/she does not even know what to look for? What if all the tests were not even relevant and my true illness is still lying undetected? What if my condition does not even show on an x-ray or in blood tests? What if my doctor is showing me someone else's test results in the attempt to hide the fact that I am terminally ill? What if I am going insane but no one is telling me?"

This list is endless, but one thing is for sure, once such worries and fears were added to your already highly stressed state and once all those worries were then added to your initial life stress, you were certainly on the road to a rapid deterioration.

2. Your medication

As explained in Step One, on going to your doctor with panic attacks, whatever diagnosis he/she gave you, whether it was: – you are just highly stressed – depression – mania – a physical condition – you are simply a hypochondriac or you are suffering with panic attacks. If you were given medication of which you are not now 100% confident in then I hope the following information will help you.

The following information is based on my understanding of the 'British National Formulary, Number 41.' The technical accuracy of the following information was verified by Dr Carmel Casserley MB., BCh, FF Hom. Having given that information I must nevertheless make clear: I am not a doctor therefore the following information is given **solely** to inform you, **not** for you to act upon. Accordingly, after reading the following information, if you suspect your medication might be unsuitable for you, or it might be inappropriate to your condition or you now want to begin the process of reduction/withdrawal, then **don't,** under any circumstance, make any changes to your medication but **do, immediately** discuss the matter with your medical doctor.

ANTI-DEPRESSANT DRUGS

1. Tricyclic and related anti-depressant drugs
2. Monoamine Oxidase Inhibitors (MAOIs)
3. Selective Serotonin Re-uptake Inhibitors (SSRIs)
4. Others

1. Tricyclic and related anti-depressant drugs

Drugs of this type are considered effective in the management of panic disorder, whilst tending not to have dangerous interactions with food and other drugs. The known side effects, of which there are many and of which many people suffer, include weight gain, weight loss, headache, tremor, rashes, drowsiness, blood sugar changes, dry mouth, blurred vision, constipation, urinary retention, sweating, behavioural disturbances, interference with sexual function, feeling jittery, shaky, decreased appetite and nausea. This group of drugs can be divided into two...

*1. Anti-depressant **with** sedative properties.*
These are generally prescribed for those suffering from depressive illness and who are agitated and anxious.

- Amitriptyline Hyrochloride (*Amitriptyline*) (*Lentizol*) (*Triptafen*) (*Triptafen-M*)
- Clomipramine Hydrochloride (*Clomipramine*) (*Anafranil*) (*Anafranil SR*)
- Dosulepin Hydrochloride/Dothiepin Hydrochloride (Dosulepin/Dothiepin) (*Prothiaden*)
- Doxepin (*Sinequan*)
- Maprotiline Hydrochloride (*Ludiomil*)
- Mianserin Hydrochloride (*Mianserin*)
- Trazodone Hydrochloride (*Molipaxin*)
- Trimipramine (*Surmontil*)

*2. Anti-depressant **with less** sedative properties.*
These are generally prescribed for those suffering depressive illness and are withdrawn and apathetic.

- Amoxapine (*Asendis*)
- Imipramine Hydrochloride (*Imipramine*) (*Tofranil*)
- Lofepramine (*Lofepramine*) (*Gamanil*)
- Nortriptyline (*Allegron*) (*Motipress*) (*Motival*)

2. Monoamine Oxidase Inhibitors (MAOIs)

It is more beneficial to prescribe MAOIs when Tricyclic and related anti-depressants have been used unsuccessfully than vice versa. And whilst these are a much prescribed antidepressant, they are known to have adverse dietary and drug interactions therefore they tend to be used less frequently than the Tricyclic and related anti-depressants. The most common, although rare, side effects include hypertension and dizziness. The less common include insomnia, drowsiness, headache, weakness, dry mouth, stomach problems, tremors, blurred vision, sweating and sexual disturbances.

- Phenelzine (*Nardil*)
- Isocarboxazid (*Isocarboxazid*)
- Tranylcypromin (*Parnate*)
- (RIMA) Moclobemide

3. Selective Serotonin Re-uptake Inhibitors (SSRIs)

Drugs of this type are considered effective antidepressants. They are thought to work faster, be less sensitive, are tolerated better and create fewer side-effects than most other anti-depressants. The known side-effects, include dizziness, nausea, headaches, insomnia, diarrhoea, anxiety, fatigue and sexual dysfunction which can last throughout the course of the medication. If taken with St. John's Wort, the drugs effectiveness can be decreased and an increase in side effects can also occur. When taken with an antihistamine or with certain other drugs that affect the action of the serotonin, then adverse effects can occur, so seek a medical doctor's advice.

- Citalopram (*Cipramil*)
- Fluoxetine (*Fluoxetine*) (*Prozac*)
- Fluvoxamine Maleate (*Fluvoxamine Maleate*) (*Faverin*)
- Paroxetine (*Seroxat*)
- Sertraline (*Lustral*)

4. Other Anti-depressant Drugs

- Flupentixol (*Fluanxol*)
- Mirtazapine (*Zispin*)
- Nefazodone Hydrochloride (*Dutonin*)
- Tryptophan (*Optimax*)
- Venlafaxine (*Efexor*) (*Efexor XL*)

TRANQUILLISING DRUGS

If anxiety is severe, disabling or if it subjects the person to extreme distress then a doctor may prescribe one of the benzodiazepines.

Whilst this type of medication is considered 'of use' for the relief of anxiety, once begun, then side effects, dependency and withdrawal issues can then become a problem.

"CSM advice

1. Benzodiazepines are indicated for the short-term relief (two to four weeks only) of anxiety that is severe, disabling, or subjecting the individual to unacceptable distress, occurring alone or in association with insomnia or short-term psychosomatic, organic or psychotic illness.
2. The use of benzodiazepines to treat short-term 'mild' anxiety is inappropriate and unsuitable.
3. Benzodiazepines should be used to treat insomnia only when it is severe, disabling, or subjecting the individual to extreme distress."

- Nitrazepam (*Nitrazepam*)
- Flunitrazepam (*Rohypnol*)
- Flurazepam (*Dalmane*)
- Loprazolam (*Loprazolam*)
- Lormetazepam (*Lormetazepam*)
- Temazepam (*Temazepam*)
- Diazepam (*Diazepam*) (*Valium*)
- Alprazolam (*Xanax*)
- Bromazepam (*Lexotan*)
- Chlordiazepoxide (*Chlordiazepoxide Hydrochloride*)
- Clorazepate Dipotassium (*Tranxene*)
- Lorazepam (*Lorazepam*) (*Ativan*)
- Oxazepam (*Oxazepam*)

The following information is the recommended withdrawal practice off benzodiazepine, as recommended by the British Medical Association and the Royal Pharmaceutical Society of Great Britain; quoted from the 'British National Formulary.'

"DEPENDENCE AND WITHDRAWAL. Withdrawal of a benzodiazepine should be gradual because abrupt withdrawal may produce confusion, toxic psychosis, convulsions, or a condition resembling delirium tremens. Abrupt withdrawal of an older drug, such as a barbiturate (section 4.1.3), may be even more likely to have serious effects.

The benzodiazepine withdrawal syndrome may not develop until up to 3 weeks after stopping a long-acting benzodiazepine, but may occur within a few hours in the case of a short-acting one. It is characterised by insomnia, anxiety, loss of appetite and body-weight, tremor, perspiration, tinnitus and perceptual disturbances. These symptoms may be similar to the original complaint and encourage further prescribing; some symptoms may continue for weeks or months after stopping benzodiazepines.

A benzodiazepine can be withdrawn in steps of about one-eighth (range one-tenth to one-quarter) of their daily dose every fortnight. A suggested withdrawal protocol for patients who have difficulty is as follows;

1. Transfer patient to equivalent daily dose diazepam 1 preferably taken at night.
2. Reduce diazepam dose in fortnightly steps of 2 or 2.5 mg; if withdrawal symptoms occur, maintain this dose until symptoms improved
3. Reduce dose further, if necessary in smaller fortnightly steps[2]; it is better to reduce too slowly rather than too quickly.
4. Stop completely; time needed for withdrawal can vary from about 4 weeks to a year or more.

Counselling may help; beta-blockers should **only** be tried if other measures fail; anti-depressants should be used **only** if clinical depression present; **avoid** antipsychotics (which may aggravate withdrawal symptoms)"

ANTI-MANIC DRUGS

A doctor who prescribes Lithium for panic attacks only does so if he/ she considers there is an underlying chemical reason for doing so. These drugs are extremely powerful, with many side effects, therefore they will only be prescribed with great caution and their effects will be monitored frequently.

Note: Regarding all Medication: Again, the above information regarding medication is given **solely** to inform you, **not** for you to act upon. So after reading the above information, if you suspect that you might be taking unsuitable medication or an incorrect dosage then **do not**, under any circumstance, make a change to your medication but immediately discuss the matter with your medical doctor.

3. Your treatment/therapy

Time and again new clients tell me horrendous accounts of how they have been messed about, made worse and damaged by both complimentary and conventional treatment and therapy. And although, at best, I do know that some treatments and therapies do help many panic attack sufferers. I also know that, at worst, many treatments and therapies have contributed to making very many panic attack sufferers considerably worse.

'Complementary' treatment and therapy

These include – acupuncture – aromatherapy – reflexology – healing – reiki – homeopathy – massage – nutrition based therapy – regression – yoga – tai chi – herbals – special restrictive diets – exercise – and stress related self-help books.

If complementary help was your choice then, over previous months or years, you might have received many of the above therapies. However as the whole area of complementary practice is so broad and my knowledge of it so limited, all I feel able to say on the subject is: Speaking personally, I am one of the greatest advocates of 'some' complementary practices. Over the years, I have seen incredible work done by my Homeopathic Physician (Dr Carmel Casserley MB., Bch, FF Hom) and my Clinical Reflexologist (my daughter Mandy) giving hugely beneficial results on both myself and countless others regarding the reduction and even eradication of pain and debilitation. That now being said, however, I must also add that I do know of many other people who have been damaged greatly by some unethical, and very unscrupulous people who like to call themselves complementary practitioners; some actually qualified and some not.

So whether or not this type of therapy or treatment helped you is very dependent on a) whether or not the medication, therapy or treatment was appropriate to your condition and b) the integrity of the practitioner that treated you.

'Conventional' treatment and therapy
These include: – medication – de-sensitisation therapy, including flooding therapy – three-day home/hospital supervised sleep – stronger or different medication to that initially prescribed by your own doctor – being admitted into hospital for observation or mind rest – attending a therapeutic day centre – home visits by a psychiatric nurse – deep seated psychological counselling – attending a professionally supervised group – "Try going on holiday" – and "Come back in three months time and we'll see if you feel any better."

Alongside or perhaps instead of medication, if your doctor thought you needed more specialised help then you were probably referred to a psychiatrist, psychologist or counsellor. And if you believed, at best, the referral would help you and, at worst, it would not, you probably readily agreed. On the other hand, the mere suggestion of a 'mind' specialist might have totally shocked you into thinking, "Oh my goodness, even the doctor thinks I'm crazy. Have I really come to this? What is to become of me? What is to become of my family?" But whatever your initial fears, if you were desperate enough then you would have agreed to see whoever was recommended. That being so, there are a few points that you need to be aware of…

Despite there being numerous avenues of treatment and therapy offered to panic attack sufferers, there are **two** particular therapies that do cause the most damage to panic attack sufferers, those being, 'flooding therapy' and 'deep seated psychological counselling,' and I fully realise that making such a statement will need qualifying, so I will immediately do so…

Flooding therapy
'Flooding therapy' is an extreme form of de-sensitisation. So before going any further, I will clarify that I fully recognize that de-sensitisation therapy is extremely effective for a number of conditions (particularly phobias) therefore I do not, in any way, criticise it. My issue is, however,

that when flooding therapy is practised on panic attack sufferers, it will often cause tremendous unnecessary suffering and damage.

'Flooding' is a therapy during which the therapist will encourage the sufferer to make ever closer contact or experience their particular fearful stimuli and to do so until they can tolerate no more. Once the sufferer has reached their tolerance level they are then allowed to back off until their high sensations of fear have calmed. Once calm, the sufferer will then be encouraged to try again to make contact and repeatedly try until they are eventually comfortable with full contact to whatever they were fearing.

The reason why flooding therapy can work for many phobia sufferers is that, during the therapy session, although the sufferer is put into a place or situation where they feel particularly vulnerable, they still feel safe: – they always have the security of knowing that their level of contact is under their direct control – they are always allowed to start, stay within and never go over their own personal tolerance level – when things get 'too much' they are always free to back off, take time out to collect themselves then try again – and they know, they will never be pushed too far 'out of control.'

Of course, during a normal flooding therapy session, if the sufferer felt extremely unsafe, ie: – no control over their level of contact – no say in what they personally had to tolerate – no sanctuary of a 'comfort zone' – no security of a 'safety net' – no escape when their fear and symptoms get 'too much' – and no luxury of knowing they will never be pushed to the point of being too far 'out of control.' Then this form of therapy would be much too stressful for the person to endure. Enter the panic attack sufferer!

When a panic attack sufferer undergoes flooding therapy and is put into a situation where they feel vulnerable to panic attacks, once their fear begins and spirals into full-blown terror, they feel extremely unsafe: – they do **not** have control over their degree of contact because the fearful stimuli is inside them – they are **not** able to start and stay within their own personal tolerance level; they just have to tolerate whatever the attack throws at them – they have **no** sanctuary of a 'comfort zone' and **no** security of a 'safety net' – they can **not** simply back off, have a breather, take 'time out' to collect themselves then try again – and they **do not** have the luxury of knowing they will never be totally 'out of control.'

Flooding therapy is a form of 'facing your fear,' 'hanging in with gritted teeth and determination' and saying to yourself, "You have to fight this! Don't let it beat you! And don't give in to it!"

Do you see? Although flooding therapy does help certain conditions, it serves only to feed panic attacks. Indeed I have worked with many panic attack sufferers who, directly due to flooding therapy, had been literally dragged around their neighbourhood, into shops and supermarkets or onto buses, trains and motorways and then been forced to stay there for hours. Then despite them experiencing the most harrowing terror and begging to be taken home, they were dogmatically told by their therapist, family or friend, "You have to do this otherwise you'll never do it." Which obviously served only to stress and distress the sufferer even more and further convince them they were surely heading for madness.

At this point, you might say, "But as part of their recovery, every panic attack sufferer must go outside sometime." And you are correct. But no one would throw a non-swimmer into the ocean before they were taught how to swim properly. So why drag a panic attack sufferer outside before they are taught how to deal with a panic attack? You don't! Also, at this point you might say, "But in its own way, this 'five-step' programme is a form of de-sensitisation." Again you are correct. But this de-sensitisation is different from all others. It is designed solely around panic attacks. It knows exactly how the sufferer is feeling. It teaches the sufferer how to defuse their own terror. It waits in stillness. It does not ask the sufferer to go anywhere, do anything or suffer any sensations of terror until thy are mentally, emotionally and physically equipped and ready to do so. And it does all that in the sufferers own timing. That's the difference.

Deep-seated psychological counselling

Deep-seated psychological counselling is obviously a form of counselling therefore again I must emphasise that I know certain forms of counselling are of the greatest benefit to many people; including a member of my own family after being brutally attacked and raped. Indeed whenever I suspect a panic attack client has elements in their life that might be causing them emotional disharmony, I always advocate, without exception, that once they feel able, to then go for counselling. In fact as long as the counsellor is client centred, qualified, competent and compatible with the client then I believe most people living in this crazy day and age would benefit greatly from ongoing counselling in whatever form is relevant to them.

Might I just add here that Client Centred Counselling does not offer advice to the client but rather, it helps the client to weave their own way through all their brain clutter and emotional baggage.

Despite my high regard for certain forms of counselling, I know that whenever deep-seated psychological counselling is used as the first line or sole therapy for panic attacks, it can be extremely traumatic for the panic attack sufferer on **six** counts...

1. The panic attack sufferer does not need their mind invaded to recover from panic attacks!

2. From my many years working with panic attacks, I know that, in the main, panic attacks are caused when a person's general lifestyle has caused the person to live against their own true nature. Less often are panic attacks caused by deep-seated emotional trauma.

3. Whilst most panic attack sufferers are emotionally distressed, their distressed state is often not primarily due to deep-seated emotional trauma but rather, to them experiencing panic attacks.

4. For a person to undergo the long task of psychological counselling, it is beneficial for them to have the luxury of time, time to ponder over, work out and adjust to whatever issues surface. But the panic attack sufferer does not have time. To them, time is of the essence, time is precious and time must not be taken for granted. Indeed, every single day, week and month of 'time' the panic attack sufferer spends in such psychological counselling, they are enduring a living hell, probably deteriorating and losing all hope of ever recovering.

5. When a person is trying to deal with traumatic/painful memories, it is beneficial for them to hold their concentration for a few consecutive moments. But the panic attack sufferer, particularly the more severely affected, is not in the state of mind to hold any consecutive thought at all. After all, as both the conscious and subconscious mind of the panic attack sufferer is continuously 'on-guard,' looking-out for the next panic attack whilst trying to avoid crumbling into a trembling heap whilst also trying to cope with life. For them to then concentrate and wholly participate in any meaningful conversation is virtually impossible, let alone psychological counselling.

6. To suffer panic attacks is to experience pain, confusion, worry and fear whilst knowing that, at any moment, a sudden wave of raging terror is likely to strike. Therefore for a panic attack sufferer to get through even one day they need every ounce of strength, courage and determination they possess. That is enough in itself! But to then expect this sufferer to also endure psychological counselling and be loaded with even more emotional pain and trauma is, in my opinion, both cruel and dangerous. Indeed, as those suffering severely with panic attacks will already feel 'at the end of their tether,' to then put them through psychological counselling, will very often prove to be

similar to the extra straw being put on the camel's back; it being just too much to deal with.

So, if you have endured psychological counselling and was encouraged to bring out and relive your most painful memories, whilst also trying to cope with panic attacks and the related symptoms. Don't blame yourself if the whole experience left you confused, distressed and significantly worse. It has done so to countless others.

Of course if you think you might benefit from psychological counselling then, once you have recovered significantly from panic attacks, it might be helpful for you to then look into the matter but we will discuss that later in the programme, when the time is more appropriate.

Professionally supervised self-help groups

In comparison with the above two therapies, the number of sufferers who are damaged by these types of groups are relatively small. Nevertheless, I do know that much damage can be caused by the genuinely well-meaning people who supervise these groups. So I will simply say one thing.

If you were or are involved with a professionally supervised self-help group then, yes, it probably was a tremendous emotional support for you. However, if your counsellor was not 'fully' knowledgeable on panic attacks (whether they were a nurse, a health worker, any form of therapist or even a person titled 'doctor') then your recovery from panic attacks could have been put at great risk.

Just a personal footnote

During the early stages of panic attacks, when symptoms of stress are first presenting themselves, if the sufferer is then given 'time,' their panic attacks will be short-lived. However as 'time' is usually at a premium for most professionals, the actual time given to the panic attack sufferer will, in most cases, fall short of that required. And for that reason I now ask the following...

- How can any initial time-saved be of long-term benefit when, over subsequent weeks, months and years, as the panic attack sufferer spirals into ever deeper fear, terror and desperation, they are then forced to spend endless hours with the very same doctors?
- How can any rational person justify the enormous amount of 'time' being spent on attempting to mend anxiety disorders and depression

whilst, in comparison, only a minimal amount of time is being spent on prevention?

- How can so many 'treatments' be justified when the results are so ineffectual, irrelevant and, for many sufferers, actually damaging?
- How can anyone be expected to believe that 'finance for prevention' is not available when in 2007, England only and when just referring to those suffering anxiety disorders and depression, the cost of formal services and lost employment were considerably over £16 billion; that's £16,000,000,000 = Sixteen thousand million? How mad is that? Even more so when the estimate is that only half of those suffering anxiety disorders and depression actually receive such services.

If those suffering anxiety disorders and depression were given the necessary support, just imagine what benefits could be gained: – a massive reduction in expenditure on formal services and lost employment – every sufferer and their family would receive the relevant information, help and support – every local doctor would be free to give their genuinely precious and valuable time to illnesses and health conditions to which they are trained and best suited – every professional, working with those suffering anxiety disorders and depression, would attain a much higher recovery rate and greater job satisfaction – and every person in the medical profession itself would benefit due to more money then being available in the proverbial pot.

Re-cap:
To Take Your Fourth Step
To Freedom

1. Whilst a few people complete this step within only a few days and most people do so within a few weeks, sometimes one or two people need a little more time, even one or two months. Even so, I absolutely promise you and every other sufferer, as long as you hold your desire to recover then your full and permanent recovery will come.

2. A major part of this step is to re-educate your automatic responses how not to overreact to even the slightest stimulus. And as you have already let-go once, you know that you can do it again. Therefore, when the next panic attack strikes or tries to strike, despite all the shakes, sweats, palpitations, dizziness and whatever else is happening to you, with every fibre of your being, with every ounce of courage left in your heart and with the limited degree of ability left in your mind, let-go: – do not move or at least move very slowly – focus your thoughts onto your calm, comforting, reassuring 'words of sanctuary' and cocoon yourself in their emotional shelter – and take a giant leap of faith. If you manage to let-go every time, good! If not, that's OK, just keep on trying until you can.

3. During the early part of this step, the 'boulders' of symptoms of stress, panic attacks, flashbacks and worry could be constantly present. So if you feel you are being dragged along on an emotional roller-coaster: – acknowledge every panic attack, ache, pain, twinge, discomfort, mood swing, worry, fear and boulder – recognise them as being merely sensations of arousal – let-go of them by focusing your mind onto other things – and allow the sensations to pass in their own time.

4. Don't force yourself into places or situations where you feel overly vulnerable to panic; you are not a gladiator so don't force yourself into the arena. Believe me, you will go out and put yourself everywhere

when you are ready. In fact, when you are ready there will be no stopping you

Also, as a major part of this step is in letting-go of panic attacks, if you are a panic attack sufferer who only rarely experiences them then you will need to put yourself into places or situations where you do feel overly vulnerable to them then take it from there.

5. If you are not suffering any mental or physical symptoms of stress **outside** the times of your panic attacks then, if you have not already done so, please read and familiarise yourself with 'Arousal Creating Prolonged Physical Symptoms of Stress,' which begins on page 75. Also see 'Arousal Creating Prolonged Mental Symptoms of Stress,' which begins on page 104. And also see 'To Ease Prolonged Mental Symptoms of Stress,' which begins on page 191. Although those chapters are not directly relevant to you, the knowledge and insight you will gain from them might be useful to someone else.

   I am, of course, assuming that if you are suffering any mental or physical symptoms of stress **outside** the times of your panic attacks, you will have already read the relevant chapters.

6. Throughout the day and night, continue to find sanctuary in your stress-buster as often as possible.

7. Continue to work on the philosophical approach: "OK, I know what is now happening to me. So I will just shakeout my arms and legs, relax my jaw and focus my mind on life. And, during the course of the day, if a panic attack strikes or any acute moments occur, I will use the refuge of my 'words of sanctuary' then get back to life."

8. Don't carry even one drop of guilt or shame because you are suffering panic attacks but rather, know that you are a person blessed with both sensitivity and an exceptionally strong strength of spirit.

9. If you are of a sensitive nature, hold onto the fact that sensitivity really can become your greatest asset. We will discus the matter more fully a little later.

10. Know that if any blame is to be apportioned for your prolonged suffering of panic attacks, the fault was never yours but rather, it was the system.

11. Remember, panic attacks are like bullies, if you fear them they pick on you all the more but when you don't fear them, they will avoid you.

12 After one of your best days, you might have one of your worst and. after one of your worst days you might have a truly golden moment.

13. If someone is bullying you or trying to guilt you into 'fighting your fear' or if someone is literally dragging you outside insisting, "It's for your own good" then explain to them that, whilst their support and encouragement are truly invaluable to you, you must now be allowed the mental, physical and emotional freedom to venture forward in your own time, at your own pace and to your own level of satisfaction.

14. Stay on this step until you know that...
    • you can let-go of every panic attack during your normal day.
    • your ongoing mental symptoms of stress have calmed to where you are no longer at the point of nervous exhaustion or breakdown.

15. Whether you have read this step yourself or someone has read it with you or to you, do not have your befriender reading it and then giving their interpretation of it to you.

16. If you had any difficulty understanding any part of this step then read the relevant section or sections again and even a further time But after your third attempt, if you still have difficulty understanding any part of it or if you don't identify with it, then please discuss the matter further with both your befriender and doctor.

17. If you have not read, understood and thought about the information in this step (irrespective of whether or not you think it relevant to you) then you have not yet taken this step.

18. Once you have read, understood and thought about the information in this step then move onto Step Five.
    Step Five will offer you freedom: – it explains how the last mile can sometimes seem the longest – it asks you to put yourself into certain places and situations where you previously avoided due to panic attacks – and it suggests that, to protect yourself in the future, you need to re-evaluate all aspects of your life.

Step Five

Free yourself... and thereby see, smell, taste, touch, feel and know freedom

The last mile can sometimes seem the longest

Beyond panic attacks

Re-cap: To take your fifth step to freedom

The Last Mile Can Sometimes
Seem The Longest

You are now on the final step to freedom and, my goodness, you have come a long way: – you are more informed than you were at the beginning of this programme – you are calmer and more experienced in dealing with fear and terror – you are confident in your ability to let-go of any panic attack that strikes or tries to strike during your normal everyday life – you are confident that your chosen words are strong enough to carry you through the terror of panic attacks – and you are aware that you possess a strength of spirit far greater than you ever thought possible. So yes, you have come a long way and are well on your way to recovery. That being so, you are now ready to claim back your freedom.

Claim your freedom from actual panic attacks

At this point, whilst every person will be confident in his/her own ability to let-go of any panic attack that strikes or tries to strike during their normal everyday life, there will still be a great variation in the ability and confidence level of each individual person. Some sufferers will still be experiencing panic attacks during their everyday life, others will not be. Some will still be afraid to venture into specific places or situations such as lifts, escalators, planes or crowded places, others will not be. Some will still be looking for excuses as to why they can't yet join 'life' whilst others will be so confident there really is no stopping them.

And so, if you are still experiencing panic attacks during your everyday life then, despite knowing that you have the ability to let-go of any that do strike or try to strike, wait until they are not striking anymore during your everyday life before you move on. If you are no longer experiencing panic attacks during your everyday life then you **are** now ready to move on.

To move on: Now you can begin to 'go for it.' Go into every place and situation where you have avoided because you where too afraid that a panic attack might strike; such as lifts, open spaces, public areas, crowded places, etc. However before you do that, seriously consider the following...

Panic attacks or Phobic attacks
Being a panic attack sufferer, it might be difficult for you to determine if all your fear belongs to panic attacks or if some belongs to a phobia. After all, if you are in a lift and experience a wave of panic, whether you are a panic attack sufferer or claustrophobic, the degree of your fear, your symptoms of fear and the severity of your symptoms would all be the same. Therefore, along with panic attacks, consider whether or not you are also experiencing a phobia to the specific places or situations to which you feel overly vulnerable.

However, irrespective of whether or not your vulnerability to specific places or situations is due to panic attacks or phobic attacks, 'controlled de-sensitisation' is certainly the way to go.

Controlled De-sensitisation

This therapy allows a person to, very slowly, repeatedly, put themselves in contact with the specific stimuli to which they are overly vulnerable. By doing so, they are able to gradually reduce their vulnerability to it and also build up their capacity to cope when faced with it. Below is an example of how you might use 'controlled de-sensitisation.' You will, of course, need to adapt it to suit your own personal situation.

Golden rules...
***Before** putting 'controlled de-sensitisation' into practice*
- Only when you are not experiencing panic attacks in your everyday life should you venture into places and situations where you feel overly vulnerable to panic. So don't try to run before you can walk.
- Base your decision on whether or not to go into places and situations where you feel overly vulnerable on the following 4 criteria...
  a) your state of health, b) your ability to let-go, c) your desire to go into such places and d) your time demands.
- List all the places and situations where you feel overly vulnerable then prioritise your list by putting your least feared at the top, number 1, and your most feared at the bottom.
- Ensure that throughout you have absolute control over your level of contact and that you can escape whenever you choose.
- Always ensure your safety, so seek medical advice before you begin.
- Arrange for someone to be with you when partaking in the following.

Golden rules...
When putting controlled de-sensitisation into practice

- Take someone with you.
- Begin with number 1 on your list of identified places and situations.
- Use a scale of 1 to 5: – 1. apprehensive – 2. anxious – 3. frightened – 4. very frightened – 5. terrified. When your level of fear is on or below level 3, try to focus beyond it by distraction, using your senses of sight, touch, taste, smell or hearing. When your fear is on level 4 or 5, try to let-go by focusing onto your 'words of sanctuary.'
- If you achieve your goal, good! However, if it all gets too much for you then just walk away, slowly.
- Ensure that you do not put unnecessary pressure on yourself and that you always feel in total control and comfortable with your level of contact.
- Live to no one's yardstick but your own: simply do the best you can, whilst working in your own time, at your own pace, within your own ability and to your own level of satisfaction.
- Repeat each of the following stages as often as necessary until you feel absolutely confident and ready to move on to the next stage.

An example of how you might put controlled de-sensitisation into practice: supermarket shopping
When putting the following suggestions into practice, always ensure that you feel completely comfortable with your level of contact, if you do not, then terminate it until you feel calm.

1. With your befriender, decide which supermarket you feel would be best for you to use; taking consideration of size, volume of customers, the entrance and exit points, the distance and ease of parking etc
2. With your befriender, work out 'a plan of action,' again considering the quietist and most appropriate time of day, the actual days of the week that suit you both and what you will both do if you don't manage to let-go and so on
3. With your befriender, familiarise yourself with the outside of the supermarket and observe the people going in and out. ... Repeat this until you are totally comfortable with the situation.
4. With your befriender, literally stand outside the supermarket then watch, listen and mix with the shoppers. ... Repeat this until you are totally comfortable with the situation.
5. With your befriender, get familiar with the inside of the supermarket: Go into the foyer about 10 metres (about 32ft) all the while trying to distract yourself by listening to the sounds around you, or watching

and mixing with the people shopping (worldly distraction) or use your 'words of sanctuary' or your 'words of reassurance.' After 2 or 3 minutes, both you and your befriender then walk out slowly. ... Repeat this until you are totally comfortable with the situation.

6. With your befriender, now go into the store itself but don't invite problems: don't take a bag with you, don't wear clothing with pockets, don't pick up a basket or claim a trolley and don't touch or pick up any items; we don't want oversights or accusations of shoplifting at this point. Just get a feel of the place but with no intention to make a purchase. That is very important. Just wander around, going wherever you feel like going: perhaps – go into the gardening department and browse around – stand at the butcher or bakery counter and (knowing you can just walk away at anytime) experience queuing without the 'pressure to purchase' – or stand at the customer services desk and enquire into the price, availability or location of a certain item. Stay in the supermarket with your befriender for as long as you can. Of course, if a panic comes on then try to let-go but if it proves to be too much for you then just walk out slowly. ... Repeat this until you can stay inside the supermarket, dealing with any panic that strikes.

7. With your befriender, go into the store with the intention to make a purchase, even if it's only a bar of chocolate or perhaps make a few purchases and even queue at the checkout. What a triumph! ... Repeat this until you can stay inside the supermarket, dealing with any panic that strikes.

8. **Whilst on your own** and your befriender standing a comfortable yet significant distance away from you, repeat all the above.

9. **Without your befriender,** so whilst being totally unaccompanied, repeat all the above.

When forethought and assurance are paramount...

Two of the above guidelines are to ensure you always feel in total control and to ensure you can always escape from any situation whenever you choose. Having said that, there might be an occasion when you could be tempted or bullied into ignoring that advice. Airplanes, trains and on motorways are all places where you would not be in total control and so would not have the means of immediate escape. So if you are tempted or bullied into going into such places or situations then I strongly suggest that you do not go anywhere until you know you are ready.

Dealing with the remnants of panic attacks

As you move through this step, you might become a little frustrated, as if recovery is not happening fast enough. If so...

1. Assess your stress-buster

Realising that a) the stress-buster can be very time consuming, b) the enormous difference in peoples' need to de-stress and c) the possibility that you might now be tempted to stop your own stress-buster routine, I ask you to consider the following...

Whether or not you are still experiencing panic attacks, phobic attacks or symptoms of stress, and whether or not you have reached the point of knowing that your nervous system is now totally calm. Remember, as we are all now living in exceptionally stressful times where living with stress and symptoms of stress have become a normal way of life, an ongoing programme of relaxation is advisable for everyone. However, no one knows you better than you know yourself and, at this stage, I am sure you are capable of determining your own means of relaxation.

2. Give your symptoms of stress time to fade

If you are still experiencing symptoms of stress then try not to become frustrated with them as, even at this stage, worry or frustration will only make matters worse. Remember, they are only remnants of a previously overstretched and oversensitive nervous system and, like all other 'after effects' of nature, your symptoms of stress will fade in ever lessening degrees until eventually they are no more. Cast your mind back to a few short weeks ago and remember how wretched you felt then, then ask yourself, are your symptoms of stress (sensations of arousal) really so bad as to warrant you being throw back into negative thinking? I think not!

3. Deal with any unresolved symptoms

If you are still suffering symptoms that have not significantly reduced, whether or not you think they are related to stress then, a) discus it with your medical doctor, b) look at the conditions below that have similar symptoms to stress and c) if you identify with any of those conditions, go to my website, www.LMbookshop.com for relevant information.
Unstable blood sugar
Chemical/food intolerance
Candida albicans
Chronic Over breathing
Seasonal Affective Disorder: SAD (lack of daylight/sunshine)

Unstable blood sugar

Physical Symptoms: Headache, light-headedness, feeling faint, insomnia, blurred or double vision, incoherent speech, palpitations, body weakness, excessive craving for sweet food especially between meals, hot and cold sweats, fatigue, trembling, pain in joints, leg cramps, restlessness.

Mental/Emotional Symptoms: Anxiety, irritability, restlessness, a lack of mental aptitude, drowsiness, depression, mental confusion, suicidal thoughts and extreme behaviour.

Possible Solution: The only advice here is to seek medical advice.

Chemical/food intolerance, Candida albicans,

Physical Symptoms: Feeling faint, headache, pressure pain in head, distorted vision, floaters in one's vision, chest pain, breathlessness, over breathing, light-headedness, nausea, vomiting, stomach pain, raised blood pressure, diarrhoea, constipation, painful muscles and/or joints, muscle spasms, frequency in urination, extreme fatigue, irregular pulse and/or palpitations, especially after food.

Mental/Emotional Symptoms: Anxiety, memory loss, rage, irritability, depression, inability to think clearly, 'a foggy mind,' hyperactivity, restlessness, insomnia, brain fatigue, crying and feeling unreal.

Possible Solution: As stated above.

Chronic Over breathing

Physical Symptoms: Light-headedness, feeling faint, dizziness, dry and tight throat, pain or dull ache in chest, especially around the breastbone, palpitations, breathlessness, inability to take a deep breath, yawning a lot, tingling limbs, 'jelly legs' and muscular body pain and/or weakness.

Mental/Emotional Symptoms: Anxiety, lack of mental ability, depression and a feeling of unreality.

Possible Solution: As stated above. Also read the work and given advice on breathing by Doctor Konstantin Pavlovich Buteyko.

Seasonal Affective Disorder: SAD (lack of daylight/sunshine)

Physical Symptoms: Various pains in joints, lowered immune system, stomach problems, lethargy, not refreshed on waking, falling asleep during the day and finally, excessive craving for sweet and/or carbohydrate food especially between meals.

Mental/Emotional Symptoms: Anxiety, depression, impatience, no libido, wanting to be alone and behavioural problems.

Possible Solution: As stated above.

4. No more - No more - No more - No more

I have heard it said, by many who should know better, that some people with a longstanding health condition, remain unnecessarily ill because the 'pay off' from it offers more benefit than does recovery. And whilst I do realise that, on occasions, such things do happen, I must state clearly that, for the vast majority of people, the mere suggestion of them malingering is an outrageous insult and very, very hurtful.

Having said that, when a person has recently suffered a prolonged illness (any illness) then the illness and any resulting debilitation will have become a very real part of their life. And sometimes, when recovery does come, whilst it is obviously welcome, the person involved can feel a little lost, as if a part of them is missing, from which they are left wondering, "What do I now do with all this life." Therefore sometimes, people can unconsciously hang on to the remnants of an illness in the attempt to hang onto what is, to them, a familiar element of their life. So not wishing that to happen to you, during this step, you might need to make the deliberate effort to let-go of the condition of panic attacks itself. Here are a few suggestions on how you might do this...

No more fighting: No more spurring yourself on, psyching yourself up and keeping yourself 'on guard' just in case 'something' should strike.

No more running: No more keeping yourself permanently occupied, never allowing yourself one moment of mental breathing space for fear 'something' negative will somehow find a way through.

No more hiding: No more finding excuses why you cannot attend social events, or trying to convince yourself that a full life is not that important anyway, or resigning yourself to living a life of restraints, constraints and restrictions or using the fact that you once suffered panic attacks as your reason why you cannot now live life to the full.

No more seeing black but gold: No more allowing your mind to wallow in the negativity of how much you have suffered and lost through panic attacks or how people let you down, abandoned and betrayed you. Instead, re-focus your thoughts onto the positive elements of your newly found strength, your new life opportunities and all the inspiring, reassuring and pleasurable elements of freedom waiting just for you.

5. Never assume you are invincible

Having nearly recovered from a stress-related condition, don't assume you are now immune to stress. You are not!

We are all now living in very difficult times and often the outcome of a potentially life changing situation is simply out of our hands: perhaps we are facing a major medical operation, or fighting for the custody of our children, or awaiting exam results or perhaps our partner is very ill and our future is uncertain. Therefore, when a situation next occurs from which you feel under considerable stress, remember, everybody has their own individual vulnerabilities. No one ever gets it right all the time and sometimes even the most courageous and stable person feels overwhelmed and frightened. And that's OK, we are, after all, human beings not robots.

So the next time you find yourself in a particularly stressful period, as you surely will, put AARRR into practise…

• Acknowledge that you have a problem.
• Ask for help or delegate.
• Respect your sensitivities and vulnerabilities
• Re-organise your workload and time.
• Re-establish or increase your daily stress-buster routine.

Do you see? The next time a situation arises from which you experience stress, if you don't put AARRR into practise, then, sooner or later, you will experience symptoms of stress. The really good news being: Now that you have unveiled the Wizard and you understand how the trick of panic attacks work, you should never be tricked into panic attacks again.

Are you ready to move beyond panic attacks?

What was your life like before you developed panic attacks? Were you truly happy and fulfilled or were you frustrated and lacked direction? Did you find happiness through selflessness or self-servitude? Were you a giver of love or were you a taker of whatever you could get, in whatever way you could get it, from literally anyone? Were you always angry with someone, anyone, everyone? Were you dissatisfied with how your life had turned out but, of course, it was not your fault? And were you always living in hope for a better, more complete, more satisfying life?

If you are truly ready to look at how your life was before panic attacks, if you are truly ready to look at your current life, assess it and work on all required changes and if you truly have any desire to become 'all that you can be' then please read on.

Beyond Panic Attacks

You asked God for strength that you might achieve;
but was made weak that you might learn humility.
You asked for health that you might do great things;
but was given infirmity that you might do Gods' things.
You asked for riches that you might be happy;
but was given poverty that you might be wise.
You asked for all things that you might enjoy life;
but was given life that you might enjoy all things.
You are, amongst all men, most richly blessed.

Henry Viscardi (amended)

A healthy approach to life

Speaking very personally, I believe that we are all on a continuous journey in pursuit of true happiness. But as that precious state is attained only through selflessness, many people tend to settle for the lesser, fleeting, negative state of self-gratification. And as negativity, of whatever nature, will ultimately cause stress, any pursuit of self-gratification must be viewed as a potential boulder to your future stability and happiness.

So, if you are a person who finds happiness through gratification then, whilst not wishing to offend you but realising that, over time, you might have developed tunnelled vision on your life, look at how some other people approach their life and then, whilst being totally honest with yourself, compare their approach to yours, for example, in their pursuit of happiness...

Some people look to materialism and spend their whole life in pursuit of money, even to the point of living with partners they detest, working to the point of collapse, in employment they hate and in a lifestyle of pretence. But what these people fail to realise is that, whilst relentlessly striving to acquire more and more possessions, they become ever more brainwashed into believing that true happiness really does equate to the amount or size of one's trinkets. And even of those who have attained sustained wealth, many will invariably lose its full value due to them never really feeling satisfied with what they have. As a result, they will inevitably spend the remainder of their life still in the pursuit of wealth.

Some people glory in the adoration of themselves or praise from others; living their whole life adorning and preening themselves and changing their appearance. But whilst these people become ever more obsessed with both how they look and how the world views them, they completely lose sight of the real person behind the public persona.

Some people lean on feeling superior; forever basking in their own high IQ, their large bank account, their high position of authority, their one act of glory, their religion, the colour of their hair, teeth or skin. But whilst these people continue to live their self-obsessed, self-focused lives, they eventually become blind to 'life' itself.

Some people become human ostriches; forever burying their head in procrastination, living in the mentality of, "Although I know this situation is not right, I don't want to hear it, see it, face it or deal with its hassle." But whilst these people continuously:– close their eyes to their accounts– put off leaving their incompatible or abusive partner – choose to work more hours despite not needing to and despite knowing their children need to spend more time with them – disregard their own intuition – dismiss their unhappiness – deny their own moment of truth by avoiding what they know to be right – and refuse to make the supreme effort to change their life. The resulting mental, physical and emotional strain of keeping things buried is so damaging, it becomes an ever-tightening 'noose of negativity' around their neck that eventually destroys or kills them.

Some people don't even try to find happiness today, they simply put things on hold until tomorrow; until all their problems are resolved, until everything comes together and is sorted. But what these people fail to grasp is that, by putting their today's happiness on hold until tomorrow, come tomorrow when their today's problems are resolved, tomorrow's problems will then be upon them. Therefore, in reality, as their lives are never problem-free, they invariably stay unhappy all their life.

Some people believe they don't deserve happiness at all; perhaps due to something they should have done but didn't or something they should not have done but did. But even if these people stay unhappy for the rest of their life, it would not save one tear that has already been shed, or undo one word that has already been spoken, or bring back one moment of a life that has already been lost or indeed change any regrettable situation that has already happened. So their staying unhappy is totally pointless.

Some people find instant euphoria in the 'extra buzz,' perhaps in the form of romance, food, alcohol, sex, drugs, exercise, shopping, risking life and limb or whatever. But whilst the extra buzz might feel euphoric, it lasts for only the moment, it is temporary, fleeting, transient and, when over, the fall can be all the greater.

And some people try to find their happiness by actually cutting off their own sensitivity; believing that by lying, stealing, raping and killing they are somehow cheating life. But whilst these people become ever harder harder, become ever darker, fall ever further and reject their gifts of compassion, empathy and love. The internal void then created leaves them wide open to negativity. So even when standing face to face with 'life,' looking it straight in the eye and seeing its pain, suffering, diseases and death. These people stand with hearts of stone, emotionally numb and spiritually void: – never showing vulnerability or distress by flinching, crying or running away for fear the world will think them a coward – never showing gentleness for fear the world will think them weak – never saying they can't cope for fear the world will think them incompetent – never getting involved with the sick, lonely, hungry or homeless unless, perchance, there is something to gain for themselves – never reaching out a hand of forgiveness for fear the world will think them soft – always repaying spite with spite, hurt with more hurt, pain with more pain, one hurtful word with a blow, one blow with a maiming, one maiming with a killing and one killing with many.

If you recognise yourself in any of the above examples, you are not on your own, for in this modern age, many people will, in one way or another. So for that very reason, I ask you to consider the following…
Self-respect – Understanding the self – Freewill – Anger and your need to control – Forgiveness – Guilt – Anxiety, worry and fear for the future – The fact that life isn't fair – Procrastination – Bereavement.

Self-respect

Many therapists tell their clients, "Before you can love other people you must firstly love yourself," and yes, they are correct. But as many of those in therapy don't even like themselves and some even hate themselves, then the enormous task to love themselves will often prove so daunting that they give up even trying. So at this point, ponder over the following…

Whether you are fat, thin, rich, poor, intelligent, unintelligent, young, old, black, white, able-bodied, disabled, self-loved or self-hated. Life/God deemed that you **were** of significant value, either to yourself or others, to warrant giving you life in the first place and Life/God deems that you **are** of such significant value, either to yourself or others, to warrant you having life now. And whether or not you like it, agree with it, embrace it or hate it, the fact still remains. Life/God deemed you to be of such significance, either to yourself or others, that you are here, now, to play your own unique part in carrying and affecting the 'vibration of life' forever. And, of course, come the day when you die, the same fact will stand. Life/God will deem that your death will be of such significance, either to yourself or others, that it also will be needed to play its own unique part in carrying and affecting the 'vibration of life' forever.

Also realise, this law of life is the same for everyone. Even when a child dies (whether through miscarriage, abortion, stillbirth, misadventure or murder) Life/God deemed the child to be of such significance, either to itself or others, that its life and death was needed, each to play their own unique part in carrying and affecting the 'vibration of life' forever.

Understanding the self

What goes in will eventually work its way out and make itself known in one way or another. As a result, when a painful issue is not dealt with and 'put to rest' but is either left open to fester or suppressed and buried. The ongoing energy then required to keep the pain festering or buried will sap the body and mind until eventually, like an erupting volcano, it will explode, spilling over everyone and causing utter devastation.

Therefore, if you are experiencing any type of 'frozen feelings' or unresolved deep-seated personal issues: – an unhappy or broken marriage – bereavement – a domestic issues – a weight issue – child abuse (mental, physical or emotional) – rape – infirmity – impotence – trauma – pain issues – ill health – drug or alcohol dependency – the responsibility, loneliness or resentment at having to raise a family single-handedly – or a lack of confidence. The resulting mental, emotional, physical and spiritual strain will need resolving.

And yes, bringing deep-seated emotional issues out from the darkest corners of your psyche and into the light might be extremely painful, embarrassing and stressful for you. Even so, if you do have any deep-seated emotional issues, whilst taking into account that I am not a doctor and I don't know you but simply putting forward an opinion for your consideration...

Now that you are virtually free of panic attacks and symptoms of stress, might it now be the perfect time for you to fully discuss with your family, befriender and/or doctor, whether or not you are now genuinely, emotionally up to dealing with your deep-seated issues?

And irrespective of whether or not you feel it is the right time for you to begin resolving your deep-seated issues, remember. Darkness is always weakened in the presence of light. Pain is always eased when shared with an empathic soul. And when a person of tremendous strength of spirit (as you have shown yourself to be) is at the point of seeking empowerment and growth, their own authentic light will always come flooding through, strengthening them, empowering them and enabling them to face any darkness within.

Also realise, whilst your personal issues might cut very deeply into your emotional psyche, where burying them seems your only way of coping, avoidance is not the answer! It is an illusion! It is trying to avoid the inevitable! It is also building up massive problems for the future. In which case, the only safe and sure way to deal with deep-seated emotional pain is to release it in a controlled way, with the help of a competent, compatible and fully qualified **'client centred'** counsellor or therapist.

Free will

You are your own person; you are not your mother, father, husband, wife, friend or anyone else. You are you! You have your own unique path to walk, contributions to give, mistakes to make, lessons to learn and wisdom to offer. If life wanted you to be a carbon copy of someone else then you would now be that person but it didn't, it wanted you! And it wanted you purely because of your uniqueness.

So as you journey through life, if others try to bully, persuade, trick or contort you into being what they want you to be, know that, just as life values their uniqueness, it values your uniqueness also. Indeed as no other person has ever, and will never, walk in your shoes, think your thoughts, feel your emotions, experience your pain or know your soul's journey. No other person can ever possess your uniqueness or know your true intended path of life. Also, as you journey through life, of course listen to the wisdom of others with an open mind, for such insights can sometimes be invaluable to your own life journey. But remember Life/God needs you.

You have intuition, and that intuition (a 'gut-feeling') can guide you safely through life, indeed your intuition it is as integral to you as the air you breathe. That being so; – You have every right to only take advice from other people when it 'feels' right for you to take and you have every right to leave behind what does not 'feel' right to you. – You have every right to take full control of your life and thereby make both your own life choices and your own mistakes without the need to satisfy others; obviously accepting all the consequences. – You need no one's validation or approval to be yourself, for you already have the full validation and approval of life itself. – Just as you have every right to take full control of your life and make your own life choices and mistakes without having to satisfy other people. Other people have every right to take full control of their life and thereby make their own life choices and mistakes; and to do so without having the need to please you.

In short, just as you don't need anyone's approval to be you, other people don't need your approval to be themselves!

Anger and your need to control others

Anger is a choice! It is a deliberate response to your frustration that the world is not as you would have it be. It is a reaction that you choose in the attempt to get what you want. And whilst anger can indeed be righteous when used in a positive way against evil, all too often it is used in a negative way against the good. For example…

Are you a bully? Does anger serve you well? During an argument when you feel you are losing the higher ground, do you think that slamming the door, smashing crockery, breaking furniture, lashing out or giving 'the silent treatment' actually makes your opinion right? Then after your outburst of anger, do you then try to justify your actions by saying, "I just can't help it! Someone just says or does something and before I know what's happening, anger has taken me over and I just see red!" If so, you are wrong!

Anger is not something that just happens to you, as though you are an innocent bystander with no control in its making. Anger is controlled by thought! You control your own thoughts. Therefore you control your own state and degree of anger! In which case, if you experience bouts of anger, it is because you are choosing to hold onto it! You disagree? If you had the incentive of going through a 24-hour period without becoming angry and, by doing so, you receive one million pounds. You would change your approach within a heartbeat for that one day and gain the million.

That being so, why are you choosing anger today? Why do you want to control another person or indeed the world? Why do you find it so difficult to accept that other people have their own choices? And why are you not open to learn from a difference of opinion? The answer is, of course, fear. You fear loss and rejection. The reason why you fear loss and rejection is because you feel a lesser person without certain people and possessions in your life and sadly, you also feel the only way you can hold onto those people and 'things' is by force. Therefore if your way of trying to control life and people is to display anger...

1. Work on finding your own self-respect because until you have self-respect you will never truly respect others.
2. Work on finding your own inner strength, your own 'rock of stability', your own integrity because until you do you will remain a vulnerable human being whose only strength is found by stealing it off others.
3. Work on attaining authenticity, that is, when the body, mind and soul work in unison, for only then will you come to know your own true self.

    You will know when you have reached authenticity when you can say to those who don't conduct themselves as you would wish them to, "Whilst you are not the person I would have you be, my respect for you is such that, mentally, emotionally, physically and spiritually, you are free to be the person you want to be."

Forgiveness

Forgiveness is not a weapon to hold over a wrongdoer in an attempt to gain an apology, nor is it a reward given to the wrongdoer for atonement. Forgiveness is, however, a gift to help the victim.

You have seen throughout this book how negativity saps the life-energy from the body and mind but not only that, it also brings very destructive energies to the person carrying it. Indeed, when a person is wronged but holds onto the negativity of not forgiving, it will, in due course, destroy them, not the wrongdoer. For example...

If you were burgled, mugged, beaten or raped, your negative feelings of outrage, unfairness and injustice will not affect your abuser in any way but such feelings might destroy you. If you discovered that your partner was having an affair, your negative feelings of betrayal and abandonment will not necessarily shame them but such feeling might destroy you. If a person stole your most precious and irreplaceable possession, your negative feelings of frustration, anger, outrage and revenge will not affect the thief in any way but such feelings might destroy you. Even if a person hurt, maimed or killed one of your children with deliberate intent, the gamut of your potential negative emotions will not affect either your deceased child or the perpetrator in any way but such feeling might destroy you.

Do you see? The only person drastically affected by you carrying destructive, negative feelings is you. And the only way you will ever be able to avoid or eradicate such emotive, damaging emotions from every sinew of your body, mind and soul is to forgive: **totally.** In other words, totally forgive everyone for absolutely everything!

And realise, to forgive is not to condone, overlook, excuse or forget! To forgive is **not** to allow the wrongdoer to walk away free. And to forgive is most certainly **not** to withhold justice. To forgive is, however, to let-go, to release the darkness within oneself that was created from the hurtful deed. To forgive is to prevent the body, mind and soul from being dragged down by the destructive, negative forces of injustice and the hunger for revenge. To forgive is to become emotionally empowered, energised, free to live and, if required, free to pursue the full measure of justice. And to forgive is to physically, mentally, emotionally and spiritually find peace.

Once it is realised that to not forgive is destructive, one then needs to begin the actual process of forgiving, which is not easy, particularly if one has been carrying the 'so-called' justification for not forgiving for many years. Nevertheless, if a person wishes to live a full and happy life then forgiveness must begin

Some people say that, for an injured party to forgive their wrongdoer, they must firstly understand either the mind of the wrongdoer or, at least, what led him/her onto their dark path of destruction, and yes, that can certainly be useful. But what if the wrongdoer is never caught? What if the crime is so evil that it is beyond all reason and comprehension? What if, for whatever reason, any understanding of the wrongdoer is impossible? Does that automatically give consent or subject the injured party to a life of hate? No it does not!

Forgiveness is **never** about the wrongdoer; whether or not they were caught, are sorry, understood, had a traumatic upbringing, addicted to something or even if they remember the incident at all. Forgiveness is about you! It starts from you, it is controlled by you and it ends with you. Yes the wrongdoer might have shamed you, lured away your partner, cheated you out of your home, raped or maimed either you or a loved one. And yes they might have caused you untold pain, heartbreak and brought your life to an absolute stop. But by you not forgiving, you are making the conscious choice to allow the damage done to continue. You not forgiving is both inflicting damage onto yourself and purposefully choosing to spend the remaining part of your life in negativity. And you not forgiving is allowing the wrongdoer to literally dictate and determine how you will spend the rest of your life.

So yes, understanding is the foundation stone of forgiveness but not necessarily understanding either the mind of the wrongdoer or what life circumstances led him/her onto their dark path of destruction. The foundation stone of forgiveness is, however, to realise that you will **never** understand. You will never understand the workings of the world and why pain and suffering has to be endured. You will never understand why the world is structured in such a way that one man has good health yet his fellow man is dying in terrible pain, one man lives in a mansion yet his fellow man lives in a hovel and in this world of wealth over 30,000 people die every single day through abject poverty. And whatever explanations, justifications or excuses you are given as to why the wrongdoer did what he/she did. In truth, the real facts will always be bent and contorted into whatever shape befits the wrongdoer. Therefore you will never really understand the true facts of the situation and why you personally were victimised. That being so, yes, forgiveness is in the understanding; the understanding that you will never really understand.

Another factor in forgiveness can be in one's belief. If you believe in God then trust God to serve out a true level of justice. If you believe in 'life' then trust 'life' to return the karma. And if you believe in 'you' then trust in 'you' and give yourself the chance to be 'all that you can be;' for that is the true empowerment of forgiveness.

Guilt

'Least said, soonest mended,' so people say and yes, in many circumstances, that is surely the case. However when one person has caused pain to another, 'least said' is not necessarily 'soonest mended,' as that can often be seen as ignoring or dismissing the hurt caused. So when one person has caused pain to another, whether or not it was deliberate, rather than taking the easy way out by leaning on old adages such as, 'best let sleeping dogs lie,' 'best not rock the boat' and 'least said, soonest mended,' they need to talk to each other with an open mind, a warm heart and a spirit desiring peace. For even if the person wronged is strong enough in spirit to deal with the hurt caused and indeed forgive the wrongdoer. It is for the wrongdoer's own spiritual integrity that they take responsibility for their actions, acknowledge the pain caused, say "I'm sorry," mean it and atone.

Once an action is done, it is done and a lifetime of stagnant guilt will help no one and undo nothing. So in the aftermath of a wrongdoing or a foolhardy act, the strong feelings of guilt are not meant to be negative but rather, they are meant to be the force that persuades the wrongdoer to face the fact that he/she has done wrong and, as such, they must do whatever they can to try to make good. Yet all too often, those feelings of guilt are not used by the wrongdoer to make good or aid the victim in any way but rather, it becomes a negative, ineffective, stagnant place from where the wrongdoer turns onto him/herself. Accordingly, this type of approach really is a useless, self-indulgent waste of both time and energy.

If you have said or done something which you now regret, then use the 'gift of guilt' to make good: admit your mistake, accept responsibility for it, feel the sorrow, apologise profoundly, beg for forgiveness, atone and ensure that from your wrongdoing comes good. And if you wish to atone but don't know how to or if your victim rejects your offer of atonement then perhaps give your time, energy and money to a charity; as they will gladly receive and benefit from any genuine act of atonement that you can make.

Atonement is relevant and absolutely crucial. If you have caused harm to another person, whether or not it was of deliberate intent or a foolhardy act, then, for your own sake, you need to atone. And even if that means dedicating the rest of your life to helping others, so be it. But whatever your wrongdoing and whatever your act of atonement, ensure that you do not waste another moment of your life feeling guilty but rather, use your 'gift of guilt' to help others.

Anxiety, worry and fear for the future

Many years ago in a remote area of China there lived a wise farmer named Tak Ying Chan. Tak Ying had lost his wife many years previously through tuberculosis but now, with his son Kai, the two men worked the small farm and, aided by their farm horse, were able to eke out a living.

However one day, whilst on his way to market, a dog savagely attacked Kai resulting in his left leg being badly maimed. Realising the severity of his injury and knowing how integral he was to the farm, fear for the future overwhelmed him to where he said to his father, "Father, what a disaster." Tak Ying quietly replied, "The sun is warm, the grass is green and all is, as it should be." – A year of strife then passed for both men but with support from his father, Kai learned to walk well enough to again help work the farm. – War broke out and to the dismay of local villagers, all able-bodied men were conscripted into the army; of which, most perished. But as Tak Ying was old and Kai was infirm, both men were allowed to continue to work their farm. Things seemed to be well enough...

However one day a windstorm struck, lashing the farm and uplifting sections of fencing which allowed the horse to escape. And as the dire realisation struck Kai of how they would never be in the financial position to buy another. fear for the future overwhelmed him to where he said to his father, "Father, what a disaster." Tak Ying quietly replied, "The sun is warm, the grass is green and all is, as it should be."– Two days of rest and quiet reflection then passed for Tak Ying whilst two days of worry passed for Kai. But on the third day, as Kai walked over the field to mend the last section of broken fencing, he saw the horse had made its own way back home and was happily chomping in the field – A few months then passed, at which point, both men were overjoyed to realise that, as a direct result of the horse escaping on the day of the storm, somehow she had returned 'in foal.' – A strong and healthy foal was born and in due course was sold, making a good profit, from which Kai invested all the money in more land. Now things seemed to be going well…

However one day, now very tired, Tak Ying explained to Kai that he could no longer work the farm. A farmhand was employed who proceeded to cheat them, throwing them into debt. Shame then fell on the farmhand and his family, disgrace fell on both Tak Ying and Kai, resulting in Tak Ying having a stroke. Kai, now faced with nursing his father, working two plots of land and repaying their debts, did his duty to the best of his ability. But as Kai became evermore exhausted and the farm fell ever deeper into poverty, fear for the future overwhelmed him to where he said to his father, "Father, what a disaster." Tak Ying quietly replied, "The sun is warm, the grass is green and all is, as it should be."

Word gradually spread of the two men's strife eventually reaching the family of the disgraced farmhand. And in an act of atonement for the wrongdoing of their son, the family sent their daughter Ling to take care of Tak Ying. Ling was very hardworking, taking care of the old man and also helping to work the farm. Now things seemed to be going well…

However one day Tak Ying died. Duty bound, Ling returned home but promised to write to Kai. – Time passed and as Kai and Ling continued to correspond, love developed and they married. Kai was now growing older and desired a son to continue his line. So despite their lack of money, Ling and Kai had three children; all girls. Years of strife then passed and as Ling misguidedly blamed herself for having three girls but no son, fear for the future overwhelmed her to where she said to Kai, "Kai, what a disaster." Kai quietly replied, "The sun is warm, the grass is green and all is, as it should be." – Time passed, the girls grew strong, and ironically the two eldest turned out to be very good farmers, lovingly tending the farm and producing crops in abundance. Now things seemed to be going very well…

However one day, like her grandmother, the eldest daughter developed tuberculosis and died. The youngest sister, blaming herself for not helping more, became overwhelmed by grief and became very ill. The doctor was called, herbs and potions were administered but as Ling watched another of her children fading fast, fear for the future overwhelmed her to where she said to Kai, "Kai, what a disaster." Kai quietly replied, "The sun is warm, the grass is green and all is, as it should be."

Time passed and gradually the youngest daughter began to recover whereupon, as it transpired, due to her then newly found experience with herbal medicine, she had developed such an interest and aptitude for it that her doctor recommended she should train to become a doctor. That she did and made a good doctor too. Now financially secure, the youngest daughter, being a doctor, proudly turned to her father and assured him that the family would never again go hungry. Now things were going exceedingly well.

However one day...

From this snippet of the story, I hope you see that despite pitfalls, life does go on, blessings do come in many guises and what initially appears to be a disaster will often turn out to be a blessing.

Accept that life isn't fair

To repeat myself slightly: In this world, one man has good heath yet his fellow man is dying in terrible pain. One man lives in a mansion yet his fellow man lives in a hovel. In this world of affluence over 30,000 people die every single day through abject poverty. Fairness?

Life is not fair, and the quicker we accept it the better we will be. Of course, that does not suggest that, whenever we witness unfairness we sit back and do nothing about it, absolutely not. But it does suggest that when unfairness is presented to us we then need to separate the issue itself from our emotional and physical response to it.

We all witness on television, the starving people of the third world but how would we help them by becoming emotionally hysterical? We often witness criminals walking away from court, freed by an incompetent and out of touch legal system but how would we change the legal system by becoming emotionally hysterical? And many of us have someone in our life enduring tremendous suffering but how would we ever help them to cope by us becoming emotionally hysterical?

Whenever we witness suffering or injustice, whether to others or our self, must we then carry resentment, bear a grudge, hate the world and become mentally, physically and emotionally hysterical? Of course not!

But should we passionately care and do everything we can to help make right the injustice, perhaps by giving whatever experience, time and/or energy we can. Of course and feel honoured to do so whilst remembering, even if we can't do everything required, we can certainly do 'something.'

Therefore, whenever we see injustice, of course we feel sadness for the victim, mixed with a great desire to help them and of course we feel anger towards the wrongdoer mixed with a strong desire for revenge or justice. But rather than allowing our passionate feelings to render us ineffective, revengeful and bitter, we need to separate the issue itself from our strong passionate feelings to it, and once separated, we then use our passionate feelings to spur us into 'doing something positive about it.'

And so, whenever we witness injustice of whatever kind, rather than becoming reactive and negative we need to become proactive and positive which, in turn, will allow us to feel 'of use' and know that we are truly 'doing something about it,' which, in turn, will enable us to think about it in a more positive way. So whether our only course of action is to write a letter, make a donation or say a prayer, we are still responding proactively, reaching out to the victim in the only way open and appropriate for us personally at that particular time.

Having said that, if an injustice has struck you personally, maybe: – the work position you wanted was given to someone of a lesser aptitude, or you developed a serious illness despite always looking after yourself, or you had an accident only to find that you were denied compensation, or you were born with an illness or disfigurement whilst your sibling was born strong, healthy, handsome or beautiful, or your sibling inherited a fortune whilst you were left penniless, or you endured many years of imprisonment whilst knowing your innocence or you having spent countless years building up a business, tending a garden or even raising children only to have now lost everything…

- Remember, any negative feelings at all, of whatever type, will serve no one and undo nothing.
- Identify the issue then separate it from your emotional response to it.
- Be positive, proactive and constructive in whatever way you can.
- Know you are doing your best to make good come from bad then 'let it go.'
- Recognize that unfairness only seems unfair when taken relatively. If the wrongdoer causes you to lose an eye remember, 'In the land of the blind the one-eyed man is king.' In other words, whatever little you might have, it is everything to some people. For sure, if you look hard enough you will always find someone considerably worse off than yourself and who would swap places with you in a heartbeat.

Procrastination

Imagine you are on your deathbed, you're not in any pain, your mind is stable and alert but you are nevertheless in your last few moments of life. And as you lie there, helpless, your mind reflects over your life…

Initially you think how lucky you were to have had life; not that it was 'a bed of roses' for you, indeed you endured many adversities but you were given 'life' and the opportunity to experience the awesomeness of it all.

So now, as you lie there, with thoughts flooding through your mind, you slowly begin to realise that, whilst you were given life and the same life opportunities as everyone else, you never appreciated it or fully lived it, you never: – walked through a woodland, in spring, filled with bluebells – lay on a beach listening to the sea whilst looking up at the stars – swam in the open sea with dolphins – made love outdoors – fully appreciated the majesty of the mountains, the wonderment of the stars, the power of the oceans, the beauty of the seasons, the miracle of a buttercup, the drama of a piece of music and the glory of love – nor had you done any one of a thousand things that would have sent your spirit soaring.

With your life now fading fast, bereft by your lost opportunities, your mind drifts over all the life challenges that were open to you but which you didn't risk, you didn't: – leave the partner who scarred your heart and depleted your spirit – moved to another part of the country or indeed to another country – accepted the position which paid less but which would have given you great satisfaction – or loved again after being hurt.

And as you take your final few gasps of air, now slowly fading away, you grieve over the lost benefits you could have made to your fellow man and to this wondrous planet earth: – all the worldly pain you could have eased but you simply couldn't be bothered – all the people you could have influenced for the good but you were too complacent – all the disharmony you could have calmed by saying, "I'm sorry," but were too proud – and all the peace you could have given by saying, "I forgive you," or, "I love you," but were too defiant. Now it is all too late and there is absolutely nothing you can do about it but feel the dreadful waste and regret seep into your soul, and not for the many things you did wrong, for everyone makes mistakes but rather, for all the things you could have done but didn't.

Death is inevitable! Whilst you have life, live it! For if a butterfly in the Brazilian Rainforest can flap its wings and the effects be felt in the Sahara Desert, just imagine what effect your awesomeness could have on the world!

Abandonment

One can feel abandoned in many ways but for many people, such feelings are from the abandonment by one's parent, partner or child. Rejected, bereft and soulfully lost, mixed with resent to the point of hate; that is how I felt many years ago when abandoned. It was undoubtedly one of the most potentially destructive times of my life. How did I get through life without it destroying me? By the very long slog of working on myself, which included me coming to realise that everyone has the right to make their own life choices.

Bereavement

If you are recently bereaved then you need to mourn, you need time to mourn and you need to give yourself permission to mourn. If you don't, the energy then required to keep your grief buried will exhaust you to where, sooner or later, it will stop you in your path.

If you are not recently bereaved but are still mourning the death of a loved one then perhaps you need help with coming to terms with your loss. And I realise that no two people ever feel grief in the same way, to the same degree and for the same amount of time but everything does have its time, even grief. For sure, whenever grief is allowed to become entrenched, it can turn very negative indeed. Therefore if you are not recently bereaved but are still mourning the death of a loved one, then you might find it helpful to identify for whom are you still in mourning; for your loved one, for your family and friends or for yourself?

Your loved one?
Whilst your loved one would benefit from your prayers and from a good deed done in their name, they certainly will not benefit from your wasted life. You don't need to cling onto grief to prove your love for them: – you can now let-go of your grief yet still share your innermost feelings with them – by holding onto grief you are not holding onto them – your degree of grief is not the indicator of how much you love and miss them – your feelings of guilt for not being ill or dying with them are not needed or wanted – letting-go of your grief is not forgetting them – and you wanting to live, love and laugh again is not being disloyal to them. Indeed a life lived to the full because of knowing them is a far greater testament to them than a life wasted.

Your family or friends?
Your family and friend don't need your grief. Why would they? What possible need would they have in seeing you distraught? Of course your

sadness might be due to you seeing your family and friends still grieving, in which case, empathy might be a more appropriate description of your sadness than grief.

Yourself?

Are you perhaps grieving for your own loss? Was your loved one also your best friend, your companion, your lover, the one who needed you, the one who you needed, the one who listened to you when others were too busy, the one who gave you cuddles when the world didn't care and the one who has now left a gaping, raw hole in your life and your heart? If so, I am so sorry. I do know how cold and frightening the world can feel. When my Mum died, for years after, I felt as if I had been cast down, alone into a very deep, pitch-black, soulfully lonely and very frightening pit, with just enough air going in to keep me alive. How did I get through it? My love for my children and my desire to help others 'in my Mum's name,' that's how I got through it. And no, I will never forget her. In fact I think of her virtually every single day and think how extremely grateful I am to have had her in my life and also how determined I am to now pass that love on to others who need it. Please know, love is never weakened by sharing it; love is actually strengthened when shared.

If you are not recently bereaved but are grieving, then please consider bereavement counselling. (You will find contact details on my website, www.lmbookshop.com)

Find you

You suffered panic attacks and symptoms of stress, yet didn't give up. You stood face to face with terror, yet didn't yield. You lived in rooms of the mind where others never dare enter. You have been thought of as weak, yet had the inner strength to survive. You endured a degree of suffering that has driven others to suicide, yet have survived to become even stronger. And you have perhaps been taken to your limit, stripped of everything, even of yourself, yet have come through ever more enriched. Yes you have indeed shown yourself to be richly blessed and possess a great strength of spirit. Yet I now ask even more from you. That is, for you to determine if your experience with panic attacks is going to be a negative force in your life or will it be the making of you.

By this point, you might have returned to your normal life and think that you once had panic attacks, you don't anymore and now you just want to forget the whole experience, as if it had never happened. And if that's what you wish for yourself then OK. But is it? Is that really what freedom means to you; you simply being free of panic attacks? Is that really what all your suffering has been for; you merely being the person you were previously? And is that really where your journey into and out of panic attacks has led you, you being right back to where you began? Surely you deserve more!

Why have eyes if you never really see? Why have ears if you never really listen? Why have suffering if you never really grow from it? And why have freedom if you never really use it? To be sure, your freedom from panic attacks need not be the end of the matter but the beginning: the starting place, the opportunity to begin the search for who you really are and the open door that invites you to become the person you were really born to be. In short. Your freedom from panic attacks will only be freedom if you embrace it, otherwise you are still living in bondage. So, as part of this final step to freedom, please consider the following...

Make the best of your suffering panic attacks
Don't look at your experience with panic attacks as a negative experience, don't think of yourself as being robbed by them and don't just sit back feeling satisfied with yourself for merely surviving them. Instead, actively use panic attacks as your own personal tool for positive growth: – feel blessed for having suffered them – open yourself up to the 'life lessons' they have given you – let them strengthen your resolve to live a fruitful and happy life – be grateful to them for the insight they have given you – be thankful to them for the strength of spirit you found within yourself – and appreciate them, for they have given you the chance of a new life.

Live your own life; not the life that others want you to live
Live your life as you want to live it: – identify the people in your life who take your time, energy and money and, when in their company, you feel drained in mind, body and spirit then, as soon as you can, emotionally, mentally, physically and spiritually walk away from them – identify those who are so warped, cold hearted, cruel and greedy that, if given the chance, they will find their happiness by feeding off you, then walk away from them also – don't take to heart other peoples' cold and hurtful manner; for they probably have problems too – identify those who give you time, energy and, when in their company, you feel good, empowered, energised and stronger in mind, body and spirit then know them to be your friend – seek out and mix with like minded positive people – and 'go with your own flow of life' by living your own life and allowing others to live theirs.

Find your own 'rock of stability'
Think back over all the anxiety, pain, distress and terror that you have experienced: – when your panic attacks were at their worst – when all your hopes and dreams had abandoned you and your reality was worse than any nightmare – when the raw, frenzied terror of panic attacks felt so powerful and unyielding, it left you feeling totally helpless, exhausted and alone – and when your despair was so crushing that death itself seemed a real alternative. Then ask yourself, a) what was inside you so strong and powerful that it lifted, supported, inspired and gave you the strength to endure and b) what exactly carried you through and beyond all the pain, suffering and distress? If you don't know then get to know!

Get to know who you really are and why you are really here
If need be, get some counselling and rid yourself of all emotional baggage. Don't live to please other people or contort yourself trying to be what they think you should be but rather, listen to and be guided by your own intuition, your own small voice of truth and protection sitting inside you. If you don't know your roots, or you dislike your roots or your roots have shamed you or let you down, know that you now have the freedom and right to be whoever you want to be and thereby make your own roots. Rejoice in who you are and be thankful for your own personal sensitivities and vulnerabilities. Don't merely aim to be the person you were previously because that person developed panic attacks. Realise, the person you were yesterday was not half the person you are today and the person you are today is not half the person you can be tomorrow.

Purposefully seek enlightenment and personal growth
Go in search for the spiritual part of you: – separate your worldly wants from your worldly needs – learn to appreciate simplicity and know that, very often, the more materialistic cultures of this world are the most unhappy – never be afraid to fail, for failure is simply an opportunity to grow – read books, meditate, pray, look into the great religions (sifting out the manmade dogma) and find your own personal truth – go outside and breathe life into your body, mind and spirit, feel life in the water, see life in the sky, touch life in the trees, smell life in the grass and flowers – and use your own strength of spirit to walk your very own path whilst allowing others to walk theirs – when life's adversities strike, don't just endure them with a resigned heart but instead, try to look upon them as a gift, a tool for growth – know that to worry about death is to die a million times before death finally arrives – realise that the mark of a life

lived well is not based on the absence of mistakes but rather, on how the mistakes were dealt with and what was achieved with the knowledge gained from them.

Be a catalyst for change

Understand that whatever you achieve in life or however successful you are, none of it matters if it's only done for yourself: – refocus your heart, mind and soul from serving yourself to serving others – stand up and be counted, for the only thing needed for evil to flourish is for you to do nothing – never doubt that a mere handful of men can change the world, for that's how it has always been – be proud to be an example of sanity in this insane world – and obviously although you can't do everything to heal this world and its people, you can do 'something.'

Find peace and joy

Allow peace and joy into your life by keeping your life as simple as you possibly can: – take time out of each day to mentally and physically calm down and relax – know that peace and joy will not be found in the vastness of your possessions but in the smallness of your wants; that is, not to have what you want but to want what you have – realise that neither peace nor joy is found at the expense of others but rather, when reaching out and serving others – for every good deed done to you, pass three onto others – 'wake up' and know that you are not here on earth to be an insignificant, ineffectual and dull being, merely surviving life but rather, you are here to radiate joy, love, light and happiness by serving others – live on a deeper level of life by relating to people 'soul to soul' and thereby feel true peace and joy.

Find you

Please realise, you are not upon this earth to be a dull flicker but a shining beacon So after reading the above, do try to live as many of the suggestions as you can, in whatever way feels right for you. For when you seek positive growth and begin to utilise both your sensitivity and strength of spirit, you will then be on the path of enlightenment, you will then be on the path of serving 'goodness,' becoming 'all you can be,' embracing true freedom and experiencing sustained contentment, peace and joy.

**To read more on this theme, please go to
'Embrace True Freedom,' page 267.**

Re-cap:
To Take Your Fifth Step
To Freedom

---

1. At the start of this step: If your symptoms have not noticeably eased then please return to your medical doctor and discuss the possibility of your symptoms being those of another condition.

2. Throughout: Regarding any panic attack and symptoms of stress – acknowledge them – recognise them for what they are – let-go of them by focusing your mind onto other things – allow the sensations to pass in their own time – and get on with your life.

3. Evaluate everything in your life that you feel has a negative influence on you. Don't carry even the smallest unnecessary chain around your neck.

4. Remember, recovery is only the beginning, the open door to 'life' and the opportunity to become the person you were really born to be. For your freedom will only be freedom if you embrace it; otherwise you will still be holding yourself in bondage.

5. For the final time, ensure that you have understood this entire step. If you had any difficulty understanding any part of this step then read the relevant section or sections again and perhaps a further time. But after your third attempt, if you still have difficulty understanding any part of it or if you don't identify with it then I urge you to discuss the matter further with your befriender and doctor.

6. If you have not fully understood any part of this step, whether or not you think it relevant to you or if you have only glanced over it then you have not yet taken this step.

Embrace True Freedom

The following section is placed separately from my 'five-step' programme because it has absolutely no connection to panic attacks, or to the recovery from panic attacks or indeed to anyone involved in the publishing of my 'five-step' programme. It is, however, connected to my own personal belief that we each can become truly free in mind, body and soul by connecting to the spirit within us. Whilst the text in the following section is easy to read, the subject matter might not be appreciated by everyone, particularly those who are not of a spiritual nature or those who strictly follow a particular religion. So read it if you wish, omit it if you wish, take from it what feels right for you to take and leave behind what does not. I simply offer it to you with love for you to do with as you wish.

I will also add here: The only reason for me writing the following chapter was because, years ago, I happened to be in conversation with David Lawson, the healer, course leader and spiritual author. And during the conversation David said he felt that many people would benefit from my sharing certain elements of my life. So although, at first, I was extremely reluctant and questioned why anyone would be interested in my private life. After many months of discussion, encouragement from others and deliberation, I decided that if I was going to do this, I would still speak in total honesty. That I did, from which I truly hope you will gain some degree of comfort and strength.

Affairs Are Now Soul Size

The human heart can go the lengths of God,
dark and cold we may be but this is no winter now.
The frozen misery of centuries begins to crack,
break, move.
The thunder is the thunder of the floes, the thaw,
the flood, the upstart spring.
Thank God our time is now,
when wrongs come up to meet us everywhere;
never to leave us.
Till we take the longest stride of soul man ever took.
Affairs are now soul size.
The enterprise is exploration into God.
Where are you making for?
It takes so many thousands of years to wake,
but will you wake, for pity's sake?
                                                      Christopher Fry

My friend, to have life is to have problems! Life, by its very nature, is cruel, for where there is life there is also death. Life on this planet can often be uncompromising, with its diseases, famines, droughts and pestilence. Life in general can be relentless with its wars, health worries, financial issues, domestic strife, personal issues and relationship heartache. Yet amidst all the pain and suffering, when we choose to connect to who we really are, we are then able to rise above life's struggle and embrace true freedom.

In the above verse, Christopher Fry, taken from his play, 'A Sleep of Prisoners,' profoundly expresses how, although the human heart can go the lengths of God, the human heart alone, without God, is no measure to deal with life. After all, man is merely man but 'affairs are now soul size.'

The age of enlightenment, sensitivity and spirituality is now coming to this planet; fast. However, as you have probably seen within your own circle of friends and family, some people have become confused, stuck. They have lost their way. They are mistakenly trying to fill their **inner** spiritual place of peace and joy with external worldly gratification. But as that can never be done, these people never really attain either peace or joy.

True peace and joy is a state of mind. It depends not on a high IQ, a pretty or handsome face, a body beautiful, a certain shade of skin, a high-powered career, 'pots of money' or even good health. Indeed many of those who have such things often prove to be very unhappy people indeed.

Personally speaking, I believe that we are all spiritual beings, in earthly bodies, working our way to Godliness. In which case, whilst living on this earth, this worldly coil, we each have a choice to make. Do we connect with God (whomever or whatever God means to us personally) and fill the spiritual place within us...thereby lead a balanced, positive existence, where we are suitably prepared to face the rawness of life, recognise it for what it is, see its darker elements, stand face to face with them, look them straight in the eye, feel touched, feel saddened, feel outraged and feel frightened, yet all the while feel a deep inner sense of contentment, peace and joy. Or do we disconnect from God and allow the spiritual place within us to be empty...thereby lead an negative, unbalanced existence where we, as 'mere man,' blindly go looking for happiness in worldly places but all the while, in truth, feeling lost, alone, vulnerable and never really feeling true happiness, peace or joy at all. The choice is ours.

"It's OK for you to talk"

After reading the above, you might think, "It's OK for you Lorraine to talk of connecting to spirit, rising above life and finding true peace and joy but you are not me and you don't have my life problems." And you are right, I am not you and I don't have your life problems but believe me, along with the abundant blessings bestowed upon me, I also have been given many testing life problems. In fact if I should chose to ignore all the good things in my life and focus solely onto my past and present problems, I could find plenty to wallow in...

"What kind of person can best endure suffering?
He doesn't exist.
For I could handle your problems easily.
You could handle mine with a yawn.
But it didn't happen that way.
I got the ones I couldn't handle: so did you."
Adapted from Psalm 44

Do you see? Whatever your life problems, every single one of us has had or does have, at least one issue capable of bringing us to our knees. Which brings me to David Lawson's suggestion (as explained previously on page 267) of how he believed that some people would benefit from my sharing certain elements of my life. If there is a possibility that opening and sharing my personal life could help someone else, in any way, then how can I say no? So here goes...

This little girl felt very alone: I was raised Roman Catholic but due to my being placed in the hands of an exceptionally tyrannical and bitter nun (who had me as her own personal lackey) every single day of every year throughout my primary years, I genuinely believed that, as I hated and feared her so much, the all-powerful wrath, judgment and damnation of a very angry God might fall on me at any second. That damaged me greatly.

I also had great difficulty reading and spelling, but as dyslexia was unheard of in the 1950's, from my early schooldays to my late twenties, I genuinely believed that I really was one of life's 'no hopers.'

Also during my primary years, when aged about 7, I was told in an exceptionally destructive way that I was adopted! What a shock! Suddenly, as the realisation struck that my beloved Mum, Dad, Grandma, Granddad, Aunty Gertrude, Uncle Bill and my three cousins were 'not mine,' my whole world literally turned upside down. Indeed, within that one brief moment, to my young mind, the family 'rock of stability,' that was supporting every aspect of my life, was certain to crumble beneath my feet at any moment; certainly at my next wrongdoing. And so, from that day onwards, more so as I got older, I began to develop very deep emotional scars of insecurity, abandonment and lack of worth, along with carrying the one question seemingly carried by many adopted children. "Is my real mother a princess who was forced to give me away or is she just someone who didn't want me?"

My lost and damaged youth: I failed my 11+ exams, as a result, I was separated from all my school friends (they went to either Grammar School or Art College) and I went to a Secondary Modern School and was placed just one class above the very bottom.

Also at 11 years, whilst playing in a local park, a boy from outside my circle of friends stabbed me, causing me to lose so much blood, it forced me to face my own mortality.

One particular day, when aged 14, after falling out with a 'so called' friend, she told me in a very cruel way, that the one person I despised most in the entire world (an aunt) was my real mother. "Total shock!" Again my whole world overturned. Yet later that same day, once my Mum and Dad had confirmed the fact, I realised that, although half my family were still 'not mine,' the other half were my real family. In fact, I was actually 'blood related' to my Mum, my Uncle Bill and even my three cousins were my real half brothers and sister. Wow! However, in those days, family secrets were always hushed-up and my situation was no exception. So from that day onward, and for the next 21 years, nothing more was ever said on the matter, by anyone, which left me feeling somewhat lost. For whilst I knew that all my adoptive family loved me very much, I felt myself becoming emotionally separated from them, and held particular resentment towards those who were my real family for not explaining things sooner and thereby saving me years of feeling an exile. All of which put me onto a very destructive course (lasting for many years) to prove my worth.

Finally, throughout my early teenage years, whilst having developed the flattering features of long golden-red hair, lovely straight, white teeth, a good figure and great legs, to my horror, my nose began to grow longer by the day, there was simply no stopping it, which, over the years, led me to become the butt of many jokes, "Great legs, shame about the face."

Someone, please love me: At 17 I became involved in my first abusive relationship. During that time, like many women involved in domestic violence, I was physically, emotionally, mentally and sexually abused, from which I felt abject shame, I became lost in fear and grew to believe that I was an extremely ugly and weak woman whose only chance of keeping a boyfriend was secured by doing whatever he wanted of me. Yet amazingly, I still chose to stay with him, in fact on my eighteenth birthday, I even became engaged to him. However six months later, after he had hit me in the mouth so hard it irreparably damaged my beautiful front teeth, in desperation and needing to feel safe from him, I joined the British Army.

I joined the army for a three-year term but after two years I married a soldier and was automatically discharged from the army. I then became pregnant, realised my husband was having an affair, had my son, started with panic attacks, crashed into full-blown nervous breakdown, separated from my husband and, with my son, moved back to live with my parents.

Four years of mental torture then passed only to be followed by torture of the emotional kind. For although I was still suffering the remnants of panic attacks, I actually moved in to live with a man (taking my son with me) with whom I had fallen spellbindingly in love, and with whom I was having a totally unplanned and, at the time, very unwanted pregnancy. The consequences of that were huge: – my being pregnant by a man to whom I was not married – the guilt of bringing utter disgrace onto my Catholic parents – my being made a social outcast – my fear of the wrath of God – the dread of panic attacks returning – and doubting if I could mentally, physically and financially cope with another child. Yet, in 1970, once I had given birth to my beloved daughter, I immediately felt an all-consuming sense of love and protection for her.

Within weeks of me giving birth, the man left me and abandoned his daughter, so again, then with my two children, I moved back to live with my parents. What a massive disappointment I must have been to them.

When my children and I had been living with my parents for about two years I was given a council house situated a little way from my parents home. However, along with independence came a very testing time of high emotions: – outrage at the injustice of it all – exhaustion due to the never-ending toil of being the sole breadwinner for my two young children and myself (no child maintenance off my husband and no state help for single working mothers in those days) – loneliness also was a really big issue for me mixed with a crushing and overwhelming sense of foreboding at not having the physical support of a partner – and feeling soulfully daunted by the task of living a life of sheer misery in financial and social deprivation.

Also during this time, as if life was not difficult enough, my beloved Mum died, God bless her. From which, and for a few years thereafter, I carried such agonizing feelings of guilt, loss, loneliness and belief that never in this world would I ever feel safe or loved again.

The end of my loneliness yet the continuation of misfortune: Two years after my Mum died I met Brian, the kindest, gentlest, most loving, caring and selfless man that God ever put upon this earth (my lifesaver) and one year after our meeting we were married.

In 1976, when married for only a year, I began to experience acute bouts of fatigue, so exhausting they put me to bed for weeks. Yet despite my knowing my symptoms were physical, my doctor insisted they were 'all in the mind,' thereby leaving me to argue my mental stability whilst physically pushing myself far beyond my ability.

Around 1980, along with the chronic fatigue, I then needed a cancer related gynaecological operation. Also, due to my dire health situation, a family member finally informed me of certain facts regarding my blood family linage. And so, after twenty-one years, I finally knew where I came from, which, again, threw me. For although I was born and raised in England and thought I was of English descent, I was, in fact, not English at all but rather, of Irish/Scottish descent mixed with an American/Canadian Airman, called Jack, who was serving with Bomber Command during the Second World War.

When recovering from the operation and also from the revelation of my family linage, rather than being sensible and taking stock, Brian and I made a financial investment with a company who proceeded to deceive and betray us; from which we lost everything, even our home. And, as if things were not difficult enough, after seven years of trying to live within my physical ability (whilst continuing to run a business and work with my panic attack clients) my whole bodily system broke down. Resulting in me suffering severe breathlessness, acute muscle pain, extreme fatigue and reacting to virtually everything relating to the twentieth century. On my few good-days I could talk a little and walk a few yards but on my many bad-days I could not even get out of bed, as all my energy was then needed to focus beyond the pain in the attempt to attain each breath.

Without labouring over the following decades but just skimming over them: At 40, I had a hysterectomy. At 44, it then being nearly fifteen years of battling fatigue, a reputable hospital consultant finally diagnosed my health condition as Chronic Fatigue Syndrome. At 47, I had an allergic reaction so severe, it brought me to a complete stop for a whole year. When I was 49, my husband Brian was diagnosed as suffering angina. Two years later he had a heart attack. The next year, Brian had a second heart attack. Two years after that he had a quadruple heart by-pass operation. And in 1999, when I was 54, after many years of helplessly witnessing my Dad becoming lost to dementia, he finally and mercifully died.

A little battered and bruised but never beaten: Over the years, I have undergone six medical operations and, due to the nature and severity of some of them, have felt the anguish that I might never see my family again nor they see me. Throughout my late forties to my mid fifties, whilst willingly giving every single ounce of time, energy, love and support that was in my capacity to give, my heart felt broken many times as my two precious children had their own extremely testing life issues; including illness, betrayal, divorce, being raped, post-natal depression, alcoholism, drug addiction, systematically battered by a partner, broken hearts and spirits. Yet through my late fifties (up to today) my heart sang with relief and humility at seeing each of my children, in their own incredible way, find the strength and courage to work their way out of their 'lost years' to become exceptionally loving, loyal, hardworking and stable parents, added to which, they are each an absolute blessing to life and God.

Which brings me to today. Now almost 70 yrs of age and having lived a more spiritual and holistic life for just over sixteen years, my life has been absolutely transformed on many levels. Even so, I am still sensitive to many chemicals and foods. At all times, I carry two adrenaline injectors with me in case I experience an anaphylactic attack. Everywhere I go has to be free of all chemical and cleaning odours, scents, smoke and fumes of all kinds. Everyone I meet has to restrain from smoking or using any sort of scent, hairspray, body products or anything with a fragrance. Virtually all my food is organic, chemical free and known to be a safe food for me. Yet still, whenever I push myself over my physical capability, my body then calls stop and, yet again, I am forced to rest for weeks.

So you see, whilst I have never experienced child abuse of a sexual nature, suffered depression, been driven from my homeland, lost a child, been widowed, been completely alone in the world, endured paralysis, witnessed a loved one suffering a painful, terminal illness nor have I experienced any number of terrible life adversities. I have nevertheless had my share. And whilst I clearly realise that my adversities have been, and are minimal compared to those of many other people, they are severe enough to restrict my life greatly. Yet despite everything, I hold no ill feeling towards anyone but rather, I feel a deep and unbroken sense of contentment and peace, along with countless moments of pure joy; which is due to my wondrous, ongoing journey towards enlightenment.

The path leading to enlightenment is often found in the most unexpected places

In 1992, whilst enduring months of bed rest due to an allergic reaction, I was forced down on my knees so far that, despite my then not believing in God, 'out of my depths' I cried out to God for help and mercy.

Was God listening? I certainly didn't think so. I definitely didn't gain an instant feeling of relief or connection to God. In fact, I began to feel an overwhelming sense of disconnection, as if I had somehow rejected God and made myself a total outcast from all 'goodness.' And although I still didn't think that I believed in anything spiritual, the very thought of me rejecting God and all 'goodness' filled me with utter despair.

Weeks then passed of my experiencing what I now know to be a period of, 'The dark night of the soul,' that is, to emotionally and spiritually feel the raw, all-consuming pain of being separated and separate from God. During that time, for most of the time, every fibre of my being felt lost in a dark and sinister world of disconnection. On a few other occasions, I felt such a sudden yet intense degree of compassion for Mother Earth and all life upon her that I was completely overwhelmed and driven with the need to help her. On other occasions, I felt such fear and despair at not knowing what on earth was happening to me that again I cried out to God, only that time, not for my life problems to be resolved because, in comparison to how I was then feeling, they paled into insignificance. My cries were then 'of the soul,' begging God to allow me to feel connected to 'goodness' again. Of course, on reflection, I now realise that my cries were begging God to come into my life but, at the time, I certainly didn't see it that way.

After weeks of enduring my 'dark night,' although it was a spiritual awakening rather than a mental health condition, I felt myself becoming mentally exhausted. So intuitively, I began to say the words used by David, one of my panic attack clients, "The desire for God's presence is proof that He is already there," which proved to be invaluable, as it rested my mind and carried me safely through until the 'dark night' had lifted.

That was the start of my spiritual awakening; my desire for an ever deeper connection to 'goodness,' in other words, to God. That experience put me on a path of soul-searching, reading and listening to the opinions of others; some plausible and some totally 'off the wall,' some with great insight and some completely brainwashed in dogma, some were made so bitter by their childhood religious experiences, they had completely lost all faith in the power of 'goodness' and some having found their own 'rock of stability' to where they were highly spiritual yet totally grounded.

As my spirituality developed, I realised that, although I had spent most of my life bulldozing my way through, pushing myself far beyond my physical capability whilst dragging others along with me; all to prove I was 'of worth.' I then needed to stop, to bring calmness into my life and to loosen my tight grip on things and people. I also needed to de-clutter my surroundings, to make peace with certain people (even when I was the wronged) to be still and to try to differentiate between my own thoughts and feelings and those when God was speaking to me.

And amazingly, once I genuinely tried to listen to God, or rather, once I genuinely tried to 'be still' and wait in love and patience for God to speak to me then, like many others who have also done the same, coincidences or what seemed like coincidences, began to happen to me quite frequently and in astonishing ways. Environmental issues developed on my doorstep, which motivated me into campaigning. Fascinating people came into my life, from which inspiring and intriguing conversations took place that completely opened me to new approaches to spirituality. I happened to watch television programmes, which introduced me to books, tapes and videos that 'blew my mind.' My work with panic attack sufferers brought people, conversations and insights into my life at the most opportune and relevant moments, that changed my life forever.

All these life events and more were being guided to me and I to them, whilst being gently, yet profoundly, given the discernment to recognise what was spiritually right for me and what was not. This ironically took me further away from the religious dogma that had brainwashed my mind for so many years, yet it took me ever closer towards enlightenment, life, spirituality, Jesus and God.

So here I am today, filled with a deep sense of purpose whilst always trying to stay open to and be guided by 'goodness,' enlightenment and change which, for me personally, involves being in service to others in the name of 'goodness;' for which I feel blessed and honoured to do so.

Insights gained, up to now, from my ongoing, exciting, challenging and ever-changing spiritual journey

My outlook on life, spirituality and God has completely changed from my earlier years; which I would love to share with you. However, when thinking about how to put all my thoughts, feelings and insights into some sort of order for you, the only way that made sense was to group them all into the following four sections…

1. God
2. Mans' relationship with the earth
3. The connection between The Holy Spirit and the Soul of Man
4. My life today

1. God

At this current point on my journey, I believe that God is the 'goodness' found in and flows from selflessness, truth, compassion, empathy, charity, hope, courage, forgiveness and love. God is truly alive, living, breathing and working through the vibrating, bright life-energy of The Holy Spirit. This life-energy flows through all life, from 'man' to a mustard seed and from an atom to this planet, the universe and beyond. To me, whether a person's belief is in God, or 'goodness,' or life itself, or the higher self (the part of oneself that is not of the flesh but of the spirit) or even if they feel they do believe in 'something' but they don't know in exactly what, God is still 'goodness' and 'goodness' is still God, whatever the term used.

'The Holy Spirit' is the entity through which God/goodness works within us, it is our sense of what's right and wrong, it is our conscience and the nucleus of our intuition. In truth, The Holy Spirit is both the greatest of all message bearers and also our own, personal best friend. Just imagine if God was an 'independent being of goodness' somewhere out there in the universe and 'man' was just another species down here on earth but neither God or 'man' knowing of each other, so no communication between either. Imagine 'man' roaming the earth with no feeling of empathy, compassion, forgiveness, truth or having a conscience.

'Jesus Christ' was and is 'The Way,' the example of true 'goodness' in an earthly form. And despite knowing His earthly fate, He lovingly and selflessly came to earth, not for self glory but rather, to teach mankind that, whilst living here on earth, if we live as God asks us to then a) we will live a contented, peaceful and joyous life and b) when we die, we will then be spiritually enlightened enough to move up to the next level of life.

We each have a 'Soul,' which itself is a unique spark of God. Our Soul lives to serve God and to communicate with God through the majesty that is The Holy Spirit.

The Hypocrites

I believe, with all my heart that, 'man' (individually and mankind as a whole) has the potential to be incredible spiritual beings. There are, however, many people today who, under the pretext of guiding and teaching us laymen about God/goodness, do not do so in the service of God but do so in their own self-interest...

To my thinking, any religion, following, cult or belief that 'claims' to work in the service of God but instead: it demands, frightens, guilt's, shames or brainwashes one generation after another into following it – or it charges for what Buddha, Krishna and Jesus happily gave to us freely – or it's an obscenely wealthy, landowning religion, with its jewel clad hands and fine robes, pontificating from its gilded cathedrals, mosques or other, so-called, palaces of worship, to its brain-washed God-loving/fearing followers – or it outcasts those who stray from it – or it demands that 'its' God, Profit, Guru or Belief is the only true way – or, with deliberate intent, it disparages debate, it refuses free-thinking, it encourages its indoctrinated brainwashed extremists to annihilate those who disagree with it – or within its practise, and even sanctioned by the practise, the male of our species are given more rights and thereby more control than the female. Then, in my opinion, that religion, following, cult or belief and the 'so-called' teachers involved in its interpretation and practise, do not walk, with humility, in the footsteps of 'goodness' such as The Christ Jesus (The Anointed One) – Gautama The Buddha (The Enlightened One) – Tenzin Gyatso, His Holiness the Fourteenth Dalai Lama – The Mahatma Mohandas Karamchand Gandhi (The Passive Resister) – Thomas Moore – or the more recent Martin Luther King. **Instead**, the religion, following, cult or belief and the 'so-called' teachers involved in its interpretation and practise, certainly do walk in the footsteps of darkness; the dense, negative entity that is born from and feeds off manmade, man instigated and man manipulated fear, separation, self-servitude, deception, hatred and control.

To walk in the footsteps of Buddha, Krishna or Jesus, and thereby serve 'goodness' is not a matter of how fanatical a person follows his/her chosen **man-interpreted** form of dogma, or how much money they donate to it or how much time they spend worshiping it. To walk in such Holy footsteps is, for each one of us to make the conscious choice to serve 'goodness' over serving ourselves; by openheartedly and humbly giving ourselves in service to others in the name of 'goodness;' God.

2. Mans relationship with the earth

I know there is more to life and the universe than we could ever imagine I also know that the earth and all life on her is formed of wavelengths/vibrations. I believe that as we spiritually grow, our wavelengths/vibrations change from a denser, lower level to a lighter, higher level. I believe that each individual man and woman is here for a specific purpose. And I also believe that the earth itself and **all** life on her, are an integral part of life.

The partnership...
I think the relationship between 'man' and the earth is that of a partnership, we help each other. I also think that every person living on earth is a spiritual being trying to work his/her own way back to God; and the earth is a place where 'man' can do that...

For her part: To help 'man' physically survive, earth provides all 'mans' needs: water, food, heat, shelter. However, to help 'man' spiritually grow, earth is also a place of temptations, diseases, pain, suffering and adversities, all of which gives 'man' the opportunity to learn, endure, resist temptations, spiritually grow and turn to God.

For our part: During our time on earth, we are to treat her with respect; to be her caretakers. We are also, to ask questions, to seek spiritual truth rather than just blindly following the manmade dogma. And we are also to learn how to access our discernment (intuition – 'gut feeling' – The Holy Spirit) then allow it to guide us, help us and protect us through our good times, bad times and all those times of uncertainty when our earthly thoughts are telling us to do one thing but our 'gut feeling' is telling us, "Be careful, you know this is not really for you." In fact, whilst living here on earth, if we can trust and follow our 'gut feeling,' it will make our life on earth significantly easier, it will certainly aid our spiritual growth, it will take us ever closer to enlightenment and, most importantly, it will carry us back to God/goodness.

So yes, whilst living on earth, we are to 'live life to the full;' dance, sing appreciate beauty and embrace all the good things that life offers yet, at the same time, we are to **spiritually grow:** we are to get to know God and build a relationship with Him and we are also to live as He asks us to. Then, as we serve God/goodness and spiritually grow, our wavelengths/vibrations will begin to change from a dense, low level to a lighter, higher level and, over time, we will become the selfless race of beings who put the needs of others before their own wants and, very often, before their own needs. Truly Gods own beings.

3. The connection between The Holy Spirit and the Soul of Man
Some people say that by living a truly spiritual life, by meditating, praying and thinking only positive thoughts, they can actually avoid adversity; illness, pain and life problems. And they say such things as if illness, pain and life problems are a punishment but, in many cases, they are wrong! Yes, what goes around comes around and illness, pain and life problems can indeed be due to karma but not always. In fact illness, pain and life problems are very often instigated by a much higher spiritual element…

In its own desire to serve God/goodness a Soul will sometimes ask for or agree to endure an adversity. By doing so, the Soul is attempting to help strengthen its own or another Soul or Souls. Indeed, in the desire to serve 'goodness,' especially through adversity, a rare Soul can actually touch and move the whole world, as we have seen so often in the past.

When a Soul has agreed to an endurance, once on earth, as the weeks, months, years or decades pass, the Soul, might become a little lazy, as if half-asleep, complacent, just drifting with no purpose. And although the Soul certainly loves God, even to where it initially asked for or agreed to endure, it now needs a little nudge, a small reminder of why it is here. In which case, initially, working through The Holy Spirit, God will gently and lovingly speak to the Soul in a whisper…

"**Soul** wake up, you have been asleep for too long. You have forgotten who you are, where you come from and why you are here. … **Soul** wake up, your light is no longer shining brightly. You have become dull and cloudy. Remember, you are more than this; far more than this. … **Soul** wake up, open your eyes and see me, see how brightly Spirit shines. Open your heart and feel me, feel how much love Spirit has for you. And open yourself to me; know that you and I are one. … **Soul** wake up, wake up, know that I am here within you, never to leave you. Lean on me when you feel weak. Trust in me when you feel lost. And have faith that I will never let you fall. … **Soul** wake up, **please** wake up, I need you to become 'all that you can be;' the bright shining beacon that offers light to all those still sleeping."

Once The Holy Spirit has tried to wake the Soul in a whisper, if, by then, the Soul has become too caught up with 'matters of the world' and chooses not to listen, Spirit will then try again but that time stronger and dramatically. For often, just as we are only able to appreciate the light of the day when we have experienced the dark of the night. Our physical mind and body are often only able to break free from the trappings of life through mental, emotional and/or physical adversity. In which case, again working through The Holy Spirit, God will give us a 'lovingly push,' which can come in a number of ways, it will start gently and will not be nice…

When a 'lovingly push' begins, The Holy Spirit will gently place a small pebble (a small adversity) in our path. If at first we don't see the pebble or if we choose not to see it, Spirit will then put a stone in our path. If we are too caught-up in 'life' or by the trappings of life to notice the stone, Spirit will then put a rock in our path. And if we are still too caught up in 'life' to notice the rock, Spirit will then present us with a mountain, from which we feel we can't go through, round, under or over: as perhaps you experienced with panic attacks.

Assuming our Soul has indeed asked for or agreed to an adversity with the intention to help strengthen either our own or another Soul or Souls. When the adversity actually strikes, particularly if it is so traumatic it brings us to a complete stop, we could then very easily feel overwhelmed, as if it is all just too much for us to carry. And if that does happen, we are then wise to remember, we are never given an adversity that is too heavy for us, in which case, we must try to endure with a good heart and make from the adversity whatever we can for the 'good.'

Jesus Christ, Buddha, Gandhi, Thomas Moore, Martin Luther King and many thousands/millions of people have all accepted adversity to serve God/goodness. By doing so, each, in their own way, guided us away from self-servitude and the misguided mentality of 'taking a life for a life' and instead they taught us love, peace, forgiveness and 'let the one who is without sin cast the first stone.'

During adversity, we can choose to serve God by digging deep and enduring with 'goodness' in our heart or we can serve ourselves, by living shallowly and enduring with self-pity and resentment in our heart. Either way we are still enduring but one way will take us closer to being 'all that we can be' and thereby strengthening our connection to God/goodness and the other way will take us away from being 'all that we can be' and thereby losing that particular opportunity to become spiritually stronger and closer to God.

When a Soul is asked or volunteers to endure, whilst the endurance will be difficult, if done with a willing heart, then nothing is more sacred...

- "The steel of a healer is smelted in the fires of hell."
  Harry Edwards
- "A nervous breakdown is often due to a spiritual breakthrough."
  Marianne Williamson
- "We turn to God when our foundations are shaken, only to learn it is God who is shaking them."
  Charles C West
- "If you are going through hell, just keep going."
  Winston Churchill
- "Things are often stronger where they have been broken."
  Louise Penny

Do you see? Those who have been given significant life adversities are often those who have been given significant tasks to perform for 'goodness.' And if that is you but you now feel it's all too much and you just can't carry on then, I absolutely promise you, if you turn to God/goodness and, from the depths of your Soul, ask for the strength to endure with a good heart, you will be amazed at the outcome.

Furthermore, even if my suffering and your suffering was not and is not given to strengthen any other Soul but rather, it is a Karmic endurance in order to strengthen our own Soul. And if that is the case then we have certainly been blessed and given the golden opportunity to 'right a wrong' and do so with a good heart. For sure, if we do our best to endure with a good heart, we will then turn all our suffering into righteousness; which itself will enable us to live deeper, become spiritually stronger and serve 'God/goodness.'

4. My life today
On a spiritual level
Sadly, at birth, I was not blessed with absolute faith, in fact for most of my life I tended to need proof before I believed. And even though I have been on my spiritual journey for many years, like many people, I still have a few days of doubt when I don't feel any connection to God at all, so on those days I just put all my trust in 'goodness.' After all, in this particular instance, it is the feeling of love and peace that matters not the name.

Most of the time, by trying my best to be a servant of God/goodness, I feel a sustained level of deep peace but when I fail I am so very disappointed. I occasionally feel pure joy when I experience a strong connection to God. I am daily comforted by my personal 'rock of stability' which, of course, is my belief in 'goodness.' I am, by the moment, guided by The Holy Spirit within me. I am often truly inspired by those who have lived in the Spirit of 'goodness.' And because life can be so terribly cruel, every time I hear of or see an act of human kindness, I know that God/goodness is truly alive and working hard on planet earth.

Jesus Christ lived in the Spirit of 'goodness'. As such, for me personally, He is 'The Way.' He is my Saviour, my spiritual shelter, my strength, my guiding light and my living example of true 'goodness.' And yes:– The Buddha shows me mental balance and calmness – The Dalai Lama shows me humility – Judaism shows me the importance of ritual, family, that no man or woman, of whatever creed or colour, should ever be considered less than another and even, for the most innocent people, blame can so easily be cast – and all religions show me that, whilst some people do deliberately misinterpret much of the Holy teachings to serve their own self-interest, there are indeed 'many mansions in my Father's house.' Yet, speaking very personally, my heart, Soul and life itself still belongs only to Jesus.

On a grounded, personal level
I now realise that every one of my life adversities was a gift from God and although I didn't realise it at the time, each gave me much strength...

Although I was adopted, I was not disconnected from my roots, as my roots are those of Spirit. Adoption was simply the means by which Spirit entrusted me to a loving, courageous and very forgiving family. In truth, I was raised in love, my whole adoptive family were good, honest people of integrity. My parents, Elizabeth and Frederick, my grandparents, Charles and Polly and my aunt Gertrude (all dead now) nurtured me, protected me, cherished me and selflessly stood by me through all my turbulent years, each showing me such abundant love that, over the years, it was, and still is their love for me that carried me through life.

Although I was abandoned by key people in my life, I know I deserve both love and life because the love and life of God vibrates through the very Soul of me. Although suffering panic attacks was not of my choosing, it was the catalyst that started me helping other panic attack sufferers. And although experiencing chronic fatigue is certainly not of my choosing, it was the catalyst that guided me to write this book; and in doing so, help far more panic attack sufferers than I did when I was fit and working on a one-to-one basis. Indeed with my hand on my heart, I tell you truthfully, if I was given the choice to have never suffered panic attacks and chronic fatigue against my never having worked with panic attack sufferers nor written this book then I would choose panic attacks and chronic fatigue every time.

And although my hair is now very short and grey, my own teeth are all gone, my figure is fuller, my legs are always covered by either trousers or a long skirt and I still have a prominent nose, I know my Soul (just as your Soul) is beautiful to behold and treasured throughout the kingdom of God.

On an philosophical level

I am now becoming my own true self. I acknowledge my weaknesses alongside my strengths. I am fully aware that to be on a spiritual journey is not simply to float through life untouched and unaffected. Absolutely not! In fact I know that, being both spiritual and human I still have many vulnerabilities to overcome. So at times, although my heart and Soul do passionately desire to serve 'goodness,' I often fail miserably. I never try to be someone I'm not. When I'm hurt and frightened I cry and try to lean heavily on Jesus. I do try to appreciate my vulnerabilities and sensitivities by making the most of them; after all, it was both of them that brought me to this point of serving God; by helping you.

My priorities in life are helping:– my family – those suffering panic attacks – ME/CFS sufferers – this planet – and like so many people, I'm just doing whatever I can to lift the spiritual consciousness of people, to turn darkness to light, adversity to triumph; panic attacks to peace.

When I have physical strength, I talk, walk a little, write a lot, travel and do all the things that I can do. When I lack breath and strength I rest, read, listen to the radio and watch television. And yes, being human, I do sometimes feel frustrated, vulnerable, frightened and literally plead, "Holy Father, whilst I do seek enlightenment, please spare me its lessons today."

And yes, it would be great to have the breath and energy to run, dance, sing and do all the things we humans like to do, but for now I can't and all the frustration and resentment in the world will not change that. So why should I waste even one second of my life or one ounce of my energy on futile negative thoughts and emotions, after all, I could be struck down tomorrow, and what a wasted life that would have been if it had been full of futile negative thoughts of resent and hate. Moreover, come the day when I lie on my deathbed, I will then be consoled and perhaps even rejoice in the fact that this world is a little better for me having had this life. And come the day when I die, if I am to be so blessed, I then hope to kneel before 'The One Holy and Almighty God' and say, "**Thank you** for giving me life. **Thank you** for guiding to me those people who truly loved me, for it was their love alone that carried me through my endurance's till I found you. **Thank you** for every person and event that could have broken me but only made me stronger. **Thank you** for allowing me those truly precious moments of pure joy, when I actually felt in my Soul that I was working under the guidance of your mighty hand; what an honour. I did my best for you with what I had."

Sending you spheres of love and light on
the golden strands that unite us all
in the one heart

This book
and all the peace gained from it,
is dedicated to the source of love, peace,
joy and human kindness

web: www.LMbookshop.com – email: info@LMbookshop.com

Lightning Source UK Ltd.
Milton Keynes UK
UKHW02f2145190218
318132UK00005B/191/P